J.B. Priestley

The Last of the Sages

by

John Atkins

JOHN CALDER · LONDON
RIVERRUN PRESS · NEW YORK

First published in Great Britain 1981 by
John Calder (Publishers) Ltd.,
18 Brewer Street, London W1R 4AS
and in the U.S.A. 1981 by
Riverrun Press Inc.,
175 Fifth Avenue, New York City 10010

British Library Cataloguing in Publication Data
Atkins, John, *b.1916*
  J.B. Priestley
  1. Priestley, John Boynton — Biography
  2. Authors, English — 20th century — Biography
  823'.9'12   PR6031.R6Z/   79-41354
  ISBN 0 7145 3804 3 casebound

Typeset in Janson 10/11 by Alan Sutton Publishing Limited,
Gloucester
Printed and Bound in the U.K.
by Mansell (Bookbinders) Ltd., Witham, Essex

Contents

List of Illustrations

Preface

J.B. Priestley is a major though neglected writer. In this he resembles
G.K. Chesterton, and both suffer from the same circumstance;
although they both produced a wealth of extraordinarily interesting
and competent work, neither has produced anything which is undeniably a masterpiece or even a work which, though flawed, seems
to mark a moment in the history of English Literature. (As can be said
of James Joyce, T.S. Eliot, D.H. Lawrence and even, to a less
obvious extent, of G.B. Shaw and H.G. Wells, who were closer in
spirit to both Chesterton and Priestley than they were to the others
mentioned.) Because both these men were writers and not mere
word-polishers, each produced a considerable volume of inferior
work. Priestley admits he has written 'too much' (whatever that may
mean and anyway, it's hardly a thing for a writer to be ashamed of)
and in too many forms. I think this is unacceptable to anyone who
loves writing and knows something of the writer's life. Did
Shakespeare or Byron or Dickens or Wells write 'too much'?
Certainly they did; much of what they wrote was unworthy but it
should never be forgotten that the good usually climbs to its eminence
on the back of the bad. In my youth I had a friend who refused to
publish anything unless it reached a certain standard he had set for
himself. The result was that he published very little and what he did
publish has been forgotten. This is a pity because he was a man who in
fact had something to say.

We have been through a very silly time in the Arts since the last
War, aided and abetted, unfortunately, by what are usually referred
to as the 'posh' Sundays and certain elements in the Arts Council.
These are influential people and they seem to have come to some kind
of joint decision that values were old hat and that the main aim of
literature was sensation and shock. The result might have been
expected — it is no longer possible to shock anybody, for effing and
blinding has become fucking and buggering. Perhaps in the long run
this will be all to the good for it will be necessary to establish values

again. Discipline will no longer be stuffy, a succession of tricksters will no longer be hailed as geniuses and Priestley's work will again be considered and evaluated. I hope so. If I were asked to recommend just one of his books as a taster I would find it difficult, for the reason already given — there is none that really stands out from the rest like *Sons and Lovers* or *Ulysses* or *Passage to India*. But this is not sufficient reason for keeping quiet and so I would recommend *Midnight on the Desert* which is as good an evocation of contemporary society (even if largely American) that we are likely to find. It should be kept on the shelf for our posterity.

I hope I will be excused for using the abbreviation JBP throughout. It implies a blend of public recognition and affection. It is an accolade not easily won. Priestley's Order of Merit was well deserved and it was the correct honour to distinguish him from the hordes of time-servers and honest but unexceptional servants of the public, but to be known by one's initials is an honour few of us gain. GKC had it and HG (without the W) and also GBS — but who else? When one considers the possibilities one knows the answer. For example, Evelyn Waugh never became EW, for his undoubted brilliance as a novelist was accompanied by his equally undoubted unattractiveness as a public figure. JBP has at times been famed for his grumpiness and prickliness but no one can deny him what we understand by the term 'stature'.

A few words about my treatment of the subject. A major difficulty in writing about JBP lies in the great range of his work, both in form and content. This presented a considerable problem in management. To deal with it in strict chronological manner would be chaotic. To divide it rigidly into subjects or forms would be boring. What I have tried to do is to illustrate his development on several fronts, and at the same time devote sufficient attention to each front to give it character. In essence this involved a kind of leap-frogging method; its drawbacks are that there are areas of overlap and a certain amount of repetition, but I hope these have been more than offset by the advantage of illustrating both trend and variety together.

In books of this kind there are often several pages of Acknow-ledgments. I don't know who reads them or what function they perform, except perhaps that of gratifying one or two people with the sight of their names in print. As usual I am dispensing with this item in favour of a comprehensive Thank-you to those who have helped. But I will mention Mr Priestley himself who agreed to answer questions and usually did, and only occasionally made me feel that I was being a little idiotic. And perhaps I was.

John Atkins

Chapter 1

JBP — An Impression

J.B. Priestley is remarkable in our day because of the wide range of his writings. It is impossible to classify him simply as a novelist or a playwright or a critic. He has passed through many phases, and although one can describe these chronologically there has naturally been a certain amount of overlapping. But, as a provisional simplification, one can say that he began his writing career as an essayist, continued as a novelist, then as a playwright, then as a publicist and later passed through the role of critic to end (if he has ended) as a social historian. In his own view this parade of his ability has done little to enhance his reputation with those who are mainly concerned with making and breaking reputations.

> If you want to achieve a solid lasting success in authorship (he once wrote in the Introduction to a selection of his work called *Four-in-Hand*, 1927), at least in this country, the thing to do is to write the same book — for example, the same sort of novel about the same sort of people — over and over again. Then the booksellers, reviewers and University Extension lecturers all know where to find you.

Priestley is a professional writer in the full meaning of the term. This means that he has always had to write to live, and this in turn means that he has never been in a position to be hypersensitive about what he wrote. I mean this in no derogatory sense. A writer knows that excellence can never be commanded. One of his more friendly critics, Susan Cooper, claims that he always writes best when he writes quickly; this is particularly true of his plays. In fact, it is doubtful if a form that must be translated into nervous and physical reaction could ever survive repeated review and cogitation. But this point can be illustrated before he ever wrote a play. All his early works, before *The Good Companions*, 1929, which relieved him of financial worry for the rest of his life, were written under pressure. In the three years 1926-8 he produced nine books! Among them were his studies of Meredith and Peacock which were even praised by academics and also his *English Humour*, 1929, which is one of the best books written on a particularly difficult subject.

Priestley feels that his theatre reputation has suffered in this way more than the others. In a late book, *Outcries and Asides*, 1974, he suggests that if he had written only eight plays instead of over thirty he would enjoy greater esteem now than he does. This is not the whole of it, he admits. There are two kinds of versatility, one within the discipline and the other that straddles disciplines. If he had worked harder at being a theatre man, attending every important first night and spending most of his time with theatre people, while missing no opportunity of presenting himself to the public as a dramatist, and intervening as often as possible in any discussion of the theatre — then he might have been referred to grandiloquently as J.B. Priestley, the Dramatist. The theatre is suspicious of anyone who doesn't give himself to her entirely. All this business with novels . . . Versatility does not enlarge a reputation but reduces it.

But this is a mean-spirited, cramping attitude, and Priestley is unrepentant. In *Margin Released*, 1962, he addresses aspiring writers, and he throws caution to the winds.

> Perhaps . . . it would better not to be a writer, but if you must be one — then, I say, *write*. You feel dull, you have a headache, nobody loves you — *write*. It all seems hopeless, that famous 'inspiration' will not come — *write*. If you are a great genius, you will make your own rules; but if you are not — and the odds are heavily against it — go to your desk, no matter how high or low your mood, face the icy challenge of the paper — *write*.

And although JBP does not actually say it, we can be sure that he would agree with this addendum: write what you want to write, not what professors or reviewers say you ought to write.

Just as Priestley is a writer who turns to whichever form takes his fancy or which he thinks will best express his mood or thought, so he ranges widely in his choice of subject. In one sense his subject is simple because it is, when all is said and done, people; but people are infinitely various and he thinks of people in their variety, not in their cribbed and cabined sociological classes. There is a fashion these days for speaking of the 'essence' of a writer. If I were to look for JBP's I couldn't do better than excerpt a passage from one of his less regarded novels, *Daylight on Saturday*, 1943. The manager of the aircraft factory, Cheviot, takes Lord Brixen, the visiting Minister, on to the stage to address the workers during the lunch hour. He stares at the hundreds of faces turned towards him, and then follows a thoroughly characteristic piece of Priestley:

> There were faces of every kind down there: worn aging faces, smooth
> young faces, the massive blackened faces of experienced craftsmen, the
> painted little faces of foolish girls, the plump or lined faces of mature
> married women, the sullen faces of disappointed men, the impudent bright
> faces of boy apprentices, faces just beginning life and faces that had nearly
> done with it, brave, stupid, cowardly, clever, hopeful, merry, sick, de-
> spairing faces. Here were the people. Here was humanity.

And here is JBP's subject matter, the faces of the people and the
worlds that lie behind them.

For one of the main driving forces of this writer is his overmastering
curiosity. He is a writer, a novelist, a dramatist; but he also paints,
and paints well for an amateur; and his love of music is unquestion-
able. Whatever man does is something he feels impelled to investigate. Sometimes he stops to wonder why, as he does in *Particular
Pleasures*, 1975, when he wonders why he is attracted so strongly by
Smetana's Piano Trio in G Minor. It is no masterpiece, so why should
it haunt him so strangely? He admits he doesn't know and goes on to
say that there's a great deal about himself and life in general he doesn't
understand. He asks himself if he is linked to someone who knew
Smetana in 1855, and out of this question and others like it comes his
fascination with time which has dominated so much of his life. Does
the significance of this piece of music belong to the future, 'so that the
fatal heart attack will arrive in the middle of the third movement? Am
I?' he continues, 'Will it? But why go on? I don't know and neither do
you.' This kind of questioning lies at the base of all his best work. It is
the mystery about personality that drove him to his conjectures about
the significance of dreams. And oddly, it may be a writer who appears
to exist at the opposite pole of sensibility to JBP who may have had a
glimpse of the answer. Could it be William S. Burroughs, with his
conviction of the programmed mind?

He thinks of himself as a writer who has deliberately created his
own challenges. 'I did this by offering myself hard nuts to crack. The
kernels can be found in my best plays and novels. In these I am quite
original, not imitating anything done before . . . ' (*Instead of the Trees*,
1977). But his achievement has been ignored, he feels, because he has
not been wilfully eccentric, doesn't go in for self-advertisement like
Shaw, doesn't ask his wife and friends to regard him as a genius. It is
quite clear that he has been hurt by not having been taken more
seriously.

Apart from these rather meretricious reasons, is there a more solid base for the unfriendly attitude that has at times been adopted towards him? My feeling is that JBP is a very personal writer and has a way of referring everything he writes about to himself. This can have its dangers. It may attract some and repel others. We can see the process at work as far back as 1927 when he brought out a volume of essays entitled *Open House*. In an essay about the Yorkshire and England opening bat, Herbert Sutcliffe, he wrote:

> I remember once bringing out a book of strictly personal essays, in which it was avowedly, my intention to write about myself, yet one newspaper chided me for being egotistical and having so many I's to the page. That newspaper would complain that Sutcliffe used a bat too much during his innings. ('Sutcliffe and I')

A justified reproof, one might think, and yet it is possible that the reviewer did sense a degree of egotism that was likely to break bounds one day. And this happened in some of his later writings, where he has thrust his own tastes on the reader to an extent that is often more than acceptable.

I would like to illustrate this tendency from one of his recent books, *Trumpets Over the Sea*, 1968. The sub-title makes no bones about his intention: 'Being a rambling and egotistical account of the London Symphony Orchestra's engagement at Daytona Beach, Florida, in July-August, 1967.' One must admire the enterprise of this initiative whereby Priestley, well into his seventies, uproots himself and his household to accompany the LSO on the Daytona Beach Festival. The account is highly personal and his criticisms and valuations are equally so. JBP is the last man to accept any notion of absolute standards that can be experienced by the individual. Between the standard and the experience lies the psychological accident. Note his attitude to Bartok. 'Narrow, intense, fanatical, he isn't my kind of man; I keep my affection for broad, expansive, humorous and tolerant men,' adding that he isn't always very tolerant himself.

Well, he has warned us, but does that make us love him the more? Whatever he discusses, whether it is music, books, or the condition of England, he immediately refers the matter to himself, his state of mind at the time. He makes no attempt to exclude external influences — they are there and must be taken into account. When he caught his hand in a slamming car door he knew it affected his judgment for the next few days 'and it may help to explain some of my grumpier judgments.' At times he just wasn't in the mood to appreciate music that at other times he would have enjoyed immensely. For example, 'for various reasons, vague but probably faintly disreputable,' he didn't want an uplifting experience when he was present at a performance of Beethoven's Ninth; he wouldn't be 'hammered' into acquiescence and so he recoiled into boredom or irritation.

This is very honest but at times it becomes mere crotchiness. Perhaps he couldn't avoid it but was it worth inflicting on the reader? His curiously ambivalent attitude towards Sir Arthur Bliss (whom he refers to as a friend) is revealing. Bliss had told him he knew nothing about music and wouldn't discuss it with him. JBP affects to take this as a joke but his repeated reference to it suggests that he was hurt. Where musical taste is concerned, JBP can vary from the sensitive to the vulgar. He admits that he is an idle listener, 'too fond of large dramatic effects and lush sounds' — the very title of the book is revealing. I think it was this that Bliss probably picked on. When they were performing together on a Panel, Bliss said it was necessary to have a technical knowledge of music to appreciate it, 'otherwise you merely wallowed in sound like his friend Mr Priestley.' His friend Mr Priestley replied that he loved wallowing in sound, though he also had some technical knowledge. The result is that too much depends on his mood. He was not touched by Gervase de Peyer's playing of Mozart's Clarinet Concerto because — 'I was not in a good temper.'

At its worst, this tendency takes control of the author and becomes unnecessarily embarrassing. He begins one paragraph: 'But who cares what I was feeling on Friday 28 July 1967? I do. And you should do, if you have read so far in this book . . . ' He goes on to distinguish between the critic, attending in a kind of vacuum, and those who don't want to listen to classical music anyway, and to pinpoint his own kind, 'you and I, my friends, eager to listen to music but aware of ourselves and the world around us.'He enjoys writing about himself but he is seeking the *ambience*. It is scarcely the best way to do it. The root trouble, I feel, is a lack of charm, a matter to which I will return later.

Now there is one very important fact in JBP's life that cannot be omitted from any consideration of him and his career. He served through the greater part of the first World War, and we know how irrevocably many men were affected by that experience. We might reasonably believe that JBP found it a shattering experience. This is not the impression he gives, however. He did not react like Hemingway and Aldington, who were marked for life, nor like Valentine Avon, the popular novelist in his play *People at Sea*, 1937,

J.B.P. in the First World War

who had been badly wounded in the war.

> After my leg was shot to bits in the War, when I was still only a boy, I spent
> a long time in hospital, and there I began to amuse and console myself by
> living in a little dream world. Pure escape, of course.

But JBP, who joined the Army while little more than a boy and served
right through the horror, made no attempt to escape into a dream
world. In fact, he gives the impression of a man who is demonstrating
how he can master events and not be mastered by them. Hemingway
never recovered psychologically from his war wound. If I were asked
what Priestley's war wound was, I would reply that it was the
traumatic events of a single day, undoubtedly 1 July 1916. (It was also
Aldington's.) In one of his radio *Postscripts* Priestley said: 'On the 1st
July 1916 there were whole towns in the north — my own among
them — that lost at a stroke the fine flower of their young manhood.'
He has said much the same thing in an essay entitled, 'The Other
Christmas', which appeared in 1937: 'Most of the boys I played with
are dead, and not a few of them all died on the same day, July 1st
1916.'[1] One is struck by the calmness and lack of heroics with which
he makes this horrifying statement. It speaks out more powerfully
than many a complete book by other writers about the war. Among
the very few references he has made to his war experience we find this
one in *English Journey*, 1934. Saying that he didn't go down a mine, nor
did he want to, that he had been down one before and everyone had
read descriptions elsewhere, he added: 'Since I was buried during the
war I have taken a dislike to narrow little passages half a mile underground.' That's all.

'I was lucky in that war and have never ceased to be aware of the
fact,' he wrote in *Margin Released*, 1962. He was actually blown up in a
dug-out but the experience never affected him to the extent it did
Hemingway, from whom traumatically-based stories emerged as
frequently as fragments of metal from his body; nor could it be
compared with the bitterness of Aldington or even Henry
Williamson's euphoric reaction to that famous Christmas Day football match. JBP sidestepped the Wound and the Bow — he suffered
the wound but managed to throw off the complex. The significant
symbol for him was the fact of virtually unmarked survival. He says
he came out of the war divided between bookishness and an experience outside the normal one of development, and with two
opposing attitudes which he didn't know how to reconcile. People
wondered how he managed to shrug the war off. But when he got out

of the Army, only the future counted, he did not want to look back. He gave his bookish side a freer run. He was also divided between a tragic and a comic response to what he had been through. He felt the open wound of his generation's fate, of the best being sorted out and then slaughtered, not by necessity but by murderous public folly. This may be responsible for the odd sensation one receives when reading the account of war experiences which he eventually wrote down (in *Margin Released*). There is a lack of reality about his account, a feeling that perhaps he did not know how to suffer — in fact, something very much like the theatrical effect he refers to so often and to which I will later devote a complete chapter. There is no sense of doom, no catastrophe, none of the tragic sense that emerges so strongly from even the most inept writing about that war. This impression grows stronger as we read, until we hear of him reporting as a semi-fit man after his hospitalisation, to what he terms a 'lunatic labour exchange', which supplied labour of varying kinds to those who requested it. He found himself packing off comedians, baritones, female impersonators until he 'began to feel like a variety agent in uniform, or a man dreaming he was one.' And at this stage we begin to wonder whether Priestley dreams life or life dreams him.

That is one possibility, and a very weird one it is. But the more familiar one, the one that the general public has on the whole adopted, is that JBP is a very solid character who would be the last to panic in an emergency, what one of his critics, Gareth Lloyd Evans, called 'the reasosonable man's epitome' (in his Introduction to *J.B. Priestley — the Dramatist*, 1964), adding that at other times he seemed to be 'the self-conscious conscience of society.' But the popular image of a person may have two faces. The man who seems the soul of dependability to one may seem a monster of insensitivity to another. This is illustrated by the Graham Greene affair. In his autobiography, *A Sort of Life*, Greene writes that JBP threatened to bring a libel action if *Stamboul Train* was published unchanged. He identified himself with Savory, the popular novelist. Greene says he had J.H. Thomas and the pipe-smoking Stanley Baldwin in mind. All references to Dickens (Savory's and Priestley's hero) were deleted, also the pipe, 'blunt fingers' and the line 'Sold a hundred thousand copies. Two hundred characters.' This book appeared in 1971. I knew nothing of this contretemps when I wrote my book on Greene, which appeared in 1957, but nevertheless I was still able to make this comment on the characterisation of Savory: 'It might be Mr Priestley, whom Mr

Greene does not care for.' I then pointed out that Greene piled insults
on Savory and added that Greene was himself aiming at a popular
success (though with fewer than two hundred characters) and that he
'had made a fairly prolonged attempt to become a flattened version' of
Savory. ('Flattened' because Priestley goes in for rotundity.)

Whether one admires Priestley or rejects him as irrelevant, it is
impossible to ignore the pipe. It is tempting to identify him with his
pipe, to characterise him as pipe-smoking *homo*; he is photographed
with it, he writes of it lovingly, many of his characters retire to
corners to indulge in its savour (like Savory). In England the pipe
symbolises solidity, dependability, stolidity, stodginess . . . and allied
qualities. Priestley revels in it. In a chatty first chapter of his *Rain
Upon Godshill*, 1939, he admits to being a slave to tobacco. He doesn't
feel the least resentment. It appears to be a good master. Nothing in
the lower world of taste and smell has given him so much pleasure. He
quotes a New York journalist who once wrote with some acerbity that
JBP was 'the kind of Englishman who smokes a pipe.' It doesn't sound
attractive but JBP would find no fault with the description. He starts
an article ('Fifty Years of Tobacco') in the *New Statesman* of 14 July
1961 with the sentence: 'I have just realised I have been smoking a
pipe for half a century.' He has no illusions about any connection
between pipes and virtue. 'The pipe-smoker's appearance of solidity
and wisdom is of course illusory. Some of the biggest chumps I have
ever known have had pipes stuck in their faces.' He feels that much of
the medical animus against smoking derives from puritanism.
Politicians without imagination tax tobacco and let property deals go
scot-free. He gives detailed advice on pipes and their tobacco and how
to smoke them — e.g. complete the filling with the third finger, not
the first. 'Man, the creature who knows he must die, who has dreams
larger than his destiny, who is forever working a confidence trick on
himself, needs an ally. (Woman I include here in Man.) Mine has been
tobacco.'

The pipe is more than a physical comfort. It provides powerful
pyschological reinforcement. Whenever JBP wishes to present himself in person, to suggest a sense of satisfaction, or good company, or
harmony, he brings in his pipe. He said he was fortunate in the
trenches, chewing away at Army biscuits and bully beef, because 'I
was rarely out of tobacco, and if I could smoke my pipe, I could often
forget I was hungry and short of sleep.' Perhaps the Pipe neutralised
the Wound? JBP is capable of extremely evocative phrases, as I will

show later, and some of them are mingled with the smoke from his pipe. He got on well with Barrie, he says in *Margin Released*. 'I think I got by because I smoked a pipe as large as his, so that we puffed away companionably, like two engines in a siding.' I think the pipe can even give a clue to authorship where there is doubt, just as a special turn of phrase may do in other circumstances. In 1929 Priestley collaborated with Hugh Walpole on a novel called *Farthing Hall*. It is written in the form of an exchange of letters between Mark, who is twenty-five, and Robert, who is in his forties. My guess is that JBP wrote the Robert letters and Walpole Mark's, thus reversing their actual relationship.[2] True or not, it is Robert who retires 'to the fire in the bar-parlour to smoke the kind of pipe one achieves after turning a corner in a difficult chapter.'

It's in a book like *English Journey* that the homely, straightforward persona is at its strongest. He says bluntly that if he says a thing he means it, and is not trying to wrap his subject up in fanciful or unattractive paper, just to make a point.

> My standard may be rough and ready and somewhat uncertain, but you can assume it is a reasonable one. If I declare that Coketown is a horrible hole, I do not merely mean that it cannot be fitted in to some private fairy-tale Merrie England of my own: I mean that it is a damned horrible hole. And I hope you will take my word for it.

Cards on the table, then, and no welching. There are some awkward subjects where one has to tread very carefully if one is to retain the reader's sympathy. What about hunting, for instance? He doesn't understand hunting people, but they are enjoying themselves so let them get on with it, so long as they don't solemnly pretend to be doing their duty.

> The foxhunter who begins mumbling excuses, who tells you that he hunts to rid the countryside of foxes, the hunting is valuable because it improves the breed of horses (i.e. hunters), is a contemptible fellow. But I am prepared to respect the hunting man who looks you straight in the eye and declares in downright fashion: 'I hunt because I like it.'

He is even prepared to accept cruelty as an unavoidable component of life so long as it's not smothered under a hypocritical blanket.

Of course, he cannot be completely consistent. There have been times when he has dropped his guard and let a shocker through. This doesn't often happen in his writing, where it is usually possible to correct a fault (except in daily journalism) but there are other

occasions. On 4 June 1932, *The Times* reported Priestley presenting
prizes to the boys of the City of London School in connection with the
study of Shakespeare and English rhetoric. Some of the statements he
addressed to the boys were embarrassing; he actually told them that
'your schooldays are the happiest days of your life.' This is, in
ninety-nine cases out of a hundred, so utterly untrue that one can only
suppose that school prize-days bring out the worst in Priestley.[3]

But now I come to an aspect of Priestley that has been often noted
and that he has frequently admitted himself. He has a tendency to
grumble and complain to such an extent that the cumulative effect on
the reader can be actually unpleasant. In a book of short essays and
statements that many critics have admired, *Delight*, 1949, he supplies
a Preface called 'On the Grumbler's Apology.' He is renowned for his
grumbling and knows it. What is worse, he seems to glory in it. He
says it is not to be taken seriously and puts it down to 'unconscious
exaggeration.' He claims that his grumbling is often done on behalf of
others. No one, he says, can punish a writer if he tells the truth —
which is not strictly true in itself, although he is not as vulnerable as
most workmen. In extension he adds that he is instinctively opposed
to government and authority. This is all to the good but much of his
grumbling is directed at what can only be called fate and it is hard to
see who benefits from this.

I think this matter is worth discussing further because it plays a
very large part in the public view of Priestley. The day before his
eightieth birthday, Ray Gosling devoted a paragraph in *The Times*, 12
September 1974, to the Good Companion who had become a Grand
Old Man. Referring to his recently published book, *A Visit to New
Zealand*, Gosling wrote: 'It is impossible not to love him, a grumpy
Grandpa carping at failing to find a tobacconist and having to go
instead to a barber's shop.' Gosling then tried to sum up this 'old and
extremely grumpy good companion' and did it by reference to
another recent publication, *Outcries and Asides*: 'Gentleman Jack, he
says, is old. He says he does not give a damn. Yet he will not dish the
dirt. Rude, contemptuous, but never bitchy. He does not name living
names as Norman Mailer does and Alexander Pope did. He is a
generous writer, not a boxer or a Bernard Shaw. A ruminator, not a
stunt man.'

This is part of it. JBP also gives off an air of tremendous complacency. His method is to admit that he is accused of various
personal faults and to accept the charge, but always contriving to

present the faults as virtues in disguise. For example, Gosling calls him rude which he often is. But Priestley is a Yorkshireman and where he comes from rudeness is not a sin but something quite admirable, i.e. Yorkshire directness. He does this again and again, frequently repeating the same points, from book to book, wherever the personal may intrude. It is particularly noticeable in his later work.

His grumpiness has caused some critics to see in him a convinced pessimist. This he accepts. The label 'Jolly Jack Priestley,' was partly a product of the good cheer and optimism that pervaded *The Good Companions*. He has always resented what he feels is the false image projected from those early days and that early success. He says he has never been a good Theatre Man because he lacks the greasy optimism which it exudes. Now and again a temporary optimism overlays the natural pessimism, as during the Second World War when it seemed to Priestley, and a lot of other people as well, that England was at last struggling out of its deep-rooted class agony. It may seem a paradox that in his novels he is what he calls a 'happy-ending man'. It is really an attempt to defy his natural pessimism.

In *Rain Upon Godshill* he admitted his tendency to say No to every suggestion. Here he doesn't seem to be very consistent because later in the same book he says he has been snowed under with Christian, Buddhist and Theosophical publications which assume that a negative attitude of mind is the necessary foundation of genuine spiritual life, and then takes exception to this. But one should not look for consistency in JBP's thinking — he throws off ideas and opinions like sparks from a lathe and it's a matter of luck whether they cohere or not. Perhaps he hedges his bets. In correspondence with him I have found that any affirmative statement is almost always followed and qualified by a negative one. Here is just one example of his contrariness. On 9 May 1951 he attended Foyle's festival luncheon at the Dorchester Hotel. Replying to a speech by Morrison, the Foreign Secretary, he said however glorious the Festival of Britain might be, it could not compare with the age-old and glorious festival of English literature. Now this may very well be true, but his manner of saying it and the timing were unfortunate, and certainly did little to create the kind of atmosphere that was being sought. The truth is, he is irredeemably crotchety, and he knows it. He even knew it in 1927, when he wrote in an essay entitled 'Having Covered the Card Table' in his collection called *Open House*: 'If I get no praise for what I have done, then I am heartsick; but if praise does come my way, then it seems to me foolish and fulsome and I am irritated or embarrassed.' This could be a good recipe for a writer. I believe his admiration of George Meredith may have stemmed partly from his discovery in the earlier writer of certain attributes which were also his own. Meredith, he said, always worked self-consciously, seeing the critical eye upon him, and if it were not friendly, steeling himself to flout it. 'All his references to criticism and the reviewers, to his own position in the literary world, point to an extreme sensitiveness and self-consciousness' (*George Meredith*, 1926). This could apply equally to JBP who is hurt so easily by the failure of critics to take him seriously.

So he came through the War, the first of this century's Holocausts, without much harm. Reviewers and hostile critics have caused him more grief. He is a very personal man. I believe the events surrounding his divorce caused him more upset than anything else. He has married three times. His first wife died from cancer while still young, leaving him at the age of twenty-nine a widower with two small children. His second wife was granted a divorce (decree *nisi*) against him on grounds of misconduct on 29 July 1952. His third marriage, with Jacquetta Hawkes, appears to have been exceptionally successful. But the bitterness that attended his divorce seems to have remained with him and occasionally overflows into his work. The judge made an ass of himself by pompously accusing JBP of using his literary skill to seduce a married woman! In *Outcries and Asides*, which appeared twenty-two years later, he finally made a public statement under the revealing title, 'Riposte at Last.' The judge, he wrote, 'notorious in legal circles for his love of publicity,' had announced that JBP's conduct had been 'mean and contemptible.' A section of the press made the most of it, and JBP had no means of redress. He now wondered if our admiration for our Law and Press may not be rather complacent. Again his bitterness surfaced in his novel, *The Shapes of Sleep*, 1962. Sterndale's marriage had been a failure and he had let his wife divorce him, which was a mistake. 'You have to make it look mucky to persuade the judges there ought to be a divorce. Then they tell the world what a dirty swine you are, as if they didn't know, by this time, how it's been rigged.'

In recent years his writing has become looser and less accurate. Priestley has never given the impression that he takes many pains over his writing (I shall give instances of this in later chapters) but at times he becomes downright careless. There is no need to linger on this — it is a familiar enough tendency with all writers as they grow old — but *A Visit to New Zealand* might be examined bearing this in mind. He recalls an incident with Jacquetta which he says occurred forty years ago, but he has already said that he met her for the first time at a UNESCO conference. The dates simply won't coincide. The distance of New Zealand from England declined from 13,000 to 12,000 miles during the course of the book. This may sound very trivial but it is the kind of thing JBP himself would have jumped upon in his earlier days. He also says in the same book that he is not rich. Being rich and not being rich seem to be highly objective states, but I do not think the author of *English Journey* would have accepted the statement. According to Susan Cooper, who wrote *J.B. Priestley: Portrait of an Author*, 1970, he lives in 'an enchanting Georgian manor house with the most English of English meadows outside the windows and numbers of exceedingly beautiful objects scattered about the shelves and walls;' he can also retire to his flat in the very exclusive Albany, originally built for Lord Melbourne. Priestley frequently complains about the extent to which the Inland Revenue gobbles up his income, and for this he has my sympathy, but I think he has to be rich before the gobbling can start.[4]

But this is not really important, merely a minor piece of brushwork to fill out the portrait. Despite his feeling of being neglected, he has had many honours. The greatest of these is the Order of Merit, which he has richly deserved. As for the others, I will dip into the bag. Vice-President of the Conservation Society. Elected to the Council of the Royal Literary Fund, 16 March 1947. Delegate on the UK delegation to the second general conference of UNESCO, opening in Mexico City on 6 November 1947. These give an indication of his interests. There have been many tributes to him and his work. On 14 September 1969 BBC 1's Birthday Salute in 'Omnibus' was broadcast. Sir Neville Cardus, Lord Snow, Michael Foot, Pamela Hansford Johnson and Alan Dent all offered greetings, but the high spot was Sir Ralph Richardson's performance in the last act of *Johnson Over Jordan*. The speakers paid tribute to his tough adventurousness of mind, his gusto and aggressiveness and generosity of thought. As he gets older there seems a growing urge to celebrate his years. The *Times* Diary for 12 September 1973 reported a dinner to celebrate his seventy-ninth birthday and publication of his new book, *The English*. Apparently he produced a 'potent image' of what it is like to grow old.

It is as though walking down Shaftesbury Avenue as a fairly young man, he was suddenly kidnapped, rushed into a theatre and made to don the grey hair, the wrinkles and the other attributes of age, then wheeled on stage. Behind the appearance of age he was the same person, with the same thoughts, as when he was younger.

It would be impossible to produce a more characteristic example of Priestley's descriptive method.

But then there is the Prophet's Own Country. The story is sadly familiar. The *Times* Diary expressed itself flabbergasted on 28 November 1969 when it heard that only one of eight members of a sub-committee considering candidates for the freedom of the Borough of Bradford had voted for JBP, its most famous son. The committee proposed that two new freemen should be created, a business man and a neurologist, both local. Four years later Bradford, having illustrated its native philistinism, repented and commissioned Hockney to do a portrait drawing of JBP, to mark the conferment of the freedom of the city on him. The Director of the Bradford Art Gallery said, 'We thought it would be good if Bradford's most famous artist could draw the city's most famous author, and both were delighted.' By October 1975 Bradford University was naming its new library and computer centre after Priestley, who also opened it formally.

Two off-beat points before I finish this portrait. Priestley's first publication was a volume of poetry. It was a typical youthful entry on the literary scene, and it was the only one of its kind. But scattered through his prose works there is a considerable amount of verse. Some is serious, as in *Johnson Over Jordan*, 1939, and there were critics who said (with some truth) that this section would have been improved if he had been more of a poet. But most of the verse is of the kind I call Reaction Poetry, that is, it was satirical and intended to make fun of contemporary modernist poetry. It is to be found in the novel *Festival at Farbridge*, 1951, and the play *Music at Night*, 1947. (John Buchan and H.G. Wells, in their disgust with modern poetry, also introduced Reaction Poetry into their fiction.) It is therefore all the more surprising that on the 22 May 1959 he was guest of honour, with his wife, at the fiftieth anniversary reception of the Poetry Society. Of course, the apparent paradox is explained by the fact that the Poetry Society in those days was intensely traditional. Incidentally, the reception was held in the Grocer's Hall, a fact that would have delighted G.K. Chesterton!

For the other point we must go back to the war period, and look at the *News Chronicle* for the 3 June 1940. There is a picture of JBP, smoking his pipe and reading a book, 'from Photo by Howard Coster.' The headline is: ' "Take Your Own Towel" says J.B. Priestley.' He complains about the attentions of washroom attendants in expensive hotels and restaurants. They are unnecessary and should be banished. The war will compel us to do away with much of the useless frippery of our national life. 'England expects every man to take his own towel.' It is in fact an advertisement inserted by Lever Bros, who explain that they take the opportunity in their advertising to present different outlooks on today's problems by 'eminent modern thinkers.'

And has the eminent modern thinker a message for the rest of us? In *Margin Released*, 1962, he wonders why he remembers so vividly a trio that used to perform in the Lyons in Market Street, Bradford. 'I cannot imagine why they have stayed with me like archetypal images; I am writing in my sixty-eighth year of this life and understand little or nothing.' Perhaps the main reason why I am writing this book is that Mr Priestley, who has asked so many questions and delved into so many corners of life, has the courage to say publicly that he has very little idea what it's all about. No doubt one or two judges and Bradford councillors have a much clearer idea.

Chapter 2

A Provincial Comes to Town

One of the essays in his first book of essays, *Papers From Lilliput*, 1922, was entitled 'On a Certain Provincial Player.' It recalls an incident in the life of Bridge Frodsham, an eighteenth century actor who spent most of his career at the York Theatre. But on a ten-day visit to London he called on the famous Garrick and treated him as an equal rather than the dean of his profession, much to Garrick's annoyance. Such a tale is obviously very much to JBP's liking. He has never abandoned the air of being a raw but shrewd provincial who has come up to the Metropolis and finds, in his quiet way, that he could teach them a thing or two if he felt like it. (Incidentally, although he is usually called 'shrewd' by journalists he rejects the term. Naturally. It is his habit to contradict.)

The provincial theme is not an overmastering one but it is discernible and must be taken into account in any discussion of Priestley. He did not go direct to London, for his Army service intervened and then, on demobilisation, he took a Cambridge degree. During his last days in Bradford he wrote a weekly column for a Socialist paper called the *Bradford Pioneer* entitled 'Round the Hearth'. The style is that of the young journalist who thinks he is writing with sensitivity: 'Now is the time when hundreds in our midst are touched with the icy finger of that grim reaper, Death.' This is taken from the very first paragraph he wrote and fortunately he didn't keep it up. There is a strong note of assurance in this writing, his ideas and tastes seem ready formed: he is a socialist, he loves music and the theatre, and to enjoy himself he requires to be 'pipe in mouth'! We are asked never to forget 'our brothers and sisters who are being trampled down under a brutal inhuman system . . . '

A note on the musical situation refers to the Bradford Permanent Orchestra, and later in the year (1913) he praises the Halle and the New Symphony, and his readers are urged to buy piano music. Although he exhibits the usual loftiness of the young journalist and at times can be pretty scathing, there is no doubt that he was proud of his

Drawing by Austin 1925

native town, and in his later autobiographical writings he compared
Bradford very favourably with other towns of a like size. This makes

the city council's later reluctance to honour him even more repre-
hensible. It was not only Bradford he defended but the provinces in
general, and he declared them to be the source of all that was good in
the great devourer, London. Partisanship becomes local patriotism
when he compares the average Cockney unfavourably with the
average citizen of Manchester or Bradford. (One wonders how much
he knew of the 'average Cockney' at this stage. Seventeen years later
he was to demonstrate a close knowledge of and considerable affection
for him.) He admits to being a lover of 'good burlesque', and he
remains that to this day, though it is doubtful if he ever gets the
chance to see it. He deplores the average woman's periodical: 'for
sheer silly, insipid inanity, it is impossible to beat the typical feminine
periodical.' And, being very young, he confesses to world weariness,
and rarely reads a newspaper because he can guess the news of the day
from past experience. In his final contribution (by what the editor
calls 'our page 6 philosopher') he admits to being a dreamer, and
proud of it. He suggests that special colleges be set up with courses for
dreamers. Certainly a lot of the mature JBP was to be seen here in
embryo.[1]

Even when he had become famous, Priestley never let the world
forget his Yorkshire origin. A fellow Yorkshireman, Herbert Read,
who had become Londonised and partly homogenised, once made fun
of him in the pages of *World Review*. In the March 1949 issue JBP had
criticised the power in the theatre of certain critics who were 'all style
and impressionism.' Read replied with heavy irony, affecting a
journalistic style that did not come naturally to him. 'Close your
ranks, ye introverts, and advance! Banish the spectre of Shakespeare,
untelescope your images, write honest prose' and more of the same
tedious stuff, ending with the presumably hilarious 'what Bradford
applauds today, London will accept tomorrow.' Read accused JBP of
having a 'divided mind', apparently because he is a sensitive person
who appreciates character but unfortunately woos the masses. Proper
critics, we are told, reject his values. This will serve to illustrate the
hiatus that rose between Priestley and the avant-garde writers of the
thirties and forties, and I mention it here because this seems to be
another occasion, judging by a later reference in one of his books,
when JBP felt he was being unfairly attacked. When looked at objec-
tively it is certainly a rather odd confrontation. Read was the man
with the great reputation, especially among the young, while JBP was
the old dodderer, the has-been. But this is largely eyewash. Read's

reputation was largely undeserved; he wrote insipid poetry and he was a sucker for any new apocalyptic movement, writing pamphlets in support of Anarchism, Surrealism and Social Credit in rapid succession. He could also be extremely peevish in controversy. (To do him credit, he was capable of moral courage, as when he defended two anarchists in a trial during the war.) On the other hand, it was Priestley who tried to rouse English drama during a very slack period, who experimented in both manner and content, who became fascinated by the nature of Time and worked consistently, throughout his life, to involve his readers, without making a silly season of it, before darting on to Space and then, perhaps to Bionics. If this was Yorkshire steadiness, it served him well and it's a pity Read lost it.

Priestley was apparently aware, from his earliest days, of the imaginary line that cuts England in two, separating the North from the South. It is not peculiar to JBP — other writers, such as Orwell, have commented on it, and there are times when one is tempted to regard it as one of the basic facts of English life, like class division. Whether the two Englands were produced by the Industrial Revolution, as JBP believes, is doubtful. In his book on *The English*, 1973, he could hardly ignore it.

> In the smoke-blackened regions, extending North from the West Midlands, ordinary people referred to 'Down South' as if it were a foreign country, and were still doing it when I was a youngster in the West Riding. (In spite of all the more recent changes, this feeling of being different from 'Southerners' still lingers in the North.)

It is a powerful undercurrent in *The Good Companions*, where Northerners and Southerners mingle, on the whole amicably. Chapter two, which introduces Miss Trant, stresses that this is a different England from that of Bruddersford. 'Pleasant green mounds' replace 'the dark Pennines', 'clear valleys, each with its gleam of water' replace the reeking cauldrons' that had once been valleys. 'This is, indeed, another England, this green and windy outpost of Arden'. It is also the England where JBP later chose to settle. Jess Oakroyd, full of the Northern self-admitted virtues, found the Southerners rather effusive — they 'did overdo this patting you on the back and making a fuss when you did some little bit of a thing: it made you feel soft.' Southrons were affected, with too much of the 'Please' and 'Thank you'. As for Londoners, they were 'a bit of a foul lot', and Mr Oakroyd felt obliged to warn Susie Dean.

Having looked at the *Bradford Pioneer* we are prepared for these judgments. They must seem right and proper to anyone North of the Trent. It is no surprise to find them reproduced in JBP's early work, although I certainly do not wish to give the impression that they are particularly intrusive. It contributes another strand to JBP's make-up but on the whole it is muted — unduly so, I imagine, from the traditional tyke point of view. We find it in *Benighted*, 1927, which appeared two years before *The Good Companions*, and here it is put in the mouth of Sir William, who came from a little village in East Lancashire. He is asked if the people there made a fuss of him now he is rich.

> They respect the money but not me. They care about money up there, know what it's worth, and don't pretend to despise it. Now in other places, particularly in the South of England, they pretend they don't care about money and they also pretend to think a lot about me, who happen to have plenty. The other's the best way . . .

But Sir William is a fictional character, and we cannot off-load his ideas on to his creator. JBP is on the whole tolerant towards the South and when he does reproduce the Northern sense of moral superiority one feels he does it a trifle sardonically. Perhaps he gave way to it more than usual in *English Journey* and this should not surprise us for it is a book which is greatly concerned with the regions and regional feeling. He describes a re-union battalion dinner, where he meets 'Daddy', who had been a Major, and was not a West Riding man but a South Country schoolmaster, 'whose character and reputation were such that through him the whole affected tittering South Country was forgiven everything.' It seems that a child brought up in Yorkshire would have had little chance of acquiring an impartial view: 'in my time we in Yorkshire considered the Lancastrians as people worth considering as people, real folk (not like the vapouring creatures from the South Country) . . .' As a dramatist JBP felt he could embroider this: plays often opened in Manchester and 'what pleases Manchester is sure to please the easy idle set of playgoers in London.' He attends a dinner in Manchester, with speeches. 'The wooden face that they could all achieve was obviously part of their performance as droll speakers, and I suspect that the grins and giggles of the London after-dinner speakers, who want you to realise at once that they do this sort of thing awfully well, would have been frowned upon here.' It is interesting to note that JBP has stated two or three times that his own face is over-expressive, and presumably not North Country deadpan.

I have gained a certain amount of amusement from writing this chapter as I was brought up in the Eastern counties and have had occasion to be both irritated and astonished by both sets of pretension, emanating from both ends of the North-South extension. We have to accept Northern rudeness — sorry, I mean directness — and Southern triviality — sorry, I mean good humour — because we are outnumbered and colonised. But I can certainly understand JBP's complaint about the Arts Council, when it subsidised a West Riding Theatre, which proved a failure. It seemed a lot of people in the smaller towns were frightened by the very idea of an Arts Council, inevitably consisting of 'superior persons from down South, giving them fancy stuff for which they had not asked.' (*Theatre Outlook*, 1947) One could imagine them wanting *When We Are Married* and getting *Time and the Conways*. But I am not so sure about that party in Dunedin which was improvised at short notice, a fact which he attributed to the Scots background and tradition.

> But isn't Scotland notorious for mean penny-pinching and every form of stinginess? Yes — and so is Yorkshire. And, my astonished friends, for the same reason. The Scots and the Tykes can afford to have these mean and stingy jokes against them; indeed they often invent these legends themselves; simply because anyone who has lived among them knows they are hospitable and generous. Surrey, let us say, or Herefordshire or Leicester would instantly take offence at such gibes — they might, as people say, be 'too near the knuckle' — so nobody risks them. We Tykes and Scots just laugh and pass the bottle. (*A Visit to New Zealand*, 1974)

So once again, we are a very modest people, and if we *do* shout our virtues rather loudly it's for the edification of those unfortunates from Surrey, Hereford and Leicester. But all in all, JBP is a fair-minded man and no one has been more generous in his praise of Southerners when they have proved themselves than he has. What Yorkshireman could have imagined that London would stand up to bombimg the way it did? This is what Priestley said of them in one of his radio *Postscripts* in 1940.

> A lot of us, especially if we are from the North, and thought we knew everything, imagined that that old cockney spirit was dead and gone. We thought the Londoner of today, catching his tubes and electric

trains, was a different kind of fellow altogether, with too many of his corners rubbed off, too gullible, easily pleased, too soft; and we were wrong.

Not many people admit being wrong. Years of experience have helped JBP reverse the unflattering picture of the 'average Cockney' expressed in the *Bradford Pioneer*.

And now we are ready to consider the young man who set up shop in London as an essayist, after serving in a war which, if it left its marks, left them very deep.

Chapter 3

The Essayist

His first book was *A Chapman of Rhymes*, 1918, which he himself referred to many years later, in *Instead of the Trees*, as 'a collection of dubious verse, written in my teens before the first World War and sent to be published, entirely at my own expense, during that war when I felt, foolishly, I ought to leave something behind.' It need not detain us here, except to fill in the record.[1] He says that in later years he destroyed every copy he could find but has seen it priced in a bookseller's catalogue at £250.

The twenties were still the age of the essay-writer, when several weekly and monthly periodicals still printed rather artificial set-pieces on any and every subject that might spring to the writer's mind, however trivial, and publishers were still prepared to bring out collections of them at the end of every season. There was a convention of titling them *On* Something or Other, and Hilaire Belloc once brought out a collection under the simple title *On*, a *reductio ad absurdum* which should have killed the species off immediately, but didn't. It lingered up to the second War, with Robert Lynd carrying the banner.

In 1957 John Lehmann edited a collection entitled *Coming to London*, in which each contributor was asked to describe his own initiation into the capital. (These were not familiar essays, because they had a definite subject and gave specific information.) In his own contribution JBP admitted that he wrote at least one essay a week for many years during the twenties. Geoffrey Grigson, in the same volume, referred to most of the big names in contemporary writing as 'bookish', i.e., they wrote out of books and developed a kind of bookish sensibility. JBP certainly got himself entrenched in this area. Paradoxically, the bookish writers used to insist that they wrote about 'life', but it was vague and generalised concern with petty personal details, usually trivia, without any discernible passion. The only method of escape lay in fixing the mind on a definite object to which everything else could be related — it might

be architecture or archaeology or even poetry — so long as the
resultant paragraphs did not waffle on about 'life'. JBP chose Time,
or Time chose him, and thus he escaped. Much of his writing,
especially the apparent coincidences which seemed to lead him on,
suggest that Time chose him and presented an unavoidable
destiny. In various places JBP has suggested that coincidences do
not really exist but are part of a plan. For example, in the later
novel, *Saturn Over the Water*, 1961, Tim Bedford runs into 'what look
like ridiculous coincidences' but in fact he doesn't believe they were
coincidences at all — and it is he, or JBP, who supplies the emphasis.
The H-bomb was another fact or thing or object which helped jerk
Priestly out of his cosy little essayistic world. Looking back on this
early work, he sees them as literary exercises. 'There was nothing
much I really wanted to say, but for some years I took great pains
with these pieces, like a man learning how to play an instrument'
(*Margin Released*, 1962). On the credit side it can be said that they
gave him a fluency. They also gave him bread-and-butter, an
important thing for a young writer, for the weekly essay provided
an income for Priestley which is completely lacking for the young
man or woman starting today. If the reader feels I am too harsh or
unsympathetic in my attitude towards the essay he will find a
much more appreciative approach in Eric Gillett's Introduction to
his selection of JBP's essays which he called *All About Ourselves*,
published in 1956.

The first volume of essays (though in this case the term was not
accurate) was called *Brief Diversions*, subtitled 'Tales, Travesties and
Epigrams', and it appeared in 1922. A shy note paid homage to
Lord Dunsany and T.W.H. Crosland as writers of tales. The tales
in this volume are not impressive — in fact, the short story is one
of the few prose forms JBP has not been particularly happy with.
The travesties, which were really parodies, were a different matter.
It was an achievement for such a newcomer to the literary scene to
get inside and project writers so diverse as Saintsbury, A.E.
Housman, Alfred Noyes, Yeats, 'Q' and 'AE'. It is odd to think
that while it was this section of the small volume that impressed
the reviewers it was a style of writing to which JBP never returned.
Instead, during the decade of the twenties there appeared six
volumes of essays-and-nothing-but-essays, the genuine two
thousand word article, gathered from one or more of the cultural
periodicals that abounded in those days. The last in this series was

called *The Balconinny*, which appeared in 1929.

I would like to refer to three of these collections in more or less detail, and in this way try to distil the essence of JBP's work in this field. *Papers From Lilliput* based on essays originally entitled *Papers From New Lilliput*, appeared in 1922 in fact it followed hot on the heels of *Brief Diversions* in the same year. The essays were reprinted from *The London Mercury*, *The Nineteenth Century* and *The Cambridge Review*. Some also came from a series he contributed to the *Yorkshire Observer*, under the pseudonym Peter of Pomfret, and others from *The Challenge*. These latter began on 29 September 1922 with 'On Being Kind to the Old', dropped the *New* from the title in 1923, and ended with 'On the Choice of a Title' on June 1923. It is obvious from these dates that most of the essays contributed to *The Challenge*, which was primarily an Anglican review, were not included in the book.

From the very beginning JBP gave indications of a mind and a talent that would not be satisfied with the normal trivia of the familiar essay. One of the better items in this collection is 'In Praise of Hyperbole', because it treats seriously a matter of some importance rather than waffling about personal tastes and prejudices. It states that hyperbole is an essential part of artistic production because it gives a sense of the first-hand to a second-hand account. A good point. But unfortunately the Familiar Essay is apt to seize on an aspect of the writer's craft and then overdo it. So you get this kind of thing (it is the opening sentence of 'On Travel by Train') which becomes distinctly tedious after a few repetitions: 'Remove an Englishman from his hearth and home, his centre of corporal life, and he becomes a very different creature, one capable of sudden furies and roaring passions, a deep sea of strong emotions churning beneath his frozen exterior.' The less we have of that kind of hyperbole the better.

It is almost impossible to choose a meaningful title for a book of random essays, and so the authors developed a special technique. The title might be spuriously literary (with a touch of the twee) as in the *Lilliput* collection, or it might be outrageously personal, as in the next collection to appear entitled *I For One*. This was 1923 (no pause for breath) and the essays were reprinted from *The Challenge*. (In fact, they had originally appeared in the series, 'Papers from Lilliput', which illustrates how irrelevant these titles were.)

The first essay, 'On Beginning' (*sic*) discusses the task of the essayist. He need not always be melancholy, though he probably will be, because 'there is something both absurd and decidedly impudent in this business of talking about oneself for money.' The essayist has nothing to cling to, he has no compelling reason for writing, everything is spun out of himself — and this is the death-sentence of the essayist, who once flourished. He has no content, and his works declare it by their titles.[2] Priestley is as aware of the falseness of the essayist's role as his most severe critic. He knows that the essayist always wears the same mask, one which assumes fear, insolence and the incapacity to concentrate on a single subject. He smugly asserts his laziness, stupidity and fecklessness, not believing in them at all — anything but! And today the Familiar Essay has disappeared, victim of its own triviality.

In this collection we have examples of the genre at its worst and its best. Belonging to the former group is 'This Insubstantial Pageant', which is no more than froth about a single slither of a notion, a mini-idea — that London is unreal — but the exigencies of journalism required it to be stretched like bubble-gum to two thousand words. It is an inferior form, but there are degrees even in inferiority. JBP never acquired that easy balance which was occasionally achieved by GKC or Robert Lynd. It is an essayist's boast (but all his boasts are anti-boasts) that he never knows how he will last the pace, and in JBP's case he often does sound like that. 'An essayist will make open confession of his ignorance and frailties,' he wrote in 'Those Terrible Novelists', leaving it to the reader to exclaim: 'Oh Mr Priestley, you can't be serious!'

The form is exhausted because there is only one Essayist.[3]There is no such thing as an individual essayist, only one mass Essayist who speaks — or spoke, one is relieved to say — through a hundred mouths. It was inevitable that very soon he had said all he had to say, and could then only repeat himself. Where there are exceptions we find that they really transcend the familiar essay and are pieces of discursive criticism. 'The Cult of the Revolver' comes very near to being a successful piece of ironic polemic. In fact, it only falls short because there is an implicit agreement, between author and reader, that this is after all only an essay (fun) and not criticism (serious). And 'A Coincidence' is in fact a splendid piece of literary management. It slowly gathers momentum and punches its message home with its very last two words. But there you are — coincidence was a matter about which JBP had definite views.

Not that JBP was altogether writing with his tongue in cheek.

He believed, in those early days, that there was something to be said for the essay as a literary form and he expressed this view very lucidly in the Introduction to a collection called *Essayists Past and Present* published in 1925. He was very positive about the essay's value and maintained that it should be a vehicle for the author's personality and not centre on the consideration of a particular subject. 'The real essayist has no subject or, if you will, has every subject in the world at his command, for the simple reason that his business is to talk about himself or to express the relation between any subject and himself.' What he is doing here, in effect, is citing what we today usually regard as the weakness of the essay as its strength.

Probably his best known collection was *Apes and Angels*, 1928. Its title belongs to the paradoxical mode, like *Tremendous Trifles*. Like many of the essays in the earlier *Open House* and *Talking*, most of these had appeared in the *Saturday Review*. It is dedicated to Gerald Barry and 'his Saturday Reviewers'. In 'First Snow' we have the essence of the familiar essay. 'The first fall of snow is not only an event but it is a magical event. You go to bed in one kind of world and wake up to find yourself in another quite different, and if this is not enchantment, then where is it to be found?' *Magic, enchant* — these are key words in this genre. But again, they cannot be dismissed so lightly in JBP as they can in other essayists of the day because we will find that for him *magic* has a positive meaning which, though difficult to catch and put on paper, is something more than an evasion which helps to fill a page. Then there is the idle boast. In 'The School Magazine' he refers to those boys who are no more than 'impudent loafers', then adds in parenthesis: 'Being a safe distance from my school and the duty of teaching the young, I can afford to declare that these are the boys I like best.' None of the academic stuff for me, you see — down with learning and scholarship and art and all that nonsense — and this was written by a man who was devoting part of his life to scholarship[4] and learning and art, and who had been so good at it in his passage through university that he was invited (as he tells us more than once) to become a don himself. It is a pose which he acknowledges in 'Other People's Accomplishments' when he writes: 'I know that it is the fashion among men who write essays to pretend to be more idle and ignorant than they really are.' It is a profession of poseurs.

The cardinal weakness of this kind of writing is splendidly

illustrated by an essay entitled 'The Wicked People'. He takes a cavalier attitude towards facts and history, in order to justify a thesis which in any case is not adopted seriously but merely to fill out the columns Barry required by Wednesday morning. There are enough hit-or-miss statements about monarchy and aristocracy in this essay to send a serious historian raving mad — or the later JBP, for that matter.

One must ask why he never made a reputation as an essayist comparable to those of Robert Lynd or E.V. Lucas or Hilaire Belloc. I think there are many possible answers. He had some very definite things he wanted to say, when given the chance, but he came late on the scene, when the form was already fading. I doubt if his heart was ever really in the essay and perhaps he heaved a sigh of relief when this mode went out of fashion. He knew all the tricks, and could employ them skilfully, but he could not always hide a sense of strain, which was never noticeable in Lynd or Lucas. One feels that he is counting his words and sometimes, when he has miscalculated, has to double back to a theme which he had already raised and dropped. (This was all the more likely to happen in a writer who cannot always control his carelessness at the best of times.) After this collection there was only one more genuine book of essays to appear in his name. After that there are publications which are classified as 'Essay' (in the singular) but they are serious pieces of writing on serious subjects. There were also to be broadcast talks, lectures and sketches, but no more Familiar Essays; the genre was dead. There was one apparent exception, for his *Delight* has been called a book of essays, but is nothing of the kind. It is a collection of short, sharp *pensées*, with none of the casualness of the old-fashioned essay.

Priestley made a selection of his essays in 1937 which he called *Self-Selected Essays*. It is a good selection because it avoids the light-weight items, those which were obviously only written to answer a dateline and were about nothing in particular. Thus the regulation self-deprecatory, self-admiring remark is largely absent, but not entirely. For example, 'I am the kind of man who can make any suit of clothes look shabby and undistinguished after about a fortnight's wear.' The same remark was made about Hemingway, but it came from his wife, which is where it belongs. It is all part of the romantic view of the ordinary man which underlies the romantic theme in literature. He appears ordinary but underneath he is a monster or a genius, his passions rage, he tears himself and his clothes to tatters. There is an excellent example of the romantic hiding beneath a prosaic mask in one of the *I For One* essays, called 'Charles Rupert Purvison'. Purvison was, in appearance, a drab civil servant of low degree, a teacher on a small income, one who constantly made economies and took cheap holidays. But he glamourised everything.

> By merely remarking — but no, not remarking, for he never remarked — by letting out the secret that he had just been on a journey, he could fill my mind with galloping thoughts of dangers encountered and over-come, with hurrying images of lost jewels, masked men, dead bodies under the seats of railway carriages, anarchists falsely bewhiskered as ticket inspectors, and so forth.

This kind of writing was typical of the period, though it went back to the Victorians, who were the first to hail normal business routines as romantic. Dickens had been full of it — business men and merchants creating their empires. There was a related image in Buchan's *Huntingtower*, the shopkeeper who was a poet at heart. Chesterton gave it colour — the grocer in touch with Assam and Mandalay. Swinnerton described clerks and agents as if they were yachts scurrying across the bay. Adventures galore beat beneath the waistcoat — or, indeed, the petticoat as Maxwell illustrated in his *Spinster of this Parish*. All of this was in opposition to the other pole of the romantic extension, the love-lorn, the vampire and the grave. JBP was still inside this movement and not part of the revolt against it (which was contemporary with him) which detested business and howled against its squalour. JBP saw the squalour but he managed to divorce it from the person of the mill-owner. When he turned to the novel he could not resist allowing his characters to don disguises. For the disguise often reveals the buried truth.

Another aspect of the early work, which I think can also be attributed to the romantic view of life, is his obsession with cir-cularity, the end returning to the beginning. I have already referred to the first essay in *I For One* called 'On Beginning'. It ends with a repeat of his first sentence, plus a brief comment. 'On Hating Strangers' has these words: 'I began with Charles Lamb and I can very well end with him . . .' It suggests a desire for completeness, not only the aesthetic satisfaction of a pattern but the more psychological satisfaction of a plan. Possibly it helps account for the immense success of his most popular novel, *The Good*

Companions, which begins and ends with a football match 'on the backbone of England'. The Epilogue that follows is merely a false limb tacked on to the true story. The circular idea remained with him at least up to the war for we encounter it again in the play, *Ever Since Paradise*, 1950. It ends with a return to the beginning — or, in other words, it starts with a flashback, film-style. There is nothing mysterious or even vaguely supernatural about it, it is simply a theatrical trick, but it's indicative of JBP's obsession with repetition and renewal and, by implication, manipulation of the time-scale. Circularity involves a time-loop and, so far from disappearing from JBP's view, it merged with a concern that was to be treated far more comprehensively.

'Though I kept right on into the thirties writing weekly essays,' JBP wrote in the *Sunday Times*, 25 June 1961, 'I knew that this kind of essay, personal in tone but elaborately composed, was already almost an anachronism' ('I Had the Time', reprinted in the *Sunday Times* collection, *Encore*, 1962). Susan Cooper says he found the form too congenial and too undemanding. Also, the public changed — the essay collection disappeared from the publishing field. This was a cultural development that could not be ignored. Short pieces are still published but both authors and publishers prefer to call them just that: pieces. Here is an example of a literary style that has gone forever. It is taken from 'The Pessimists' in *Open House*, 1927. Two young friends call on the author:

> Last Sunday they were in magnificent form. They bellowed their news and stretched themselves in my sitting room, sang and splashed in the bathroom, and then came down to put away the lunch of six. My bottled beer went winking down their throats. My coffee disappeared between two epigrams. They filled their youthful and aggressive pipes, blew out great blue clouds of old matured Virginia and young raw satisfaction, and then accompanied me into the garden, where we lounged and smoked through the afternoon.

One can imagine the old clubman slapping his thigh with appreciation as he read it. Today one's feelings approach nausea and one wonders how sensibilities could have altered so radically in the space of fifty years. Such writing is as dead as Addison. It serves as an exhibit of the High Georgian style. It was formed by the society from which it came. It is robust, forthright, suspicious of nuances, it finds poetry, which it honoured, in sensations only, it deprecates thought, it is grossly satisfied, and it never questions the basis of such a cheerful existence. It believes it is incredibly clever and it never rises above the level of polished stupidity.

Priestley has left this sort of thing a long way behind. He writes now about real things and he manages to temper his confidence. But you cannot spend a decade of your youth writing in a particular way and remain unmarked. There are moments when, probably because the spirit is tired, there is a reversion to an outworn style. It may be only momentary. I sense it in one of the appendices to his *The Art of the Dramatist*, 1956, when he writes, 'It is not egoism, though I am probably crammed with it . . .' which might be seen as the last fling of the Essayist, setting before us for just one more time that quaint old rascal, The Author. But there was a more serious lapse. It occurred in 1977 and was called *Instead of the Trees*, subtitled *A Final Chapter of Autobiography*.

Priestley has stated many times that he has written too much, that he has been his own worst enemy and written more than enough for his own good. In this book he gives advice to a young writer, much of it tinged with bitterness. Don't be afraid of 'a few large golden daydreams,' he writes, which is presumably a rather coy way of saying don't be afraid of the romantic. Don't drift along, waiting for a challenge to turn up. Write too little rather than too much; play hard to get. Don't dodge about too much, keep to the same kind of thing so that you fit neatly into Eng. Lit. pigeonholes. Never oppose the Establishment, who control patronage. Don't become associated with unpopular causes. There isn't much body in most of this. Once again it is the author's personality which has become the centre of interest. The book is really a disguised return to the collection of essays, the genre he favoured in his younger days. One asks: Was this book really necessary? He is certainly catering for his regular readers, loyal souls. There is a clubbish air about the whole thing. I think Priestley might reply, as he has replied before, the book is about myself, so what do you expect? But there is something displeasing about its self-centredness. He pushes his personality at us. He pretends to be apologetic but it sounds more like self-admiration — an old dodge, as we have seen. And the self-admiration is the Yorkshire kind which can be pretty odious. One wonders why he has to keep repeating that he is grumpy but loveable. In fact, the book lacks charm — and as I have already said, charm is a major lack in all his work. Now charm is not necessary in a discussion of the political situation but it is absolutely essential in more personal matters.

The Familiar Essay has gone but the short piece remains and I would like to finish this chapter with a consideration of this later development. *Delight* is the bridge. Like so many minor books by well-known authors, it is a revealing one. It consists of 114 snippets with a Grumbler's Apology as a Preface, and the book is dedicated to the family by the 'old Monster'. Although ostensibly concerned with things that have brought him delight it has a strong undertone of things that have caused him displeasure, because so much of what he has enjoyed is in the lost past and has not been replaced. The tone is still that of the Familiar Essay (he pays tribute to E.V. Lucas and Robert Lynd); it is the fag-end of a tradition he had seen die — urbane, whimsical, nostalgic and poking fun without being malicious. But these pieces are not essay-length. They are squibs.

There is no doubt that things are getting worse all the time. Real tobacconists, who knew their commodity, have disappeared and have been replaced by 'bored pushers of packages across counters.' No one writing in today's newspapers can compare with Belloc, Chesterton, Tomlinson, Beerbohm and Lucas. The disappearance of the old children's games was 'further evidence of a decline in real living values.' Nothing has ever been able to replace the peculiar enchantment of the old stereoscope. What it really amounts to is that JBP has changed rather less than the world. Thinking of his childhood, as he does all through this volume, he writes of 'the wreck of a shining world'. There used to be 'verbal jugglers', 'illusionists of logic', when he was an undergraduate. When he asks if students are no longer fascinated by their tutors we know the question is rhetorical. It seems somehow to represent an astonishing lack of imagination; one would not have expected JBP to fall for this lachrymose view of the Good Old Days. Perhaps he was sometimes aware of this, for when he deplores the lack of comic characters nowadays (naturally they were ten a penny when he was a boy) he does qualify it by saying he has made allowances for adult taste!

The volume also hums with anti-youth attitudes. (We'll hear more of this later.) Young people are often referred to as 'clever young monkeys', and the most he will grant them is that they are probably sincere in their idiocy. He harps continuously on his age and the senility he insists is almost upon him, his fatness, the degeneration of his faculties. 'I am knee deep in the soggy world of greying hair and rotting teeth . . .' He was fifty-five! It's an odd image of delight we get. The only enjoyment he seems to find in his contemporary world comes through the family, where he seems capable of relaxing and enjoying private jokes and horseplay. But at times the reader is tempted to ask how sincere the catalogue may be. His paragraph on 'Giving Advice' invites wonder. This is a delight, giving advice, especially when he knows he has no right to give it. There follows a list of disqualifications: 'I swing violently from enthusiasm to disgust . . . I base my judgements on anything — or nothing . . . I cannot plan, and if I could I would never stick to the plan . . .' And so it goes on. But where, here, do we find the person who has the right to criticise anybody?

So it's goodbye the Essayist. But certainly not goodbye J.B. Priestley. From some recesses of his personality he dug up new resources and when he returned to the short form he preferred not to call it an essay. *The Moments* appeared in 1966 and its full title was *The Moments and Other Pieces*. Most of them had previously been printed before in the *New Statesman* and they reflected that periodical's concern with public affairs. The change from Lynd, who had been a previous regular contributor, to Priestley was radical. Here he is constantly concerned with Government policy, the H-bomb, the Communist World and the Third World. He still writes about personal matters, but he relates them more significantly to the world about him. And, an unexpected result of this change, the personal touch becomes more attractive. he's not such an opinionated old bore after all, we think. Probably the single most revealing sentence in the whole book appears before the table of Contents: 'Mr J.B. Priestley made an outright gift of this book to Oxfam.'

To complete the transition from Essays to Pieces I will quote a couple of shorts from *Outcries and Asides*, 1974. These pieces are as short as the ones in *Delight* but they are for thinking adults. A few are taken from 'The Uneasy Chair' feature in the *New Statesman* and together they comprise a kind of Table Talk, as he himself says. There is a vast amount of wisdom in this unpretentious, unheralded book. Nearly every piece contains the gist of an essay, but it is stated simply and without any of the excrescences that mar that form. There is, it is true, an occasional descent into Georgian whimsy, e.g. a piece entitled 'The Dummies' which is mere verbal-

ising about the imagined lives of ventriloquists' dummies. But this
passage (from 'Ideologies') might profitably be inscribed in stone
and set up in Trafalgar Square for every marcher, politician,
demonstrator and publicist to read:

> In medieval Nuremberg, you may remember, some wretched prisoners
> were condemned to torture or final execution by the Iron Virgin or
> Maiden. They were placed inside this hollow effigy, which had a
> number of spikes that began to inflict terrible wounds and would finally
> kill them when it was completely closed. The Iron Maidens of our age
> are the ideologies, whether of the Left or the Right. Ordinary humanity
> is forced inside them, and then begins to bleed.

And this, 'Passing Thought', is a gem which I quote in full:

> How happy we ought to be nowadays! Just consider if you can manage
> it without vertigo, the innumerable research scientists, experimental
> psychologists, psychiatrists, sociologists, who are toiling and bringing
> out reports at conferences and pronouncements in the public press, all on
> our behalf! Why, it makes me feel that I spent my childhood, boyhood,
> youth, in the Dark Ages. Only the prejudices and sheer stupidity of old
> age can account for the feeling I have at times that we don't seem to
> have arrived, after so much care and public expense, out into clear
> sunlight, illuminating the eager eyes of youth and the contented faces of
> the old.

Chapter 4

A Patriot

I thought about patriotism. I wished I had been born early enough to have been called a Little Englander. It was a term of sneering abuse, but I should be delighted to accept it as a description of myself. That *little* sounds the right note of affection. It is little England I love. And I considered how much I disliked Big Englanders.

from the final chapter of *English Journey*, 1923.

Patriotism, note — not nationalism, which he attacked bitterly in an essay written over thirty years later in *The Moments*. Note also the use of that word 'affection'. We will come across it many times before we are finished.

I am trying to build up, piece by piece, a complete and recognisable portrait of this man, J.B. Priestley. Here is another element, his patriotism, his love of England, his unashamed admiration for many aspects of the past, and the old traditional way of life. The second War formed a watershed in his life — it seems to have affected him much more deeply than the first one, in which he served, ever did — and on the whole the pre-war love came to be tempered by a post-war concern. Of course, like all generalisations, this is only partly true. *English Journey* showed his concern for what was happening to his native country before the war got going, though it was already clear to people like Priestley that it was on the way. But after the war this concern was transformed into a passion, as Susan Cooper noted in her book on Priestley: 'Through no deliberate intention of his own, at least half of the major creative works which he has produced since the end of the war have been from their conception imbued with his unending passion for stirring the English into new life.' For JBP loves the English and is exasperated by them. Stirring them is not easy — but then there are two sides to this. At times they seem unbearably stolid but this protects them from the bouts of hysteria which often assail other nations.

There are two ways in which a patriot may be alarmed by the way things are going. These are the awareness of virtues that have been lost and awareness of follies that are being committed. What I might call the traditional traditionalist follows the first path while the critical traditionalist follows the second. Here is JBP in the former role. Writing in *The Prince of Pleasure and his Regency*, 1969, about the Great Frost of 1814 and the Cockney's adaptation to it, he inserts a parenthesis positively dithyrambic in tone: 'Ah — what we have lost! Oh, to have gone to Frost Fair, to have eaten oysters at a few pence the dozen, and brandy-balls and ginger-bread, and then to have tried pricking the garter!' One of the cleavages that exist in English society is between those who are saddened by such changes, and think they are for the worse, and those who don't care a damn. One sees it at its widest between generations. A young man in the novel, *It's an Old Country*, 1967 (the title is deliberately provocative) says the whole population is living in different centuries. 'My dad doesn't understand me, and his Dad — he lives with us, if you can call it living — doesn't understand *him*. Even Sis and me's miles apart — what she wants, I don't — and what I want makes her ready to throw up.'

Publishers soon realised that JBP was a thoroughgoing patriot and just the man to write or edit those standbys of our literary scene, books in praise of ourselves and our land. Look through the Priestley bibliography and the titles will jump out at you: *The English, English Humour, The English Comic Characters, The Beauty of Britain, All About Ourselves, Our Nation's Heritage*. To dip into one at random — *English Humour*, published in the English Heritage Series in 1929, with a general introduction to the series written by Stanley Baldwin in a flurry of clichés and dead language. The humourists are the expected ones and special chapters are devoted to Shakespeare, Dickens and — Lamb! Priestley's admiration for Lamb is at first surprising but on reflection inevitable. Lamb is just the sort of writer who would appeal to him! The choice is at first surprising because Lamb must surely rank as the prototype of forgotten English writers — I doubt if even the educated Englishman would think of him as the author of anything more than a mild little essay about roast pork, with a few retold tales from Shakespeare thrown in. In fact, most of us would not think of him as a humourist at all although we might grant him a certain element of charm. Now this is just the quality that JBP's writing so often lacks, and this may explain the attraction. Lamb is again praised in the book on *The English*. I once heard that monument of jollity, Hugh MacDiarmid, state in his loveable way that he wanted nothing to do with a people that had a high opinion of Charles Lamb and one immediately felt, irrespective of Lamb's true position in the literary world, that one wanted nothing to do with someone who turned his mind into a sledgehammer. It is in the midst of these tensions that the quiet figure of Charles Lamb assumes an importance for patriots that seems to bear little relation to his talents.

The English, 1973, is 'an informal attempt to explain' them, writes JBP. 'They are not unreasonable but they are hardly ever strictly rational . . . they prefer the open-ended.' The barrier between the unconscious and their consciousness is not fixed, is not really complete. This is the essence of Englishness, the 'guiding thread in the maze.' He returns to this again and again, the refusal to rationalise is the *Leitmotiv* of the English. Live and Let Live is their motto. He tests selected men and women from different areas for their Englishness. Rather surprisingly (to me) he presents Cromwell as one who stands for 'Englishness on the largest possible scale.' He moved into the dark of his mind, its deepest recesses, to find the answer to his problems. His career is the geatest triumph of what he calls Englishness. Despite these claims, JBP never really tells us in what Cromwell's Englishness consists. He moves on to safer ground with Charles James Fox, who *knew* so many things without going through any of the usual ratiocinative processes, and usually knew them rightly: 'A prime example of Englishness.'

JBP himself, of course, is another. Writing on 'The Uncommon Common People' he says the chapter will 'wander around like an old man's thoughts.' This describes his normal and most successful literary method, relying on instinct rather than on established rules. During the thirties he was told he must decide between Communism and Fascism but replied that he didn't want either. This was called muddling along, and he was content to do this like the majority of his fellow-countrymen. A more subtle example is illustrated by his attitude to the public schools, recorded in this book. Instead of jumping on the band-wagon and deploring them and their influence he admitted their good points, which were many. For a progressive to write this is regarded as an instance of crankiness, flying in the face of truth — but it is also an instance of Englishness at work. We never know enough to be anything but open-minded in opinion. In action it is necessary to make a choice at certain times. But these times come at intervals.

He is a great admirer of John Cowper Powys and quotes from his *Autobiography*, where he describes a friend by saying he 'combined scepticism of everything with credulity about everything.' With such an attitude, one cannot accept violence as a means to an end. The English, constantly relying on what is instinctive or intuitive, would not produce either the fanatical rationality or the sudden breakthrough of wild irrationality that leads to it. He admits that this can sometimes encourage a cosy self-deception when vigilance is required. 'I am convinced,' he writes, 'that all really violent revolutions exact a dreadful price: the pendulum swung high comes crashing back, to be stained with blood again.' This is an article of faith that most thinking progressives in this country have arrived at now. And so the once despised Lord Halifax, the trimmer (George Savile, first Marquis of Halifax, 1635-95) is given high and honoured rank in the hierarchy of Englishness. He remained in the centre 'where sensible government could be carried on, distrusting all movement along extreme positions, and always determined if possible to "trim the boat".' Among the poets he singles out Wordsworth, whose 'promptings' suggest that his unconscious had been breached by consciousness.

JBP is very determined in his use of the word 'Englishness'. At times he becomes heavy-footed and by too rigid (and unEnglish?) definition gets into difficulties, as when he excludes that most English of artists, Sickert, because his father was a Dane, and includes the German Delius, possibly because he was born and brought up in Bradford. Delius was, of course, as English in spirit as Sickert. But having said this, one has to admit that the inconsistency is a wonderful example of what he means by Englishness. In his discussion of the humourists he seems to expand, for it is in humour that he finds identity. When he encounters a warm and humorous spirit he surrenders himself to the quality he calls 'delight'. The grumpiness for which he is famed is normally caused by the hypocrisy or preciousness of those who should know better — or their humbug, for he is one of the few remaining writers who still uses that word, so important at the beginning of our century. Is it merely a matter of fashion or do we now accept humbug? And then there is the repeated admiration for Charles Lamb, whose genius was so quiet and subtle that it is almost impossible for the rawer spirits of our time to appreciate him. JBP claims that the essential ingredient of true humour is affection, and it is this he finds in Lamb. And coming to our own time he mentions Evelyn Waugh as an extremely amusing writer but a man without affection.

Donald G. MacRae, Professor of Sociology in London University, once chose and introduced a selection which he called *The World of J.B. Priestley*. He begins his Introduction with this statement: 'It may seem odd for a sociologist rather than a professional critic or historian of literature to introduce a selection from the work of a man like Mr Priestley who is novelist, dramatist, critic but quite certainly not a professional social scientist.' To anyone who knows and appreciates JBP's work it does not seem odd at all. I do not value him particularly for any literary excellence, for it seems to me that his creative ability and originality are limited, but as a phenomenon that arises from and embodies a particular type of social persuasion. In him one sees a large slice of twentieth century England, emergent and active. He proclaims the life and diversity of the English, writes Professor MacRae. This is true, but there is also something more. Beyond this act of social reflection, he himself, in the variety of his work and the range of his interests, serves as a kind of social concentrate. Compared with the thin and evanescent talents that have driven JBP and writers like him from the literary pages of the superior Sunday papers, he is a cornucopia of richness.

This type of writer, social phenomenon rather than artist, had his heyday at the beginning of the century. It was the age of the Grand Old Man, the sage who knew all the answers, who wrote about any and everything. They were known by their initials (GBS, GKC, HG) which seemed to denote an honour bestowed by the populace, more democratic and yet far more elusive than those other initials, MBE, OBE. Priestley is in this tradition by right, but chronologically he arrived just too late. And if an English writer is not honoured by the people he has little chance of being honoured at all, certainly not by the Establishment. In *The Prince of Pleasure* JBP wrote: 'it has been one of the persistent weaknesses of the English Establishment that it has always tended to underrate the influence and importance of writers, so many mere scribblers in its eyes.' His social impotence has always irked him. Like many other writers he has raged against the folly of those who control our destinies. But this is a cross which every patriot must bear, if he is a true one. Only the specious patriot will please.

Chapter 5

The Turn to Fiction

In 1927 JBP published a novel. In fact, he published two novels, for *Benighted* came hot on the heels of *Adam in Moonshine*. This is typical of his pell-mell method: a sudden new enthusiasm grips him and he cannot rest until he has exploited it. It happened with the novel, it happened with drama, it happened with Time, it happened with politics. It would not be true to say that each succeeding passion completely drove out the preceding one, for JBP is a man of great energy, but it did become dominant. Thus between 1927 and 1930 he produced five novels. During the thirties, up to the outbreak of war, he produced five more but now his energies were more importantly taken up by the drama. The first five contained two of his best novels, *The Good Companions* and *Angel Pavement*, 1930. The second five contain none that rank among his best work.

I do not intend to discuss every novel in detail. *Adam in Moonshine* is a romantic fairy story about a young man who unexpectedly finds himself involved with a group of anarchists. It was the kind of novel that was already old-fashioned in 1927. In *Margin Released* JBP calls *Benighted* 'an attempt . . . to transmute the thriller into symbolical fiction with some psychological depth.' After a good start, it fails as JBP himself admits. Its main interest comes from its trying to do something that later became popular in the hands of such writers as Graham Greene and Eric Ambler. I shall say more about these novels at the appropriate time, but would now like to pass on to *Farthing Hall*, 1929. This is interesting because it was written in collaboration with Hugh Walpole, with whom JBP stayed in the Lake District. This was very helpful to JBP as Walpole's reputation guaranteed a larger-than-usual advance royalty.[1]

It is written in the form of letters. Shorn of its desire to be ultraclever and to show off, this would be a pretty entertaining novel. The design is neat and the treatment effective but every now and again there comes a passage of excruciating poetic jolliness which, it is true, was fairly standard form in the twenties but now does no more to the reader than irritate him. Some of the letters are really disguised essays; the main essay period was approaching its end for JBP, but the habit of treating ideas in an essayistic way still remained strong. Idle thoughts masquerading as wisdom came easily from JBP's pen. 'Have you ever noticed when you've been here (London) how certain faces and figures keep cropping up in the crowds and theatres and shops?' one of the correspondents asks, and there follows a page of leisurely disquisition on this theme, tedious for the modern reader. Who wrote that? There are several clues. One of them, or both, loves to describe the more sinister characters as enormous, huge, violent — seemingly ten foot tall, crazy with drink, ready to knock hell out of you. It's a line in romantic characterisation which we often encounter in Priestley's early novels. *Benighted* had had its quota.

The Good Companions, which appeared in the same year, made Priestley's name known throughout the British Isles. It was one of those enormous successes which spread far beyond the normal reading public and which, from time to time, really do turn a writer's name into a household word. Priestley's attitude towards it today is diffident and ambivalent. It has caused him a certain amount of embarrassment because he does not regard it as his best work of fiction, yet it is still the novel by which he is best known. Writing in *Instead of the Trees* of the fascination he had always felt for the big picaresque story (he has written Introductions for *Joseph Andrews* and *Gil Blas*), he says his publishers viewed the project with disfavour. To him it is 'a fairy story set against a fairly realistic background.' (*Adam in Moonshine* was probably an earlier attempt at the same target, but failed on the realistic side.) If his publishers disliked the idea they were horrified by the title, but JBP is a stubborn man and his stubbornness has often been justified. The simple, unpretentious, old-fashioned title was still capable of appeal even in an age which had learnt to accept more sophisticated or literary titles such as *Point Counter Point* or *Decline and Fall*. It was a bestseller and JBP is a bit rueful about it. I doubt if he was rueful about the royalties. 'I was blamed by the fastidious minority for writing it at all.' Afterwards he was blamed by the disappointed majority because he didn't go on writing the same kind of novel again and again. He believes he has done better things (most critics agree) and has a particularly high opinion of *The Image Men*, 1968-9, (which most critics haven't).

The Good Companions must be regarded as a literary phenomenon rather than a masterpiece and it is necesssary to consider its quality. One result of its success is that JBP is often referred to as merely a Yorkshire writer who succeeds splendidly with West Riding types but is at sea when dealing with the Southern middle class. But if the novel is read carefully this criticism can be refuted. (This type of argument is found automatically with any writer who obviously has regional roots, such as Thomas Hardy and D.H. Lawrence. It is as untrue of them as it is of JBP.) Miss Trant is sensitively observed, and the Southern artistes score well, even if not one hundred per cent successful. Inigo Jollifant is a parody at first but gains in credibility. Jerry Jerningham is not one of JBP's more successful creations. But Mr and Mrs Joe and Morton Mitcham and Susie Dean are as good, in their way (and it is a very different way) as Jess Oakroyd. And when we mention parodies we should bear in mind that some people (Jerningham is a good example) are inevitably parodies in themselves.

The fault lies in what I call criticism prepense. Two things go to make a good portrait, observation and understanding. Oakroyd is certainly understood as well as observed: JBP would not have attempted this novel if he were not. The others are all observed; it is the understanding which may at times falter. Like Hardy, JBP usually got it right, and both of them got it more right than Lawrence did, although his record is a good one. We follow certain formulae; one is that the countryman is raw and humourous, and is regarded as real, while the middle class is polite and restrained, and in itself only engenders a quiet literary mode. The aesthete exists to be mocked, and is made unreal. These conventions make a bigger impression on the average reader than the skill with which the portraits are depicted. Miss Trant is in fact just as real, just as well observed, just as well understood as Jess Oakroyd, but she doesn't appear so because she hasn't the advantage of being quaint or old-world or homespun. The convention was much clearer in the case of Dickens, a model for Priestley, because it is only his eccentrics who make much impact. Dickens didn't really give a damn for the Cheerybles but JBP gives much more than a damn for Miss Trant.

The Good Companions provides quite an intricate pattern in dualism and opposition. It is true that Jess Oakroyd represents the Old World, and Miss Trant a newer one, yet in the terms that JBP later elaborated in *English Journey* they both represent nineteenth century England as against the twentieth. Each in his way is driven from his old home by the vulgarity of the new. It is in this sense a novel of affirmation, perhaps the last great example of that type to appear. Oakroyd, Miss Trant, the Good Companions as a whole and most of them as individuals, represent the last-ditch, desperate and doomed stand of the old against the new. And JBP does not make the mistake of finding all his virtues in the past and none in the present, which is a temptation frequently succumbed to. Miss Trant meets a man in Cambridge who fiercely proclaims that the world progresses; he is thinking mainly of architecture, and he refuses the thoughtless assertion that we have lost the talent for building well. We can't build like the cathedral builders, but also we don't want to, it wouldn't suit our style of life. This is a valuable caveat which we imagine Miss Trant never forgets.

It is really a question of living with all one's faculties and not dropping off to sleep. Miss Trant, around whom the novel centres, finds herself being involved with other people, and common people at that. At first she is appalled but she pulls herself together, telling herself she must meet life as it comes and accept it. She did not want to marry but she was determined not to be 'old-maidish'. 'She must not mind being jostled by things, by people, by life; she must be ready to take hold of herself.' It also represents, as the picaresque always does, the good old tension between the Apollonian and the Dionysian aspects of life. It is constantly stressed that there are two ways in life, and the main characters are in fact deserting the life of outer discipline and restraint for the more demanding but also more exciting one of self-discipline and self-expression. The struggle receives its most marked expression when Miss Trant's sister Hilda appears upon the scene. (The name recalls Hartley's Hilda in the Eustace trilogy, and the characters are similar. Apparently it is as suggestive to the English mind as are Rose and Lily.) 'As a wife, a mother, a mistress of the house, she is a sensible and capable woman; it is only as a social being, a member of society, or rather two societies, for she is always leaving one and struggling into another, that she is somewhat ridiculous.' She is, rather oddly, not so very different in her attitude to life from Mrs Oakroyd.

But people themselves are two-sided — a recurrent theme. Miss Trant knew there were two Hildas. One was reproving, the other apparently permissive, when she can make social captital out of it, explaining away the antics of her younger sister: 'there she is, hiring theatres and designing costumes and all the rest of it. Oh, quite crazy, of course! But very amusing and original, don't you think? Exactly! Why not? That's what I say.' And in fact there had for a time been two Miss Trants, wrestling with each other, but now there was only one, 'looking boldly upon the world.'

The novel does exert a tremendous spell. The good companionship of the Good Companions makes a direct appeal to the uncomplicated emotions that lie at the heart of all of us. Speaking personally, I became really aware of this effect when Elsie got married and left the company and a replacement had to be found. What will she be like? Will she fit in? These are the questions that immediately arise. You care, as you don't care about Lucky Jim or Philip Quarles. It is because the Companions are completely real and recognisable. At first I had misgivings about Inigo. When we first meet him, as a schoolmaster, he seems to be full of confidence with his constant wisecracks and banter, and then he becomes quiet, restrained, even naive. But later you realise that this is exactly what would happen to a young man of his sort in his position; slowly the real Inigo emerges, he finds himself, for while that dreadful school had made a clown of him the concert party drew the best out of him. This is what we mean when we say a character grows. Adam has escaped from his moonshine, Mark French (of *Farthing Hall*) has got his girl and has at last grown up.[2]

Before coming to *Angel Pavement*, which appeared in the following year, it is instructive to take a quick look at a story called *The Town Major of Miraucourt*, which was given separate publication, as it illustrates an interesting point about JBP as a writer of fiction. It should be of enormous interest, for he says it is his only war story, but we very soon discover that it is nothing of the kind. Only superficially does it come out of his war experience; basically it derives from his reading, for his soldiers are quite explicitly modern versions of Falstaff and his crew. This kind of stimulus is not uncommon in Priestley's work, plays as well as fiction, and it could throw light on one of the mysteries underlying *The Good Companions*. The life of the concert party is described with enormous conviction and yet JBP had never had first-hand experience. Did he find his model in *Nicholas Nickleby?*

This is not such an idle question as may appear, as I hope to show in the course of a brief survey of *Angel Pavement*, which many critics consider his best novel. It might well serve as a model of the type of English novel that preceded the present one. The change in fictional style, which occurs roughly once in every two generations, is marked. JBP himself has followed the trend. His more recent novels, such as *Sir Michael and Sir George* or *The Shapes of Sleep*, 1962, are economically pared to the bone (and therefore shorter) compared with the affluence and exuberance and the proliferation of descriptive language to be found in *Angel Pavement*. The characters are for the most part treated humorously (even in tragic moments there is always the discernible shadow of irony), even as figures of fun, a mode which the developing modern approach rarely permitted. (I use the past tense because there are signs that this mood is returning.) The author takes the reader into his confidence and even gives an occasional nudge. It verges at times on an Old Pals Act.

Here is an instance of a device which was frequently used in the prevailing novel, starting with Dickens and probably ending with Priestley. (Wells was one of its most assiduous practitioners). Mr Dersingham, we are told, 'never did anything about it, because he was waiting — as he always said — until he knew where he stood financially.' And then we get this comment in parenthesis: 'From which you might gather that he knew where he stood philosophically or socially or politically or artistically.' It is a Pooterism that has disappeared from our literature. Characters are treated at length and with no regard for verbal economy. Before Mrs Dersingham actually enters the story, for instance, we are given four complete pages of partly psychological, partly social description. The tone is condescending, though filtered through an apparently generous sympathy. And so the character is projected through a film of authorial opinion.

I have mentioned Dickens and this brings me back to the *Nicholas Nickleby* reference. It seems possible that Graham Greene once taunted JBP with his love of Dickens, though he denies it. Modern novelists, often under the influence of critical opinion that has its origin in Central Europe, cannot bear Dickens, equating his humanity with sentimentality and his humour with social indifference. There is no doubt that the Dickensian strand in JBP is, or was, very strong. Mrs Smeeth discussing her daughter's prospects in the hat trade, for instance, would not be out of place in — *Nicholas Nickleby!*

> Millinery. You know Madam Rivoli's in the High Street, the place where I got that very nice purple hat of mine that fell into the water at Hastings that time? Mrs Talbot keeps it now. You know, her husband died of eating oysters about four years ago, and nobody round here would touch 'em for months — well, that's Mrs Talbot, a little woman, looks a bit Frenchified — smart, y'know, Dad, but overdoes it a bit. I pointed her out to you one day, and you said if you'd legs as thin as that you'd take the trouble to hide 'em and I thought she heard you.

Of course, it's not mere imitation. If it were, *Angel Pavement* would have impressed no one and would be as dead now as *Adam in Moonshine*. When JBP got to London he very quickly discovered Dickens there, still living, and in this novel he managed to plait together into one strand the second-hand of his own percipient reading and the first-hand of his own personal discovery. The passage quoted is comedy but along with the humour goes the underlying sadness, the bedrock of melancholy our lives are built on: the hopeless loves, the shabby misunderstandings, the familiar dreariness. This novel pulses with the tragic sense in a way that JBP never managed again. Without it, no fiction can reach the highest quality.

Angel Pavement may be important because it does sum up, in literary garb, a moment in our social history, as *Tom Jones* and *David Copperfield* and *Tess of the Durbervilles* and *Sons and Lovers* each did in their own times. The sheer injustice of the multiple ruin caused by the casual acts of a casual interloper is an apt prelude to the muddle JBP discerned throughout the commercial world in *English Journey*. No comment can be more apt than Smeeth's, when he considers the wreck of his life. 'Not good enough.' The ejection of the Mittys is a symbol of the necessary revolution. The reason why this is a fine novel is because it operates on the symbolic level as well as the workaday. Everyone is defeated and everyone is determined to fight back. This is the essential JBP quality and it is lacking in most of the literature that followed. The world could play all manner of tricks with Herbert Smeeth, 'but could never capture, swallow and digest the whole of him.' Since *Angel Pavement* we have become accustomed to a series of knockers but very few fighters. It is part of the English tragedy.

Priestley puts far more emphasis on the fantasy-life of his characters than most novelists, either then or now, and this constitutes an important part of the books's quality. He knows that dream is as much part of individual reality as any sense impression. He is also wise enough to know that a man's spirit is not the whole of him. The apotheosis of the mind running wild is Thurber's Walter Mitty, only dimly related to the Fred Mitty of *Angel Pavement*. JBP steers skilfully through mid-channel. At the end one expects Golspie to get his come-uppance, on moral grounds. (JBP has high moral standards, and they have nothing to do with prudery or goody-goodiness.) But he doesn't and for a very good reason. He has been dealing with Londoners, Southerners, a poor lot, and it is obvious from his conversation with Sugden, the Lancashire business man, as they leave the Port of London, that such people deserve all they get.

The remaining pre-war novels are not important enough to warrant examination in any detail, though I shall refer to them later to illustrate certain points in JBP's career. *Faraway*, 1932, and *Wonder Hero*, 1933, were followed by *They Walk in the City*, 1936. In *Margin Released* JBP admits he made a hash of it: 'it ends in melodrama and not even good melodrama.' *The Doomsday Men*, 1938, deserves a little more attention. The *Times* reviewer called it a 'good rough-and-ready adventure story' (29 July 1938). He added that Mr Priestley had written 'a satisfactory story for the holidays (which) contains a hint of the serious thought to be expected of the author of *I Have Been Here Before* (1937).' By this time JBP had started a new reputation through his drama, and it is there that he aired his more serious intellectual opinions. But the *Times* reviewer did draw attention to an important aspect of Priestley's writing which is that whatever form he is working on, even one that is apparently concerned entirely with entertainment, such as the thriller or the children's story, he can never exclude the more serious implications entirely. *The Doomsday Men*, for example, may appear to the casual reader to be concerned with the fate of a family fortune or a blonde's virginity, but for JBP and his more alert readers its subject is the fate of the world itself. Three brothers, each disillusioned in his own way, decide to destroy the world. Between them they have the capacity to do it: one is a scientist who has discovered the ultimate weapon, another leads an apocalyptic religious cult, and the third is a millionaire many times over. Always the great difficulty in this kind of book is to maintain credibility. It starts well, a sort of gentle Raymond Chandler affair, but it deteriorates — not into actual incredibility for that doesn't really matter, but into stylistic banality which can't sustain the content. The fact is that JBP writes well in the *Angel Pavement* vein and can sustain it, but cannot sustain the *Big Sleep* vein.

Let the People Sing, 1939, carries the adventitious interest of having been written in response to a BBC request for a novel suitable for serialisation on radio. It must be considered in the context of its time, 1939, and its unusual genesis. David Hughes writes: 'It remains one of the few books by Priestley that I would recommend no one to read,' adding that its laughter is linked with bombs. But it cannot compare with the later *Black-Out in Gretley*, 1942, for gloom. It is not a very good novel but as it belongs to a genre that fascinates Priestley, the picaresque, it deserves some attention.

Timmy Tiverton, a comedian, is down on his luck but he's one of those gallant pros who used to delight JBP on provincial tours and whom he was to commemorate so lovingly in the last section of *Particular Pleasures*, 1975. It resembles *The Good Companions* because it is about a travelling show, the oddly assorted members of which manage to rouse the sleepy population of a half-dead provincial town to new-found life. It is an *England, Arise!* sort of novel, written when JBP realised what was coming and hoped the English would be able to snap out of their lethargy. It is fairly stiff with symbolism: Timmy's companion in his adventure is a Czech professor and they are both on the run from a law that is either unjust or mistaken. They represent Knowledge and the Comic and they are both without a home. One wonders whether the similarity in theme with *The Good Companions* implies a temporary loss of invention or was it a cold-blooded decision to repeat a popular triumph for the BBC, who catered for the masses? In fact, there is more genuine picaresque quality in this novel than in the earlier one. Of course, it is not eighteenth century picaresque, but why should it be? Only a reader befogged by academic disciplines could imagine or demand it. The classical picaresque had a hero who was young, handsome, witty, resourceful and probably, to his own surprise, heir to a vast fortune. This new hero of Priestley's is of his own time, and verges on his immediate successor in the literary parade: the anti-hero. He is ageing, he is rather odd-looking and he is certainly not witty. Instead, he has an inexhaustible sense of humour. He is always resourceful.

Perhaps he is closer to the other form of the picaresque, the Quixotic. He goes out to do battle with a world he no longer understands and he is mildly ridiculous to the inhabitants of that world. But he tilts at more than windmills and he usually manages to knock them down. There is a great deal of exaggerated comedy in this novel, as in the portraits of the Professor and Sir George Denberry-Baxter. We know that JBP was a great admirer of the Marx Brothers and there are passages here which one feels he was consciously scripting for an anarchic team of their type — for instance, the scrimmage in the Market Hall. If, as sometimes happens, JBP is accused of being non-realistic, the critic should ask himself if he would say the same of the Marx Brothers. (Incidentally, *Festival at Farbridge*, a later novel, actually ends on a Marx Brothers scenario, a dinner given to the Festival organisers by the Ancient and Noble Order of Stags.)

There is one major weakness in this novel. It lies in the main character, Timmy Tiverton, who just isn't funny, yet is intended to represent the living spirit of Comedy. This is, of course, a major stumbling-block standing in the way of all but the greatest novelists — to go beyond telling the reader that a character is comic (or wise or attractive, intelligent or sinister) and to demonstrate with full conviction that he is comic (or wise or attractive, intelligent or sinister).

In 1938 Harvard university published a pamphlet entitled *An Exchange of Letters*, which contained a Foreword by JBP. The exchange was between the Dean of the Philosophical Faculty of the University of Bonn and Thomas Mann, on the occasion of the latter being struck off the roll of the Faculty's honorary doctors. Priestley's contribution began: 'In these pages there will be found two Germanies, addressing one another across a dreadful gulf' and it ended: 'And behind the noble melancholy of this remonstrance of Mann's, we may discover what, unhappily, so few people seem to understand, namely, real patriotism, the patriotism that brings us the duty — in our author's own fine phrase — of keeping pure the image of one's own people in the sight of humanity.'

Apart from the solidarity shown here between writers and academics in the face of a shocking example of cultural persecution, an additional point of interest lies in the fact that Harvard chose JBP to represent the writing fraternity of the democratic world.

Chapter 6

Magic and Dream

Magic is not a word the modern writer cares to use — but refer him to Yeats and it becomes momentarily respectable. He will probably try to explain himself by saying that with Yeats magic was objective, not a will-o'-the-wisp of the imagination. *Objective* is a magic word, of course. There is probably a deep-seated belief in even the most rational person that magic, that is, a force that is not amenable to the laws of science as we know them, does exist. But then the laws of science as we know them are probably fairly primitive. Priestley often uses the word *magic*. He is referring to some unknown quality which he is convinced exists. In discussing his early novels I have mentioned his deep concern with fantasy-life. It may seem odd that this concern is most noticeable in his least successful novels, but it is not really odd when we consider that he is trying to describe something that will only yield to metaphor. In this chapter I intend to illustrate his grapplings with that elusive quality.

David Hughes read *Adam in Moonshine* while in Bradford, in search of the influences that went to mould JBP. He could not understand how such a fairy-tale could emerge from such a place. Then he thought of the moors. 'To raise your eyes from a blank urban street and glimpse the hills, soft and untenanted, beyond the rooftops: that was a reassurance, an emphasis on magic, that the boy Priestley had never forgotten,' he wrote in his *J.B. Priestley: an Informal Study of his Work*, 1958. JBP himself makes frequent references to this contrast and usually relates it to this word, *magic*. He is fascinated by borderlands — between dream and wake, reality and fantasy, home and theatre, factory and moor. As a race, we are permanently straddling frontiers.

Let us take a brief glance at the kind of magic that is sensed in *Adam in Moonshine*. At one point Adam is a prisoner of the police but he is released by friends. 'As they ran, they laughed softly and crazily into the night that stretched itself out before them, wide and glittering, marvellously sweet-smelling, moonlit, magical.' I think the first question we have to ask ourselves is this: was there something about that moment that made it different from other moments (which we must call more normal moments) or is the author simply playing a trick on us? Some authors like to impose the magical as a literary device — the Georgian poets were adept at this. Very often the moment was not magical but the poet would have it so. One's sensitivity to literature is of first importance here: there is a considerable difference between a sense of magic that arises out of literary skill and one that actually inheres in the moment.

I am not going to answer any questions because I don't know the answers. Priestley links dream quality with this magical quality we are trying to isolate. It is possible, he thinks, that the strangeness that informs a dream may be identical with the strangeness that informs the magical moment. Therefore it is not surprising to find that in the other novel that appeared in 1927, *Benighted*, JBP is already trying to puzzle out the truth about dreams. Some people hate to wake in the morning to leave their dreams, which suggests they have ghastly waking lives. Penderel was the opposite, he was glad to wake out of terror. 'Ordinary life's bad enough, but it's a prince to the stuff we spin out of our rotten unconsciousness every night.' He puts forward the idea that they were all being dreamt by the unpleasant Mr Femm. Philip thought it more likely that they were dreaming Femm and his companions. (Margaret reminds them that Alice in *Through the Looking Glass* was told she was part of one of the King's dreams, and this made her cry.)

This may be idle speculation. Also it has no apparent connection with the sense of magic. But it illustrates an interest of JBP's which was later to approach the character of obsession. Accounts of dreams are scattered through his early essays. One of the most remarkable is to be found in 'The Berkshire Beasts' in *Open House*, 1927. He is walking through a large park with an old family friend, a somewhat characterless and colourless lady. They encountered a herd of remarkable beasts, of various sizes, but the largest was twice the size of a full-grown elephant. They had floppy ears but no trunks. They were all wearing spectacles, and each lens was the size of a normal dinner plate. His friend remarked casually, 'Ah, these are the Berkshire Beasts.' One experiences a sense of awe that emanates from this essay. There are no essayistic remarks about his being a very ordinary fellow, nor is any attempt made to interpret the dream. In next year's *Apes and Angels* 'The Strange Outfitter' recounts another extraordinary and sinister dream. Again no attempt is made at interpretation, nor is it used as a starting point for random comments on life, in the usual essayistic manner. It ends with this suggestive sentence: 'I wish I knew exactly where I had been.' He is beginning to wonder if there may not be rather more to a dream than an inflamed imagination.

The association of dreams with a theory about Time didn't spring up overnight. Dunne's book[1] turned out to be the necessary catalyst. Dreams do not figure in *Angel Pavement*, nor do magical moments. In fact, although we are told that Mr Smeeth used to have unpleasant dreams they are attributed to fried liver or toasted cheese which he found difficulty in digesting. There is a brief reference in *English Journey* to his 'many vivid dreams', with the arresting comment that 'the dead move casually through them.' But at the time JBP was concerned with something very remote from a Time theory.

Priestley emerged as a serious Time-philosopher just before the outbreak of war, and I am leaving a consideration of his Time plays to a later chapter. Here I am less concerned with theory than with experience and the writer's attempts to transmit it. A third quality now presents itself to Priestley's sensitised attention. It seems to him that the peculiar quality that is to be found in theatrical production has much in common with dreams and the magical moment. These three themes sometimes come together in his work to produce a concerted attack on his sensibility; or the three of them cast shadows over each other so that it becomes impossible to know which causes which. We get an example of this in 'A London Hotel' which he included in his *Self-Selected Essays*, 1937. There is a curious unreality about the meals: 'they are like those dinners that actors pretend to eat in the second act of comedies. . . It is all like eating food in a dream. . . Those liquids that the conjuror pours out of his magic kettle — I will wager that they taste exactly like hotel tea and coffee.' At this stage we might hazard that JBP's thinking ran along these lines: dream is an additional dimension of reality; theatre approaches it in quality; magic is a mysterious ingredient stirred in to complete the mixture.

In his Time plays JBP was grappling with the problem of Time, trying to clarify it in dramatic terms. Later he attempted to reproduce the quality associated with what appeared to be another dimension, rather than bridge the gap of understanding. We get an example of this in his play, *Summer Day's Dream*, 1949. It resembles a pleasant dream of the future when our contemporary rage and madness has spent itself. An international team of experts are prospecting for a precious mineral in an England that has been reduced to primitivism by a devastating war. The Russian is at first opposed to any sense of dreaming or unreality — in fact, she calls it mysticism — but is gradually affected by the charm and beauty of the pastoral life. It reminds her of the days she spent on a farm when she was a girl. What the American, Heimer, refers to half deprecatingly as 'midsummer in old England' slowly has its effect on her. 'I feel it too,' she says, ' — as if I was in a dream — a midsummer dream.' JBP has tried to reproduce that eerie quality that pervades any good production of *Midsummer Night's Dream*, but at the same time he attempts to retain the link with the world which we know and which Shakespeare simply put aside.

We talk of reality and the very word implies unreality or non-reality or irreality — we're never quite sure what to call it. In another of his self-selected essays, 'Mad Make-Believe', he describes a shipwreck scene being shot for a film, and it seems to him that the scene hovers between make-believe and reality. The crew continued for a week, shooting from different angles, and he wondered if one night things might not have begun 'to edge over towards their make-believe, reality might have quietly slipped its moorings, together with the liner.' Is this hyper-imaginative fancy? Feyness running riot? There was a time when the answer would have been a loud Yes, backed by the legions of positivism and established orthodoxy. But today, when hard-bitten pulp writers produce fantasies of similar type week after week, when large crowds visit the cinema to see transitions from one kind of existence into another, the reply would certainly not be unanimous. JBP senses a kind of no-mans's land between what has usually been called reality and what has been thought to be imagination or invention. In some of his writings he has even suggested imagination itself may be the sign of another actual dimension. As a creative writer I don't think he ever quite managed to jump the chasm that lies between these different worlds of feeling and experience, as the best surrealists sometimes did. Whereas Chirico and Magritte and Dali in his prime managed to cross a mysterious border, JBP never got further than sniffing the air on the other side. But then he was really more interested in the borderland than what lay beyond.

Do people, real people, meet in dreams? (It depends what you mean by real, Professor Joad would have said.) This is the theme underlying another play, *The Long Mirror*, 1940. The lives of two people are inextricably tangled although they have never met in the flesh. One, the woman, is far more aware of the relationship than the man. The medium could be dream or another time dimension or some form of extra-sensory perception. But at the beginning of the play Mrs Tenbury, a secondary character, remarks how real and sensible her dreams seem to be. 'I don't see how I could invent them. So much convincing detail, too. . . And all the people too, where do *they* come from?' When the two main characters finally meet they decide that they have met previously in dreams. 'It was a kind of dream,' says Branwen, 'but we were real in it' — and in that last sentence she and her creator challenge all modern theories of dreaming, apart from Dunne's.

Now let us return to the sense of magic. In the novel *Bright Day*, 1946, Gregory is greatly excited by the Alington family, their vitality and culture. Jock warns him not to make symbols of them, it is unwise to introduce magic into your relations with people. Gregory objects to this, however. Magic must come in: 'life without magic soon begins to wither.' Is this just a casual remark, without any kernel of meaning, or is Gregory implying that an actual quality, an x but a metaphysical x, is at work? The theatre seems to act as a bridge between the two mysteries. It is neither completely part of our workaday world nor it is completely outside it. In *Theatre Outlook*, 1947, JBP states that something wonderful happens in the theatre if conditions are right, some mysterious creative action is in progress, and again he falls back on the only word available to him: magic. What he is insisting is that it is not simply the importation of poetry or art or music into a play. That would be the psychological x.

> The most beautiful actress in the country, robed as a medieval queen by a superb designer, who has also done a wonderful set, may offer us a death scene in which she speaks the most sumptuous rhetoric, accompanied by music supplied by one of our best composers; and yet we may feel nothing at all; whereas, at a neighbouring theatre, against a dingy commonplace setting, a rather ugly young woman in a dirty mackintosh may mutter an apparently banal phrase or two, and yet

make us feel all the heartbreak of this life and so haunt our imagination for years.

What is the secret? Is it that the theatre is a microcosm of life? Is there a profound symbolism, rooted in the unconscious? Does the dream of the playhouse chime with the long dream of man's life? Does it hint at profound truths for which we have never been able to find the right words? Is there a suggestion of symbolic ritual? Do we feel in our lives that we are playing in a vast playhouse of rising suns and waning moons? 'And when we sleep do not curtains rise on fantastic stages, in secret deeply-hidden playhouses where we appear as audience, dramatists, directors, actors, scene-shifters, and all?' In the last paragraph of *The Wonderful World of the Theatre*, 1959, he writes: 'It is the magical place where man meets his image.' (And this last paragraph is a place where a writer tries to distil his beliefs.)

One wonders what kind of reaction JBP gets from his readers. Those of the old Georgian school will hang on his words. It is even possible at times to feel that through Priestley the Georgians are delivering a kick-back. But he is not really one of them, though he was. He picked up their rather idle love of the ethereal and discovered a hard grain of fact in it. This is what he is trying to push, the notion that there is a mystery which is subject to law — but it is not the law of the positivist, who sneers at anything that might have surprised Newton, or rather Newton's disciples, for it would have been difficult to surprise Newton. In 'Some After-thoughts' to *The Happy Dream* (which, in addition to its separate publication, he included in *Instead of the Trees*) he gave the name Dr Consensus to the man who tells us what to believe, who wishes to spread the truth and put an end to all nonsense. His real object is to take magic and mystery out of everything. But, says JBP, two things cannot be denied, and they may well be related. Dr Consensus works harder and harder and addresses larger and larger audiences; and the contemporary world shows us more and more boredom suddenly erupting into violence.

Back in 1949, in *Delight*, he had told us he enjoyed his dreams, or most of them, and unlike many people, he also liked to think about them. What were they? Where did they come from? People would say to him, 'It's only a dream!' — but why *only*? Trying to answer these questions led him into deep metaphysical waters, in which he seemed perfectly happy. In 1964 he decided to grapple philosophically with the problem of Time and the result was an interesting and important book called *Man and Time*. In it he responds to that *only* and, as is often the case with JBP, puts his clearest statement in a parenthesis. 'Long before I was interested in precognition, before I had read any depth psychology, I could not understand why so many people thought their dreams no more important than their sneezes and yawns. Our dreams are our night life.' That last sentence goes to the heart of Priestley's view of life. I intend to devote a chapter to his theory of Time, but as his approach to it was through his sense of the magical moment which seemed to have so much in common with the dream, which in turn seemed to be a product of the Time-scale, this is a good moment to refer again to his *Man and Time*, where he makes a rough classification of different kinds of dream. For he accepts the existence of different dream-producing stimuli. Discussing the accounts of dreams sent to him after a radio appeal, he writes: 'Obviously many of them feel that these dreams-that-come-true are quite removed from ordinary dreams, in a class by themselves.' (He says they are much more sharply delineated and leave a stronger impression of reality.) Discussing Dunne's theory (which we will come to in due course), he says that while it may be an adequate explanation of most of our dreams, it does not explain them all. 'For there are dreams that are outside the confusion of the three- and four-dimensional focuses — clear dreams without these jerks and disconnections, and powerfully dramatic dreams in which figures obviously symbolic play a part.'

Priestley is a creative writer and does not set out to prove anything. He has, however, given the twentieth century a nudge by suggesting that the sense of magic, which under the shadow of positivism had lost so much credibility that it was no longer taken seriously, is a real thing, ironically a positive thing, and that it is closely associated with the dream state. This insight has led to an examination of dreams, and in turn to a study of the Time factor and depth psychology. It led JBP to Jung, whom he admired tremendously and got to know. Unlike many psychologists he was a good advertisement for his profession. He never encouraged creative writers to consult him but told them their work was their therapy. JBP came to Jung because he realised that, however true his and Dunne's theory of Time might be, the unconscious was involved. Whatever causes dreams, they take place in the unconscious. In *The Happy Dream*, 1976, he distinguishes between precognitive dreams and what he calls, unsatisfactorily, 'ordinary dreams'. We have thousands of rubbish dreams and a few memorable ones. They may bring anything from terror to rich absurdity, and they belong to a different order. 'They seem to me to be definite creations just as a produced play or a film is a definite creation.' This kind of dream is designed, shaped and coloured to make a certain impression. 'It might be described as the unconscious cornering consciousness.' In the dream which gives the pamphlet its title he saw a girl walking ahead of him. He never exchanged a word or saw her face, and she suggested no particular girl — 'but the sight of her, I remember, brought a new glow of feeling to the happiness that had been there from the first. Woman had arrived. Not my woman, no woman I wanted personally, but *Woman*, essential femininity . . .' I have had the same dream, or something very close to it and truly identical in the feeling evoked, on three occasions. One cannot prove it is different from other dreams, one can only know. The dream, Priestley's and mine, had few events but a glorious atmosphere, radiating happiness. At the core of the experience was the sense of himself both young and old. It celebrated the defeat of Time because it included the whole of Time.

Is another existence suggested? In our dreams we have another body. It can move from room to room without hindrance and glide through walls. It can travel at infinite speeds. It can cope with fantastic experiences. (In my dream I experienced a more intense happiness than I have ever known waking, and it bathed me throughout the day that followed.) It can float across and observe magical landscapes. It doesn't bore us, as our ordinary bodies do.

Might we have this body after death? he asks.

Chapter 7

Introduction to the Theatre

I have an entirely technical problem here, which is my responsibility but which it would be wise to share with the reader. Early in the thirties JBP turned to the theatre. In view of his association of the magical moment, this will come as no surprise. But the natural sequence seems to lead to his Time plays, and their relationship with the world of dreams. The Time plays, however, appeared towards the end of the thirties, which means that if I discussed them first I would have to skip the earlier work. I have therefore decided to discuss his early dramatic work up to the first years of the war in this chapter and then follow up with a more detailed discussion of the three major Time plays. This is not entirely satisfactory but it arises from a recognition of the peculiar character of these plays and their importance in JBP's *oeuvre*.

David Hughes tells us that JBP's first drama was an adaptation of Peacock's *Nightmare Abbey* which was favourably considered by Nigel Playfair and J.B. Fagan but was never produced. *The Good Companions* appeared as a musical play in 1931 but the major work of dramatisation was done by Edward Knoblock. Richard Addinsell composed the music and John Gielgud appeared as Inigo Jollifant. 'No one will complain here of a dull and mumbling sub-naturalism,' wrote the *Times* critic. 'This is the theatre all out, and thank heaven for it. . . a whale of a play' (15 May 1931).

Dangerous Corner, 1932, was the first play written entirely by JBP. He tells me in a letter that it was also the first play he wrote (regarding the Peacock adaptation as not entirely his work), which means that his entry into the theatre was an unusually painless operation. It is clear, however, that he possessed considerable sensitivity towards the theatrical atmosphere. He prefers writing plays to novels, which is another indication of his natural bent. He tells us, jokingly, in an early essay that it is becoming so difficult to get theatre tickets that it may soon be necessary to have a play produced if you are to be sure of getting inside the building.

It is a curious fact that he used the phrase 'dangerous corner' in an essay called 'Having Covered the Card Table' which appeared in *Open House*, 1927, i.e. five years before the play appeared. Does this mean the phrase had been haunting his mind during the meantime? And would this signify that the idea for the play was slowly forming? In the essay, he reviews his profession of dealing in imponderables, poring over men's thoughts and dreams, trying to re-create them on paper, never knowing whether anything has been achieved or whether it is all idle vanity. 'There are perhaps a few moments of intense satisfaction for me while the work is in hand; there is a brief delight in the turning of a dangerous corner; and then nothing but fret and labour that is at once hard and yet fantastic until the work is done and I am free to juggle lazily with the next dream.' Has this any significance? Certainly the dream aspect is stressed. He is preparing to put his dreams on the stage.

Dangerous Corner has had a remarkable history. It opened at the Lyric Theatre and was nearly taken off after three days. Since then it has been in almost constant production somewhere in the world. Nevertheless, it is not a play one can readily admire. It is not even one of JBP's own favourites. The 'dangerous corner' is punctilious truth-telling and the danger is expressed by Stanton when he says, 'I think telling the truth is about as healthy as skidding round a corner at sixty.' It hardly ever departs from a single emotional tone so that not even suspense can raise the interest level. His immaturity in handling dialogue is evident — points are emphasised needlessly and he has not yet learnt that very delicate art of the dramatist, knowing exactly how much to say, and being aware instinctively of the little that is just too much. It's one of his 'unveiling' plays, where the coverings that conceal the truth are stripped away piece by piece. *Laburnum Grove*, 1934, was to be another up to a point, but there's a closer similarity with *An Inspector Calls*, 1947, a much superior play. At times it seems to proceed jerkily through a series of 'Stop it, I says' (I have a feeling that the amateur theatre has a particular regard for this sort of thing). He resorts too easily to his favourite theme of everything being a muddle, which allows him to escape (or so he hopes) through a theatrical muddle, which he has created and justified. 'Don't go thinking there was any deep laid plot,' says Stanton. 'There wasn't. There never is in real life. It was all improvised and haphazard and damned stupid.' One asks what the point of this play is, especially when we compare it with the two mentioned above. It relates some trivial events in the recent lives of some very average people. Looking back, we can see that its declaration of mystery was probably far more important for Priestley than any overt message. It is also interesting to note the circularity of the story, which reflects a similar device to that encountered in the essays and *The Good Companions*. The play ends as it begins and then makes a new start. 'Probably the most ingenious play ever written', said the *Times* reviewer, but '. . . the Caplans are gramophones rather than characters.' (20 October 1938, when the play was revived.) He draws attention to the continuous confession, leading to the sense that the sole function of each character is simply to confess. In *An Inspector Calls* continuous confession is turned to continuous accusation, and a new dimension is added to the play.

Laburnum Grove had a theme and therefore represented an advance in stagecraft. It is that the much despised suburban life can have noble qualities. The young hate suburbia, its dullness and conformity, they want excitement and a touch of naughtiness. The attitude of the young is satirised (on the whole, JBP has never cared much for the young) everything is stood on its head and suburbanism is presented as both wise and exciting. It is called an Immoral Comedy, but this aspect is not very credible. The respectable Mr Redfern, living at Ferndale, Laburnum Grove, Shooters Green, a suburb of North London, turns out to be a very successful financial crook. Suburban respectability conceals crime instead of rejecting it. It is a very chestertonian paradox. There is another version of it, in a less obvious way, in *Bees on the Boat Deck*, which appeared three years later. Gridley, the Chief Engineer on the S.S. *Gloriana*, says that things are best when they're quiet — out at sea, the engines turning nicely and not too many passengers — it wouldn't matter if nothing happened for six months. The trouble is, life never is quiet. As soon as everything is settled, there is some kind of upset — and it's often the seemingly quiet people who start the troubles. In this play, it is a scientist, a decent fellow from some very respectable suburban home, and he is testing an explosion. 'You don't want to hurt anybody,' shouts Gridley, 'but — by God! — you're going to.' No one seems to be hurt in Laburnum Grove but there is every indication that they could be.[1]

Eden End, 1934, was produced in the following year. Although not ostensibly about Time as a problem, it is very much about time as an ever-present mystery. (The mystery of time hovers over a very large number of JBP's plays without, in most cases, dominating them. I shall return to this point in the next chapter.) 'The illusory pursuit of happiness is its chief theme', JBP wrote. To begin with, though produced in 1934, *Eden End* is set in 1912, and 1912 is stressed. It belonged to Priestley's Golden Age and we are constantly being referred back to it, not only in plays like this and *The Linden Tree* but also in novels like *Bright Day* and *Lost Empires* and here and there in personal memoirs and social histories like *The Edwardians*. Again, this is something to which I will devote a chapter of its own. In *Eden End* there is a great deal of nostalgia, looking back and memory probing. Stella has left home and come back years later, and the passage of time becomes as objective in this play as the piano, one of JBP's favourite properties, which lives on time and is used to bring back an old musical comedy number (old to the audience but topical to the cast), one of the most effective of time's landmarks. We are never allowed to forget the passage of time; there is a servant named Sarah and one of her main tasks seems to be to say, every so often, 'Eh, fancy! And it only seems a week since you wor a little lad.' And inevitably someone talks amateurishly and despairingly (as we all do) of Time's insoluble mystery: Stella, meeting her old lover after the lapse of years, asks for no more than to be together, idly talking: 'There isn't anybody else. Just us. And time's stopped for us. . . Or we needn't talk at all, if you like. Just be quiet. Trying to make time stand still for us. It flies at a terrible speed really, Geoffrey.' You might say that in this play JBP is shaping up to Time but not actually taking it on. The *Times* reviewer found it static. 'Has coma set in? Has the natural power of response died? Or is this play, though written by a man who has proved himself to have a finger on the theatrical pulse, as immobile as it seems?' His complaint was that the naturalism was not naturalistic nor fluid enough.

Cornelius, 1935, is one of his better plays but it was rather depressing for the general taste. In the Introduction to Volume 3 of *The Plays* JBP called it 'a period piece'. It is that, but it is the kind of period piece that may be found worth reviving from time to time, if only for its documentary and historical value. It stresses the decline in human relationships that JBP had observed taking place — old friendships dropped, old associations terminated, at the dictate of the market. The theme is human wastage, the human cost of the social muddle. Each scene ends with a quotation from a book about the Andes, with suggestions of a return to nature, freedom, simplicity, the primitive. Cornelius's business is going downhill; he faces his creditors and unmasks the crooks who try to take advantage of him. His partner, Murrison, who it is hoped will somehow rescue the firm, commits suicide. Biddle, the loyal old clerk, says Murrison was mad but Cornelius rejects this. 'He knew what he was doing. He was sane then. That was the real Bob Murrison.' Cornelius is about to follow his example, but at the last moment flings the revolver aside and picks up a ledger and, quoting the passage from the book on the Andes, hurls it at the door, forcing it open. The passage was this: 'After a week in the Indian village — we decided to take the track into the clouds — to find — among those heights — the lost city of the Incas.' The pessimism is in marked contrast to the mood of, say, *The Good Companions*, but in the midst of it the spirit of affirmation is just maintained, especially through Judy, a lively young secretary — a more sober, business-world Susie Dean.

Dramatically *Cornelius* is a success. In 1936 came *Spring Tide* which positively creaked in its efforts to have the right people in the right place at the right time. (One curiosity about this play is that it was produced and published under the authorship of 'George Billam and Peter Goldsmith', the latter being a pseudonym for JBP.) The material is familiar Priestley stuff, with a wise old bird showing everybody how much better it is to work together rather than as isolated units. It also contains one or two ideas which were to be exploited more fully and successfully later: for example, a shop assistant and a bullying customer, and the suspicion that the former may have committed suicide, which does happen in *An Inspector Calls*; and even the virtually simultaneous marriages of three couples might have carried the seed of *When We Are Married*, 1938.

In *People at Sea*, 1937, there is a philosopher named Professor Pawlet who brings us back to the author's metaphysical concern, in direct collision. This, after all, is the year in which JBP launched his two celebrated Time plays, *Time and the Conways* and *I Have Been Here Before*, on the stage. Pawlet only draws attention to the problem in academic style by saying: 'We know that the universe is at least four-dimensional. What we see and what science investigates is merely a three-dimensional cross-section of a four or multi-dimensional reality. So we haven't the least idea of what things are really like.'

But this is not the real subject of *People at Sea*, a title that had both surface and metaphorical meaning. A ship has caught fire and most of the crew and passengers have escaped but a few remain because their life-boat was not sea-worthy. It is the sort of situation JBP delighted in — where characters were prisoners of circumstance — and he was tending to use it more and more glibly. (In fact, it was a popular device throughout the thirties and was used by others, including the novelist Anthony Thorne.) The enforced corralling of assorted and largely uncongenial men and women led to stress, hostility and new alignments. The truth was laid bare — in ringing clichés. In his Introduction to Volume 3 of *The Plays* JBP called the characters 'shop-soiled'. It is a pretty trashy play, where one cliché situation follows another in quick succession. It is one of the most political of his plays and contains the most virulent class hatred yet expressed by Priestley characters.

There is a good deal of random sociology, as when Avon, the novelist, says one's sense of security depends on one's generation.

> It's all a question of dates. You three were brought up in the age of security. You just can't help feeling secure. But there's twenty years between us, and that makes all the difference. I can't help feeling insecure. As soon as I hold something comfortably in my hands, I wonder how soon somebody's going to take a crack at it and blow it to hell.

The rebels (Boyne, a stoker, and Miriam Pick, a personal maid) talk too much. Stage rebels always did in the thirties. It sounds unreal and thirty years later their descendants would only mumble like illiterates, but perform symbolic deeds. But society was to blame for individual faults. Professor Pawlet sympathises with Boyne and admits his own guilt as a member of an unjust society: 'You are what we've made you. We have no right to expect anything better. Though I must condemn you, I don't blame you, etc., etc.' Such talk was intended as self-accusation but in fact became a social bromide for the intellectuals. It doesn't all sink to this level. The Professor shoots Boyne and excuses himself by saying nothing could have been done with him. Short sharp execution is better than the elaborate codes and punishments of established society, which make life-enemies of its delinquents. This is something that could be well said today, when we allow criminals to shelter under revolutionary labels. The Professor, despite his donnish manner, does speak a good deal of sense, as when he reminds Miriam that although there may be much wrong with society, this does not negate the possibility of there being much wrong with the individual too. Such touches distinguished JBP from the average Left-wing critic of the time.

Music at Night is both more original and ambitious. It was first produced at the Malvern Festival in 1938 and then taken to the Westminster Theatre. The dramatic critics seem to have set their faces against it as they did against *Johnson Over Jordan*, with which it bears some affinity, but both plays had a great effect on the audience. In this play a few friends have gathered in Mrs Amesbury's house to hear a new violin concerto by David Shield. He tells them the music has no programme beyond its Italian movement labels. In fact, the audience programmes the music. This method suits JBP, who is impatient of the normal nuances and delicacies of social intercourse, and likes to strip his characters down and let them speak without reservations. When they do this in the novels, which are supposedly naturalistic, it jars. But here it is acceptable as a device that is more concerned with underlying truth than surface truth. The time element is shuttled, and it is manoeuvred in parcels of different characters, ten major ones and six minor. This has its drawback. Although the aim is similar to that of *Johnson Over Jordan*, it lacks the impact that play achieved because interest has to be fragmented between ten characters equally instead of one Johnson. JBP's main concern, increasingly as he gets older is with the *quality* of the individual life. Our individual lives are really not important, he is saying, but just flickers in some greater eternal life. Each character is compelled to face his own rottenness and is sobered by the reflection and, temporarily at least, seems prepared to lead a better and more responsible life. Many years later JBP was still worrying this theme in a novella called *The Carfitt Crisis*, 1975. The *Times* reviewer tried to be kind: 'there is refreshment of spirit in watching a good craftsman struggling with courage and honesty to loosen stage conventions that for him and many others have grown oppressively rigid' (11 October 1939). JBP was aiming at a threefold impression: dramatic, poetic and philosophic. But instead of characters we are given types, and when this happens no other consideration can save the drama.

The following year, 1938, saw one of JBP's most successful and
charming plays, the Yorkshire farcical comedy *When We Are
Married*. It is in the joyful tradition of cheerful, breezy English
comedy that has been going non-stop ever since *The Shoemaker's
Holiday*. Paradoxically, despite JBP's earnest efforts to create a
thoughtful drama with philosophical content, it would not be
surprising if this play continues to be performed long after the
others are forgotten. Its main secret is a very simple one, the one
that contrasts so strongly with *Music at Night*; the characters are
living people, and not types. It is closely observed and full of
human sympathy. It has been immensely popular, especially with
amateur groups. JBP himself is very proud of having taken the part
of Ormonroyd at short notice, when the original actor was taken
ill. This study of a drunken provincial press photographer is a little
gem. It is not the kind of play you can profitably say much about.
It presents life, it does not attempt to moralise about it — and
that's that. It is not all sweetness and light but JBP is tolerant of
the weaknesses he exposes. One target is the prudery and sense of
moral superiority that seem native to the Northerner. Although
JBP is regarded as a Yorkshire prototype, he is quick to point out
their faults. Gerald, the young man from the South, is sternly
criticised by the Yorkshire councillors and churchmen — he is
naturally 'lah-di-dah'. In fact, we are given a very attractive picture
of him. The others boast of being straightforward — he *is*
straightforward. It is also interesting that the most decent and
tolerant of the Yorkshiremen, Soppitt and Annie Parker, are the
only ones without pronounced Yorkshire accents.

The fourth dimension crops up again in *Ever Since Paradise*,
which is called a discursive entertainment. As the play was first
written in 1939 but was greatly revised before it was produced in
1946, we cannot be sure when the reference originated — not that
this matters, for we know that by 1939 JBP was in the thick of his
Time researches. We follow Rosemary and Paul from their first
meeting, their blossoming love, to their marriage and then falling
out. The play starts with a scene in a solicitor's office to discuss
divorce. Helen, a commentator, mentions the part in any person
that can see ahead in a dim way and know what's coming.
Rosemary speaks of a big *Now* that is behind the little *Now*.
William, another commentator, says it's 'a question of movement
along the fourth dimension', and goes on: 'These two *Nows* — two

different kinds of time. Now imagine yourself travelling with the speed of light — a hundred and eighty six thousand miles a second — along the fourth dimension —,' but the others can't imagine it and the subject is dropped.

With *The Long Mirror* in 1940 we are into the war period, which had such a powerful effect on JBP's writing that it is a convenient place to pause in this consideration of his early work (which is in any case not intended to be complete). Later, in *Particular Pleasures*, JBP referred to this play as 'a rather thin "fey" piece written especially for Jean Forbes-Robertson.' It begins well, quickly building up a sense of mystery by that time-honoured device of strangers meeting in an isolated hotel, but it deteriorates sadly because JBP is more interested in his Time theory than in the characters. As in so many of his plays, one character has a therapeutic effect on the others, which is one of the major encouragements of life and is naturally exploited by drama. But in JBP's plays there is a strong tendency for the healing to come from the merely structural reality of another time-scheme rather than from human compassion and understanding. An external *deus* teaches people to behave better. The final act degenerates into shallow, portentous West End dialogue about feelings, loyalties, personal claims, all treated rather breathlessly. It's not the theory that's incredible but the relationships, so that in the end we get the best of neither world.

How is it, we are asked, that Michael Camber and Branwen Elder know so much about each other when they have never met? Most of the awareness belongs to Branwen. When Michael refers to an old friend who is dead, she corrects him, saying 'he's out of our time.' Branwen is beginning to understand how her experiences are gained — she calls it just *seeing* , whether at a distance or in the past, and it includes sounds and feelings and thoughts. But why was it always Michael?

> Perhaps it began as a mere accident — like — telephone wires getting crossed. Or perhaps there's some link that we can't understand, outside this world, outside time. I know enough now to be sure of one thing — that there's a great part of us that is outside this world and outside its time.

She tries to illustrate it with a long mirror in the sitting-room of the hotel — an unsatisfactory device, for the mirror is neither used nor noticed at any other time during the play. At first the two of them see themselves, then Branwen steps to one side and Michael can only see himself. But he knows she is there, nevertheless. She says, 'I think this outward world in time, where you and I are going to say goodbye and then vanish from one another's sight, is only like a long, long mirror, full of twists and cracks and corners, stretching from the cradle to the grave. All you see in it are images. What is real and true — and *alive* — is here, not in there.'

And now we can look at the three plays on which JBP's major dramatic reputation rests. They may not be the best plays but they are the most remarkable ones. Moreover, many of the plays written before them were in some ways a preparation for them, and the ideas he expressed in them continued to exercise his imagination for some time after.

Chapter 8

The Three Time Plays

It is, in a way, an arbitrary decision to call *Time and the Conways*, *I have Been Here Before* and *Johnson Over Jordan* 'the' Time plays. Why not include *Dangerous Corner* and *An Inspector Calls?* The answer is that these three are directly concerned with an understanding of time, whereas in the other two (and also some which have been quoted in the preceding chapter) a time-shuttle is used as a device. In one or two plays, in fact, there are references to Time-theory which have no organic relationship to the action of the play.[1]

Time and the Conways was first presented in 1937. Act I shows the Conways as a united, happy family. The only moment of grief comes with a reference to the father, who had been drowned. There is a suggestion by one of the girls that foreknowledge of his fate might have been possible. Could he have guessed in a dim way what was in store for him? There is also a slight suggestion of extra awareness in the character of Beevers, as though he has a faint apprehension of what the future holds. Otherwise it is a completely orthodox West End beginning — nothing unusual, in fact rather disappointing for there appears to be no dramatic development, only a continuing restlessness which is a poor substitute.

Act II ('the present time', i.e. eighteen years later) presents all-round deterioration of character in all cases except Alan, the dull one, the one who was always subject to slight ridicule because of his lack of ambition. The other characters — mother, daughters (except Carol, who is dead), the other son, family friends — all have become hard or bitchy, disappointed or frustrated, spineless or hopeless; as one direction for Robin and his wife Joan puts it, 'lost and hopeless'. Time is certainly represented as the enemy in this perspective, the conventional 'winged chariot': 'There's a great devil in the universe and we call it Time,' says Kay. Thoughtful Alan brings out his pipe (like JBP), quotes Blake, and suggests that Time is only a kind of dream — if it weren't, we would have to accept the theory of continuous creation. 'But Time doesn't destroy anything. It merely moves us on — in this life — from one peep-hole to the next.' The happy young Conways still exist, the landscape is still there, but they're seeing another part of it, a worse part.

Act III returns to the set and time of the first Act. It is in fact a continuation of the first Act, without a break — but now we are seeing the Conways through the experience of Act II, through their potentialities as expressed in another view of the same landscape. The vague premonitions now take on an extra meaning. Talking about love Kay says it wouldn't be too bad to fall in love in one's own home, much better than to be desperately unhappy and in love, miles away in a strange house. She stops and shivers, but doesn't know why; we know that this is a premonition (in normal terminology), or another view of the landscape, for this is going to be, or is, part of Kay's experience.

There is a lot of idle chatter, much of it contributed by Mrs Conway. At one point Kay rises with a terrible cry of 'Don't! Don't!' With hindsight we see the idiocy of all this chatter. Kay's outburst is a warning from what we call the future, but is more truly from another segment of an existent whole. Kay remembers Alan's lines quoted from Blake:

> *Joy and woe are woven fine,*
> *A clothing for the soul divine . . .*

But this is not precognition, although it may well reinforce it. It is simple awareness or, more crudely, horse-sense — but it is the horse-sense that comes so naturally to a poet. For Priestley the insights of art and music are closely related to an understanding of Time. In some of his plays and even in his novels he allows music to speak for him. Here it is Schubert just as in *The Linden Tree* it is Elgar. The music is much more than decoration.

Just as joy and woe are woven fine, so are JBP's plays and novels. At this point I would like to refer to an incident in *Bright Day*, 1946, one of his most thoughtful novels. Bridget suddenly talks to Gregory with unexpected urgency. He can't understand what she is getting at. 'What I saw, as I stared in my bewilderment, was Bridget herself as I had never seen her before. It was as if I saw her not only as she was at that moment but as she soon would be, with the woman added to the girl.' A little while after remembering this flash, Gregory was talking to Eleanor Nixey in a hotel in Cornwall.

She came upon him suddenly on a cliff path, but now she was thirty years older than when he had first known her, and she was Lady Harndean. As he looked at her he was profoundly stirred.

> What I perceived then, in a blinding flash of revelation, was that the real Eleanor Nixey was neither the handsome young woman I had been remembering nor the elderly woman I saw before me, both of whom were nothing but distorted fleeting reflections in time, that the real Eleanor Nixey was somewhere behind all these appearances and fragmentary distortions, existing outside time and change; and that what was true of her was of course true of us all.

He adds that while it is easy to say this he actually *felt* it; it was an experience. The effect described here is exactly the same as the one expressed in *Time and the Conways*. Each moment of time is picked out of an existent duration of time.

This play was published with *I Have Been Here Before* in the same year as they were produced on stage, with an Introduction by Priestley. In it he says some critics called the first play pessimistic, which bewildered him. 'It was my intention here to challenge and combat pessimism, that deep underlying despair about life which I believe to be one of the evils of our age.' And from this he goes on to state: 'Death is not the end but the beginning of real life.'

I Have Been Here Before plunges more deeply into theory. The ideas expressed and acted upon by Dr Görtler were taken from Ouspensky's *A New Model of the Universe*, as we are told in a prefatory note to the published play. The individual lives in a series of spirals, referred to as Recurrence, but changes can take place resulting from wisdom gained by experience, and Intervention is possible. This theory has much in common with the Reincarnation theory, in so far as the individual can rise to higher or sink to lower levels, but the aspect summed up in the title is different. Without going into detail, the play hinges on Dr Görtler's intervention in the lives of three people. He had seen them wrecked before and he wishes, through personal persuasion, to alter their behaviour sufficiently to avoid the same disaster. Some critics complained that Görtler's speech is too theoretical. It would be false if it wasn't. He is a scholar and his ideas of time and regeneration obsess him. It is a critical delusion to suppose that some modes are suitable for drama and others are not. Business men must speak like business men, whores like whores and professors like professors. Drama, like life, can accommodate any and everything. This type of reaction, of which we have far too much, is merely automatic and can be traced to a principle held by some critics, that Intellect is alien to Drama.

On the other hand, there is one point where the language discussing the Ouspenskian ideas (which are, incidentally, not the same as those of Dunne, who had the major influence on Priestley) becomes literary and therefore false — but the words are not Görtler's but Ormund's. He is one of the three people who are saved by Görtler's intervention. He is struggling to express his own newly acquired view of Recurrence, and the second and third chance it presents. Perhaps it is his awkwardness that drives him to uncharacteristic speech, which can embarrass an audience and would probably have embarrassed him if he had stopped to think: 'They've never told me yet about a God so generous and noble and wise that He won't allow a few decisions that we make in our ignorance, haste and bewilderment to settle our fate for ever. Why should this poor improvisation be our whole existence?' and so on.

In addition to Recurrence there is also a strong statement of belief in inter-connectedness, the kind of thing that is stressed even more strongly in *An Inspector Calls*. If Ormund is to commit suicide (as he did last time round) too many lives will suffer — the inn-keeper and his daughter will lose their savings, the schoolmaster will lose his job and Ormund's widow will face poverty and despair. He now has the chance to correct the mistake he made before. In an earlier chapter I drew attention to JBP's sense of what he calls 'magic', and showed how what was perhaps at first a vague though immensely strong feeling led him to deeper enquiry, especially into dreams and time. Is it here that we eventually run the positive element in magic to earth? Dr Görtler seems to express its true quality once and for all when he says, 'The creative magic of our feeling, imagination and will. These are the realities — our feeling, imagination and will — and all our histories are their dreams.'

This would seem to be pretty intractable stuff for drama. Priestley's success results in one of the most remarkable plays the English stage has seen. With it he reaches his peak as a playwright, although there were still good plays to come. In the past he had been criticised for putting types instead of real people into his plays. This cannot be said of *I Have Been Here Before*. 'Everyone in it is interesting in himself, not the puppet of a theory,' wrote the

Times reviewer; '. . . the stage becomes suddenly a place of spiritual adventure — an adventure described without pretentiousness and with a splendid moderation of language' (23 September 1937). Gareth Lloyd Evans, in his book *J.B. Priestley, the Dramatist*, wrote: 'Its attractiveness rests largely in the subtlety with which its theatrical tensions are maintained and the emotional excitement it generates . . .' It gives the appearance of being written with great difficulty. After all, it was the first occasion on which Time-theory had been presented explicitly in a creative vehicle, and yet the dialogue is not, with the single exception noted, unreal or stilted.

Johnson Over Jordan came two years later. As a result of his experiences in putting it on, JBP prepared a reading edition with a final essay entitled 'And All About It'. Johnson, a kind of modern Everyman, dies and we follow his progress after death, for only the body dies. (In fact, if we follow Dunne closely, and also Priestley in his Dunne-mood, not even that dies, for everything is in permanent existence.) Hence this play could be seen as a straight-forward case of 'life after death', although 'continuing conscious-ness' would be a better description. Freda, the daughter, wonders if the mind still operates after death, in a kind of dream experience, so that the dead person would not be aware of his body's decease (JBP mentions this possibility in his essay). The play's three Acts take place in an office, a night club and an inn. In an early stage direction we read that Johnson imagines he is back in his own office, 'a world we ourselves visit in dreams.'

Some might see it as a symbolic dream. The night club is hell, defined by thought and memory and otherwise non-existent, as Johnson clearly sees, but later he discovers that thought and memory can be used to create heaven, as in the inn. Everything depends on the use. In this hell we see a struggle between a person's two selves, with Johnson admitting that he is half-animal, half-god, yet it is not entirely the animal, a simple beast, who is gratified by the complicated lusts of the night club. A stage direction refers to the 'telescoped personalities we often meet in dreams,' another indication that JBP is linking the continuation of consciousness with the dream experience. Apart from theory, this is important because a dream is more actual than a symbol, though it may be interpreted symbolically. We create symbols as things apart, whereas dreams are as much part of our lives as pain and pleasure.

Priestley tells us that the scene in the office in Act I is 'moved by anxiety'. It is designed to make Johnson look and feel small; it spotlights the things he doesn't know but apparently should, the petty meannesses and dishonesties of which he had been guilty, his insufficiency as a citizen, an employee, a husband and a father. The nightclub scene is brutish and disgusting. Hell is always easier to portray then heaven, and is usually done more successfully; the only literary evocation of heaven which, in my knowledge, comes close to being an exception to the rule is Dante's *Paradiso*. The early part of Johnson's heaven is in this class, but begins to fail as the necessary triviality starts to pall. (And just as so many of JBP's novels begin to slacken after a good start.) But his choice of heavenly quality is full of wisdom; Johnson is given a sense of security and well-being (which no other state can give him) by an old cricketer and a music hall comedian, both of them entertainers and unpretentious men whose work was a source of happiness in others.[2] Johnson fancies he sees Pickwick and his company (it is the repetition of a similar scene recounted in one of the essays in *Apes and Angels* which, after all, is a description of Johnson and his kind) and he actually does meet Don Quixote, for it is imagination, memory and affection that create life, not in any fanciful sense but in truth. JBP has here illustrated a truth that I have argued, usually unsuccessfully, that Falstaff is just as *real* as Shakespeare and Tom Jones just as *real* as Fielding or, if you like, Henry VIII. The mere existence of a body some hundreds of years ago cannot possibly validate reality. As far as heaven is concerned, Pickwick and Quixote are creations of simple goodness, and anyone who treasures them in his memory is prolonging that quality.

JBP tells us in his essay that his notes for this play pre-date the writing and performance of the other famous Time-plays. His interest in Time had been growing throughout the thirties, as we have seen. His conception of Time allows anyone to meet anyone else at any age he chooses. On such occasions a person will have a two-fold consciousness, one in time and one outside time. People 'wander in and out' of their own pasts, recreating experiences as we do in dreams. JBP says he wanted to give an account, in dramatic form, of a man's life in a new way. He was sick of the triviality of the average biographical play, with its 'easy amble of scenes, its obvious chronology, its rubber-stamp effects' and its effete dialogue. Reading Dr Evans-Wentz's study of the Tibetan *Book of the Dead* he came across the conception of the Bardo, 'a prolonged dream-like state, in what might be called the fourth dimension of space, filled with hallucinatory visions directly resultant from the mental content of the percipient,' and adapted it for the stage.

It was an ambitious play in every way. In the complete list of people connected with the production, which he gives at the end of his essay, we find the name of Basil Dean as producer, Benjamin Britten as composer of the original music, Anthony Tudor for the ballets, and Ralph Richardson, whose acceptance of the play and the part of Johnson revealed an intuitive understanding. 'For once I wanted to make full use of all the resources of the theatre,' JBP writes. It included an imaginative employment of music and a comprehensive use of lighting, dissolves, masks, ballet, reproduction, machinery, sets within sets, in fact, all the tricks known to the theatre of 1939. Also a change of theatre after only ten days allowed JBP to make important text changes which would otherwise have been impossible. The essay concludes with a justified attack on the English theatrical system. His targets were the critics, who so often give the impression of either hating the theatre or being utterly ignorant of it; fashionable audiences; a government that milks the drama long before author and management have covered expenses; but against them he ranged the many playgoers who expressed their appreciation and admiration. In a postscript he foresees the collapse of the English Theatre unless the system is changed radically. I will return to these matters in a later chapter.

Gareth Lloyd Evans, in his book on Priestley as dramatist, calls *Johnson Over Jordan* a failure. 'It fails because, yet again, Priestley seems unable to trust himself and his audience with too much or too rich a diet of the non-naturalistic; the theme, the technique employed, cry out for a wholehearted plunge into symbolic drama.' Johnson is apparently a down-to-earth character yet seems hardly rooted in life; the 'expressionistic' scenes seem unrelated to the rest of the play. The characters slowly lose identity and at the end they are supposed to become a composite image of the human condition, but it doesn't work, as JBP himself admits. The characters are intended as metaphors but Priestley doesn't allow them to leave the earth. Certainly he tries to raise his speech, but this attempt is one of the least satisfactory parts of the play. The 'poetic' passages are slightly embarrassing to the audience. One wonders if Wales might have succeeded here where Yorkshire failed. On the other hand, his attempts at poetry are no worse than Shaw's. When we speak of *Johnson Over Jordan* as a failure we become aware of the inadequacy of our vocabulary for critical purposes. What kind of failure? Is it a failure that puts it on a level with the permanent failures of the West End stage?

It is something quite new in English theatre. There had been authors and managements that had provided specialised plays for specialist audiences but these did not come into that category. Priestley was rejecting entirely the old conception that the past is gone irretrievably, that the future is something that is still to come and that we live in a limited span of present tense from birth to death, and he was putting these ideas before a fashionable audience. No-one could accuse him of preaching to the converted. Nor were the critics particularly helpful for on the whole British critics are eager to attack the triviality of audiences and equally prepared to find fault with an author who tries to transcend triviality. So far as Priestley was concerned, the whole enterprise represented a radical change in the direction of his work. From now on he was going to return to the Time theme again and again, and especially in his more personal books, such as *Midnight on the Desert*, 1937, and *Rain Upon Godshill*, 1939. It represents a tremendous leap from the traditional nostalgic tone of his early Georgian essays and criticism (which I have still to consider). Should we regard J.W. Dunne as the midwife of this birth?

JBP paid acknowledgments to Dunne in the Introduction to *Two Time Plays*, 1937. The simplified account of Time given in *Time and the Conways* does not depend upon or pre-suppose Dunne's more elaborate theory. Dunne believed that the single and universal Time that is imagined to be hastening everything to decay is an illusion. Our real selves are our complete lives and any given moment is a three-dimensional cross-section of a four- or multi-dimensional reality. The loss and pain felt in the cross-section is no more than the grimmer aspect of a full landscape. And to appreciate JBP's later work properly we must now turn to Time-theory in greater detail.[3]

Chapter 9

The Theory of Time

Dunne's three main contributions to the theory of Time are *An Experiment with Time, The Serial Universe* and *The New Immortality.* I am not so much concerned with Dunne's own views as with what JBP took from him. The basic idea, which JBP accepted, was that 'everything which has established its existence *remains in existence.*' 'A rose which has bloomed once blooms for ever,' as Dunne asserts in *The New Immortality.* (Chapter eleven of this book is the gist of a lecture which Dunne gave to, among others, the cast of *Time and the Conways.*) JBP states that although he got to know Dunne personally he never accepted the theory in its entirety. In its full working out it became very involved indeed and moved into territory that was hardly the business of a playwright.

To recapitulate briefly: in his earliest writings JBP had mentioned the sense of 'otherness' which he had felt at certain moments which he called 'magical'; these he related to the dream experience and also the feeling of a borderland between reality and unreality which the theatre always gave him; it was while dwelling on these matters, aided by the kind of reading that most intelligent young men of the period indulged in, that he began to link up these suggestions of unknown areas of feeling, with distinctive qualities of their own, with the possibility of other dimensions of time. The fascination with Time did not come upon him at some period during the thirties. While at Cambridge, where he took a degree after demobilisation from the Army, he used to attend lectures by John McTaggart Ellis McTaggart, a philosopher who was particularly concerned with the nature of Time. The lectures fascinated and delighted JBP, who said he used to recover the old sense of delight whenever he read anything by McTaggart (*Delight*, 1949).

It was during the twenties, when JBP was beginning his literary career, that the psychoanalysts began to draw attention to their work in Britain. They were not primarily concerned with the theory of Time but now and again they were compelled to consider certain implications of their theories that involved a positive approach to the nature of Time. In *Beyond the Pleasure Principle*, for instance, Freud considered the possibility that 'repetition' might be a fundamental principle of psychic life. He noticed that individuals tend to relive patterns of events experienced in the past. Quite unconsciously, people behave in such a way that, even though they are in new situations with new people, the outcome of events follows the same lines as similar situations in the past. Man cannot inherit experiences but tendencies towards certain kinds of belief and conception can be transmitted. Some part of man's mental apparatus is responsible for the recurrence of similar patterns of thought.

Like most of the younger writers of his time, JBP was attracted by Jung more than by Freud. Shortly after Jung broke with Freud he had his famous dream about the killing of Siegfried. At the time Jung had no clear idea of where he was going and he still accepted the greater part of Freud's teaching. But in the dream, the unconscious part of his psyche seemed to be telling him of the direction in which he was going, which was a break with an analytical emphasis on personal psychological factors and a move towards a concern with man's deeper relationship to the realities of myth and religion. The archetype, he later claimed, structured the conscious material in such a way that it expressed symbolically the purpose, the direction and the eventual meaning of the process taking place. As a proto-image, the archetype was present in principle at the very beginning of the process, which is why dreams frequently reveal an unconscious foreknowledge of the path of development that will unfold. 'It is as though an acorn had a dream in which the leaves of a new oak tree were symbolised,' writes Ira Progoff in *The Death and Rebirth of Psychology*, 1956, a book which JBP knew and recommended. Jung's Self was both reality and symbol; it is the underlying reality of psychic life and at the same time it is a symbolic goal drawing the work forward.

These are theories not of Time but of the unconscious, which projects into Time — but the orthodox idea of Time, which is a single irreversible movement through its own dimension. Dunne challenged this with the notion that Time resembled a series of moving streams, and that movement was possible (and indeed took place during dreams) from one stream to another. Within each consciousness was a series of observers, and there was no logical reason why there should be any limitation on the number of these observers. (This idea gave the title to one of his books, *The Serial Universe*.) This is not the place to describe the theory in detail, especially as JBP was not concerned with the idea of infinite regression. It is a mistake to stress Dunne's influence too much — remember that it was Ouspensky who supplied the main idea for *I Have Been Here Before*. And there were other possibilities which were summed up in another book recommended by JBP to his readers: *Foreknowledge*, by H.F. Saltmarsh, 1938. Saltmarsh accepts the existence of precognition and then examines the various theories accounting for it. He rejects Dunne's serialism on three grounds: an infinite series of observers (which in fact would be different levels of consciousness in the one person) was unacceptable; a time dimension cannot be changed into a space dimension; and time does not flow over a static history at a certain rate.

Three other theories are described. Professor C.D. Broad suggested a two-dimensional time, so that fixing a position in time would require co-ordinates, as on a map, rather than a point on a line. Saltmarsh himself put forward the idea that as we experience duration (our 'now' must be more than a mere pin-point of time), perhaps the subliminal awareness of the present is of much longer duration than our conscious awareness. And then there is the 'extra sense' theory, attributed to Du Prel, according to which there is a stratum in the subliminal mind which is capable of obtaining sensory knowledge of events outside the range of normal consciousness.

I have already stated that the theory of Time put foward in *I Have Been Here Before* is not Dunne's but Ouspensky's. In one of his personal memoirs, *Rain Upon Godshill*, published in the same year as *Johnson Over Jordan* was presented and two years after *I Have Been Here Before*, JBP writes, 'Actually, I think that reincarnation is perhaps a more attractive and more plausible theory than this of recurrence . . .' This seems an astonishing statement to coolly let drop into the discussion. JBP had allowed himself to be associated with the recurrence theory and one imagines that he based a play upon it because he believed in it — and yet here he says another theory is more plausible, for the two theories are usually taken to be rivals and not explanations of co-existing processes. It is a timely reminder that we should never approach the work of a creative writer in the same way as we approach that of a scientist or philosopher. The poet and playwright play it by ear, to use modern terminology, and complete consistency is no concern of theirs. (Emerson expressed this point of view once and for all.) Although we speak of the 'Time-plays' (the critics do and I do and so does Priestley, judging by the titles of two of his collections), only one of them, *I Have Been Here Before*, is actually concerned with Time theory. *Time and the Conways* does not even involve acceptance of precognition. It uses what is really no more than a dramatic device, a method of making a judgment on life. We only include it in the canon of Time-plays because we know that its author was seriously concerned with the nature of Time. *I Have Been Here Before* is actually based on a theory which permits intervention. One doesn't have to go to Ouspensky for this kind of thing. Saltmarsh recounts cases of this type, one of the more remarkable being that where a man dreams the mooring ropes of his yacht part, the vessel is swept away by the tide and is swamped on the bar, but by taking action prompted by the dream he was able to avert the full consequences. According to this theory there is a probable future but it is not inexorable; it can be avoided by intervention. Saltmarsh gives a homely example of this 'determined yet plastic future'. Events which will occur at noon tomorrow are determined by the total state of affairs now existing. I insert a new factor and thus change the basic state of affairs. Thus a freewill act modifies the future and precognition may be only partly fulfilled, or not at all.

The major enquiry that was evolving out of this concern with Time and dreams was this: was there such a thing as precognition? It was certainly not a passing interest with JBP. Although he wrote no more plays that can truthfully be designated 'Time-plays', the subject cropped up again and again in his other writings. He also referred to books by other writers that had impressed him and two of these are worth mention here because of their relevance to his own thinking. One was *The Sixth Sense*, 1959, by Rosalind Heywood. It is more concerned with automatic writing and telepathy than with precognition but there is one revealing passage quoted from the Willett scripts that must have left echoes in his mind. Mrs Willett had been describing a visionary journey but was disturbed by noise and then wrote: 'I've lost the thread, it's all gone. I was seeing visions and I did not ever want to leave. Fred (Myers) was with me F.W.H.M. I also saw Henry Sidgwick. He

had a white beard . . . How *nothing* time is. All human experience
is one . . .' In an Appendix Mrs Heywood gives some interesting
explanations and hypotheses of the psi effect. Professor Gardner
Murphy's has the closest relevance to JBP's concerns. He adapts
the field theory which had been evolved by anthropologists and
sociologists. He believed that flashes of ESP (they are never more
than that in our experience) indicate an enduring capacity at some
deeper level to make contact with all of space and all of time. The
field principle might hold in psychics as well as in physics and a
psychic field may extend backwards and forwards in time as well
as outward in space.

The other book was Louisa E. Rhine's *Hidden Channels of the
Mind*, 1962. She is chiefly concerned with telepathy, clairvoyance
and precognition as the main aspects of ESP, or the psi faculty.
She expresses a point of view which surely appealed to JBP thus:
'In the area of precognition distinctions are not always clear-cut.
The division between present and future is often blurred; the past
and future are perceived as if they are the present. The extra-
sensory perception of these various situations seems simply to
encompass all, as if in a timeless, spaceless purview.' And
discussing Space, she wrote: 'the matter of who is where in ESP
seems to be a function of the dream imagery. As on the stage, the
scene can be arranged now here, now there, and not necessarily
according to reality.' This remark in particular must have had
meaning for JBP. When he started writing for the stage, conventions were largely rigid. Today they are extremely fluid. He
was one of the playwrights who was most influential in effecting
this transition.

Let us go back now and have a closer look at his own theorising.
I have already referred to the dream he recounts in 'The Strange
Outfitter' in *Apes and Angels*. In this dream a crowd of people dance
and sing in the street, wearing frightening masks with movable
mouths. In *Rain Upon Godshill* he noted that his dream was like a
preview of a scene from *Johnson Over Jordan*, written years after he
had forgotten the dream. He also refers to a schoolboy dream of an
uncle whom he rarely saw and who appeared suddenly and unexpectedly and glared at him angrily. Years later he was having a
drink in a crowded bar when he looked up and saw this uncle,
whom he had not seen in the bar before, glaring at him as he had in
the dream. (He refers again to this dream and its sequel in *Man and*

Time, of which more later.) Now all kinds of questions arise. Are such dreams coincidences? Are they a re-shuffling of personal experience? But some of these dreams are not like his own experience and are not at all fantastic. He cannot believe he created everything in the dreams, down to the last detail. He believes they are incidents chosen from other people's life stories. Sometimes we even seem to leave this world altogether. Is it possible that access to ordinary reality is temporarily blocked and one's consciousness goes elsewhere? He recounts an ecstatic experience under the dentist's gas; the dentist laughingly attributes it to the gas, but 'there is no metaphysical ecstasy in nitrous oxide gas, the ecstasy is somewhere in me, buried deep, buried so damnably deep that I had to lose seven teeth finding it.'

There is also the 'clear wise dream', far removed in quality from the ordinary dream. Instead of a confused reflection of ordinary experience it seems to offer us a new and superior type of experience. Things are not out of focus but are more sharply observed than ever before. 'It is as if, returning to Dunne's theory, we were for once able to maintain a concentrated four-dimensional focus on four-dimensional presentation. Or, alternatively, that for a brief while we had been attached to a mind infinitely richer and greater than our own.' When JBP writes of the exceptional intensity experienced in some dreams he comes close to the kind of vision described by Aldous Huxley in *The Doors of Perception* and *Heaven and Hell*.

In later years JBP has given us his own views on Time in some detail in two books: *Man and Time*, 1964, and *Over the Long High Wall*, 1972. The former has the appearance of a coffee-table book but it is much more than that. It is liberally illustrated but the illustrations are much more relevant to the text than is normal in this kind of book. It is massive in appearance and massive in size but it is certainly not superficial in content. (Anyone in doubt should read chapter six on 'Time, History and Eternity'.) It is a comprehensive study, the sort of thing that is becoming more and more rare, because fewer writers are capable of the effort demanded by straddling half a dozen disciplines. It is in the tradition of Arthur Koestler and Aldous Huxley but it is more personal than their essays on the same level. The personal touch has its drawbacks; JBP can rarely resist gibes at academics which are usually justified but are better omitted from a book of this kind.

The Introduction (opposite a Vicky cartoon of JBP masquerading
as a very robust Father Time) refers to 'most writers on Time, who
pretend and may even have deluded themselves into believing that
they are purely objective . . .' And later, in a petulant parenthesis,
he exclaims, 'I am often wrong, unlike most of the politicians,
editors and experts I know.' This deprecation of possible rivals is
unfortunately characteristic of JBP.

In this book he says the dreamers can see a future that exists in
some shape or other, which could be dramatically changed by an
act of will; two examples of this kind of intervention are given —
saving a baby from drowning and a boy from being knocked down
by a car. This is more like the common working idea of the future
— half made, half there — than any defined conclusions of
scientists or philosophers. 'We have in these dreams possibilities
that were actualised, the visit to the creek, the encounter with the
boy on the road — and possibilities that were prevented from being
actualised — namely, the drowning of the baby, the knocking
down of the boy.' But there are some events which are too big to
be avoided. For example, nothing could be done about the Battle of
Borodino, where Count Toutschkoff died, although his wife had
dreamed of it, including the name of this tiny village in distant
Russia.

Over the Long High Wall received the kiss of death. 'I regard this
book as the supreme flop of my career in publishing,' writes JBP.
For anyone who is interested in the rules of the universe in which
we find ourselves — and one would expect such people to be
numerous — it is a fascinating book. Perhaps it would have been
more welcome if it had appeared in the late thirties, when Time-
theory was in the air and your hostess would not be bored if you
brought it up in conversation.

Priestley believes there are three kinds of time: passing time,
which is clock or chronological; a time for slowing down of
experience, for contemplation; and a time for speeding up, creative
and imaginative. Of course, we all talk about time passing slowly
or quickly but we don't believe it. JBP believes that in some way,
still inscrutable, this is an objective fact. No exact analysis, no
sharp lines can be made or drawn. The inner feeling is strong and
he gives greater weight to feeling than does the average scientist,
including the psychologist. The evidence is difficult to project,
perhaps because the relation between the consciousness and the

unconscious blurs the issue. The distaste for conventional time is
very strong among some people, those who never carry watches,
who exhibit impatience when time is mentioned. There is a
character of this type in the early novel, *Benighted*. Penderel hardly
ever wanted to know what the time was. 'Some people never seem
to think about anything else. I don't think I like watches and
clocks. We ought to go back to hour-glasses and sundials, things
that deal with time quietly and don't for ever pester you with their
sixty seconds to the minute.' In *Man and Time* JBP refers to one of
the implications of the popular view, that things are real only when
part of Now, so that the world keeps on destroying and re-creating
itself every fraction of a second:

> There is an opposite view. Those who take it have firmly turned their
> backs on all that destruction and recreation, that endless rushing from
> nowhere to nothing. In this theory, that has gone to the other extreme,
> everything is solidly there, whether we call it past, present or future.
> We experience things in Time because our Now, so to speak, goes
> steadily forward, as if we were travelling through a dark landscape with
> a searchlight, or we were staring at a bright scene through a slit in a
> moving barrier.

He calls the ordinary view of Time Consensus-Time. In *Over the
Long High Wall* he referred to *something* in us that is not subject to
the iron despotism of passing time, or uni-dimensional time, what
Dunne called Time 1, 'the conveyor-belt to extinction.' Precognition in dreams is a glimpse of the future which is confirmed in
waking life — and 'a vast enslaving system begins to crumble.' We
are in fact wonderfully different from the prevailing consensus
notion of what we are.

In *The Happy Dream*, already referred to, JBP wrestles with the
possibility of many dimensions of time, just as there are obviously
at least three dimensions of space. Let us assume, for the sake of
argument, that time also has three dimensions. In such a case, we
cannot refer to Time as 'the Fourth Dimension', as Wells did in his
Time Machine. The fourth dimension may simply be our clock time,
passing time or world time. Suppose there is a fifth dimension,
enduring time, in which anything that has happened goes on
happening. And a sixth dimension, which would be the realm of
creative time, in which what can be found in the fourth and fifth
dimensions can be rearranged and brought to new life by a powerful impulse to create new life. He had already tried to incorporate

the imagination into his scheme of time-dimensions back in 1939, in *Rain Upon Godshill*. He calls 'the aesthetic feeling' a delightful sensation. Somebody says 'France' or 'wild horses' or 'Eighteenth Century' and he is immediately lost in a little vision of whatever it is, and feels 'happier than if somebody had just given me ten thousand pounds.' There is no obvious reminiscence, he is not thinking how it looked or felt to him, but of how it really *is*. In this selfless enjoyment of the object a four-dimensional outlook is experienced. He says it has some connection with the mysterious multi-dimensional world we exist in. But we have only hints, no certain knowledge, and the vagueness of this account reflects the groping of the mind.

Perhaps these ideas of Priestley's have a great deal in common with other ideas which have occurred to thinking men throughout the ages. There is the idea of Eternity, which he tries to define in *Journey Down a Rainbow*, 1955, which he wrote with Jacquetta Hawkes.

> Eternity is not unending time. It is outside time. It involves another dimension of things. If we think of time as a line, then eternity is a plane. Life in time is existence along the one-way track from the cradle to the grave . . . eternal life is always a new and heightened experience of Here and Now . . . all moments of noble living, the ecstasy of love, the compassion and understanding that enter into every genuine personal relationship, the creation and rapt appreciation of great art, the adventures of the mind among significant ideas, even an amazed wondering about ourselves, all demand this unknown dimension, this timeless being.

It is, incidentally, surprising that this is the only reference to Time-theory in this absorbing book. The timeless quality of Pueblo religion and the time-obsessed quality of American life would seem to invite it. But JBP let the reality stand without recourse to theorising.

The other idea of Time, which exercised the Greek and Egyptian philosophers so much, is that of Great Time. Perhaps it was their notion of Eternity. JBP mentions it in *Man and Time* as an idea that has haunted mankind, of 'the mythological dream time, that is behind and above and altogether qualitatively different from ordinary time.' We no longer try to organise it, as the ancient astronomers did — the idea has dwindled and to some has become a matter of derision, but it refuses to go away. It is the antithesis of 'passing time'. Perhaps it is the analogue of the World Mind, to which I will return at the end of this book.

Time is a mystery which we cannot crack. But only a little thought is necessary to indicate that it is something more complicated than a single dimension. The evidence points to at least three dimensions. And if you cannot accept that as fact, JBP writes in *Man and Time*, then you must behave *as if* there are three kinds of time. Nothing else will cover the facts, apart from denying their existence in the manner of the positivists.

Man and Time contains the philosophical approach. Any reader who would like a more personal approach to JBP's Time-theories, whether based on Dunne or Ouspensky, is advised to go to *Midnight on the Desert*. Here he will find a vividness of phrase that rouses the attention where a more metaphysical approach might fail. He presents Dunne's theory in a way that Dunne himself could not do.

> On this view of Time, the Past has not vanished like a pricked bubble. To understand this dimension of things we move in Time as a blind man's finger moves over a piece of carving. Our consciousness travels along this track as we might travel on a railway journey. Then the Past is the station we have just left, and the Future is the station we are approaching. The Past has not been destroyed any more than the last station was destroyed when the train left it. Just as the station is still there, with its porters and ticket inspectors and bookstall and its noise and bustle, so the Past still exists, not as a dim memory, but in all its colour and hum.

With Ouspensky he is not so metaphorical.

> He points out with some truth that so far as Time is concerned we are one-dimensional creatures, analogous with the one-dimensional creatures of Space who would have to spend their whole existence along one line and know nothing beyond it. This is true of us intellectually. We are compelled to think of the single track of Time. But intuitively and in imagination we are not so narrowly bound. In high moments of emotion we seem to feel the timelessness, the eternal Now, of that fifth dimension.

And this is where JBP and the rest of us have to leave this fascinating subject. One day there may be a break-through but we haven't made it yet.

Chapter 10
The Theatrical Parallel

Again and again in his work JBP stops and says, in effect: How like the theatre this is! The theatre seems to represent for him a link between the world we live and work in, what we sometimes call the real world, and the world of dream that may provide an entry to an even more profound reality. The theatre is the magical moment held up for our admiration. It would be easy to make a sizeable anthology of his comparisons of life and theatre — and by theatre I do not mean drama; I mean the ambience of the theatre rather than its conflict.

Back in 1927, in an essay called 'Autolycus Again' (*Open House*), a rogue comes to the house selling furniture polish and he disappears before it is discovered that the polish seriously damages the furniture. JBP's mind flies to the theatre — this is Autolycus. He 'will not make so much these next ten years, and yet I consider him the more subtle comedian' — that is, more subtle than Harold Lloyd, who was paid £8,000 a week — 'staging as he does his comedies in our very midst and compelling us to join him as minor players.' In the same collection we have 'Midsummer's Dream' (the very title is, of course, an evocation of theatre). High midsummer seems to destroy reality, inducing thoughts similar to those of Indian philosophers in a similar environment. Perhaps it is the unfamiliarity of the vivid blues and golds that brings the sense of unreality. 'It is not that I feel that I alone am real. Other people are not part of the dream, but even they are touched with fantasy, for though they still remain their solid and companionable selves, they seem to be taking part in some kind of open-air theatrical entertainment.' One of the best examples of this mingling and merging of the real and the fantastic is to be found in his essay on 'Mr Punch' in *The Balconinny*, 1929. The children in the house were completely absorbed by Punch. They talked Punch, acted Punch and seemed to have rented a house in Punchdom. 'If I were to walk out one of these evenings and discover that the beach and promenade were crowded with Punches, Judies, babies, clowns, policemen, beadles, hangmen, comic boxers and crocodiles, I should not be very surprised. The real people here are quite shadowy.'

In the following year's *Apes and Angels* there were constant references to the theatre in all its varied forms — revue, musical comedy and circus as well as 'legitimate' drama. The parallels are always being drawn. 'The Two-and-Fourpenny Fairyland' is concerned with the public's love of musical comedy which he attributes to their desire to escape into the romantic world of the rich and the beautiful. This is a platitude to us but at that time had not been repeated *ad infinitum* — and in any case, JBP puts the point very neatly by saying that 'Princess This or Lady That is to them what Plato's Republic is to an idealist philosopher.' He naturally cannot resist the comedians — he has written several books on humour and humorists; they are the only reason he goes to musical comedy and puts up with those insipid leads and empty plots. He calls them 'those dynamos of drollery and character, perhaps the most massive personalities the English Stage can show.' When he goes to the circus he becomes a child again, glorying in the fun and the excitement along with the hundreds of other kids. 'We liked the horses and the tigers and the strong men and the Japanese jugglers, but the clowns we adored. How we laughed at the very serious one, dressed in a glittering court costume of clownage, who insisted upon turning the ring into a living-room and made all the assistants transform themselves into doors and windows and chairs and tables and even central heating apparatus!' ('At the Circus'). This is bare, uncomplicated enjoyment, all sophistication set aside, and it is fundamental to JBP's art and our appreciation of it. Even the philosophical Dunne has Grock leering and winking at us behind him.

1934, and JBP is now himself a playwright. In that year *Four-in-Hand* contained a story called 'Adventure'. Hubert longs for adventure, and if he hasn't got it he dreams it. Returning from work, on top of a bus, he thinks (or his creator thinks): 'There is something theatrical about these thoroughfares when the hour is approaching midnight and it happens to be fine. They look like stage "sets". They suggest that at any moment the most picturesque drama might begin.' The same feeling overcomes him three years later, and is described in one of the *Self-Selected Essays*,

'Our *Bad*'. He describes a visit to *Bad* Tölz in the Bavarian Highlands. He goes to the fair, which is perfectly ordinary, but the people hardly belonged to this world at all. As he looked at the men and women in their folk costume he expected cardboard tankards to be distributed, followed by the order to group themselves, and then the curtain would go up. And by 1939, when he publishes one of his thoughtful memoirs, *Rain Upon Godshill*, he is prepared to be more explicit:

> I have always felt that the miniature world of action and feeling in the little lighted area of the stage is profoundly symbolic of all our lives here in this world, so that the actor may be seen as representative of our common humanity.

Note the word 'symbolic', not merely 'representative.'

The war provided countless examples of this effect. In my next chapter I am going to discuss JBP's treatment of the war in creative terms, but I would like to anticipate a little by quoting from one of the war novels, *Daylight on Saturday*, 1943. It is *A Novel About an Aircraft Factory* (the sub-title) and provides numerous opportunities for the life-theatre parallel to be made.

> The scene inside the conference room looked as if it were part of a play. Blandford, pale, compressed, icy, was sitting at the head of the table; Elrick, crimson and swollen with anger, was standing at the other end; and five or six other men were sitting around, with expressions on their faces that ranged from extreme annoyance to mere embarrassment. Angleby felt it was rather like going late to a theatre and finding yourself invited on to the stage, where a very dramatic scene, from some unknown drama, was being held up for you.

This is becoming very familiar by now — in fact, too familiar for there is a suspicion that it is becoming a method of retreat, a substitute for real feeling, with JBP reducing life to the theatre rather than discovering drama in life. But the decadence of an idea does not invalidate the idea.

In *Letter to a Returning Serviceman*, written at the end of the Second War, JBP tells us how he turned to the theatre on returning from *his* war, though it did not happen immediately. As a youth he had been involved with the Labour movement in Bradford. But now he found that movements and committees had no appeal for him. He became a typical private Englishman. It was the theatre that broke the walls down. From the beginning of his work in the theatre, he says, he took more interest in the actual production of his plays than the average playwright. First of all, he had to work with other people and he found he liked it. But there may have been more to it than that. In the theatre he experienced the coming together of so many different elements, things that were engaging his attention more and more: the magical moment, the dream sense — and was it a parody of life or was it an attempt to get closer to life? There seems to be a chicken-and-egg situation here. In *Bright Day* Gregory's aunt and uncle reminded him of 'an artful pair of comics'. But aren't the comics seen in the theatre a burlesque portrayal of aunt and uncle?

When you see a novel with the title, *The Magicians*, you prepare yourself for a story that will suggest something beyond the normal diurnal range of experience. Virtually dismissed from his executive position with New Central Electric, Ravenstreet, with no other plans, feels he is attending a comedy, a show that would have been very funny indeed if there had been life outside the theatre instead of darkness and dissolution. The comparison is extended — he was surrounded by an immense cast of comic characters, acquaintances who seemed to be hardly more than puppets. By now the theatre has practically taken over the whole of life. Theatrical metaphors occur throughout the novel. For example, 'the tottering giant and the fat waddling dwarf moved together across the lawn, a vaude-ville act again.' (JBP has a tendency to blow up or deflate his characters physically.) The Sepmans are referred to as 'two type characters in a modern morality play: the Dissatisfied Woman and the Angry Man.' When the guests come to dinner, the central event of the novel, Ravenstreet feels he is showing actors to their dressing-rooms before a performance they have agreed to stage. The sense of theatre still remained with him when he offered them cocktails and sherry: 'The cast had assembled; the curtain was about to rise; an unknown comedy or tragedy was about to be played.'

JBP drew the attention of his audience to the life-theatre link when he gave a lecture under the Hubert Henry Davies Fund on 30th September 1956 at the Old Vic Theatre, with his old friend Sir Ralph Richardson in the chair. The lecture was published in the following year as *The Art of the Dramatist*. Ordinary playgoers often remark admiringly of a play, 'It was just like life.' JBP tends to see the reflection in the reverse direction, saying of life, 'It was just like theatre.'

There are certain rare moments in our lives perhaps when we are physically exhausted but alert in spirit, perhaps when we find ourselves in great danger — when reality itself suddenly turns into dramatic experience, as if the whole world were a giant theatre and all this life a drama, so much play-acting compared with some unknown deeper reality.

It is not surprising, therefore, that his personal memoirs (books such as *Rain Upon Godshill*, *Midnight on the Desert* and *Margin Released*) should be full of such comparisons. Let us take the latter as an example. He writes here that the years of adolescence hold much more than later ones. In 1912 he was eighteen. His sixteen-year old self had been a different person. He feels he is writing while the house lights are up and there is an interval before the Second Act (opening in 1912 — as some of his plays in fact do). During the first half of 1914 he crammed so much experience into a short time that 'life was like a roundabout with the gilded cars and cockerels flashing by, the bray of the organ, the drums and cymbals, never silent, while the man in the middle wipes his hands on an oily rag and yawns.' Huxley wrote a poem with similar meaning. Again, convalescing after his war wounds, he was sent to a country house in Rutland. This was unreal — 'even Rutland itself was as near to being an imaginary county as the map of England would allow'[2] — one end of the vast military machine had dissolved into fantasy. His sky-blue coat and pants with white shirt and scarlet tie, regulation wear of the military sick and wounded, was the gaudiest outfit he had ever worn in a public conveyance. Then arrival at the country house, where there was a crisis, 'people . . . rushing in and out of rooms and slamming doors like characters in a farce.' The staff consisted largely of V.A.D. girls, county and pretty, straight out of *Tatler* and *Bystander*, looking like nurses in musical comedy. While here he organised a little concert party, which toured the East Midlands and gave shows in various mansions. They would be given tea below stairs, where the 'kitchens and pantries and servants' halls . . . were often like magnificent stage sets.' And another time, when on a train journey in France, he was the only officer aboard, with hundreds of embittered, sometimes drunk and near-mutinous soldiers. 'It was like suddenly being put in charge of eight circuses, short of pay, food and water.'

If this feeling is peculiar to JBP he himself believes it owes a lot to a quality peculiar to the English. But if it has any validity it must be universal. JBP simply feels the English are closer to it than most other races. William Hogarth, always regarded as 'typically English', makes him feel he is in a theatre. 'What he makes me feel is that in this life, to which there must be a deeper and more enduring reality, we are condemned to play our scenes of comedy and tragedy as if on a lighted stage, while our more essential selves stare, laugh or cry, seemingly helpless, in the darkened auditorium,' he writes in *The English*, 1973. And this seems proof to him that Hogarth's most characteristic work came out of his Englishness. It combines various strands in JBP's approach to life. There is the comparative unconsciousness of English mental action; the conviction of a deeper, unknown reality, underlying logic and reason; and with it goes the constant reference back to theatrical experience as an accurate image of our condition. It recurs again and again in his work, but especially in this book on his fellow-countrymen. And in the chapter on Englishwomen the most prominent presentation is given to actresses, as though they constitute the norm.

Chapter 11

The War: Plays and Novels

The Second World War caused a much greater disturbance in JBP's career than in that of most writers. It was a war that, like most thoughtful people, he had foreseen for some time because he knew it could not be avoided. He was in complete sympathy with its major aim, the defeat of Hitler and the destruction of Fascism, but he did not wholly approve of its conduct. The result was that he dropped all those concerns which had featured so strongly in his recent work: time, dreams and magic, and devoted himself to the one overriding cause. It was a remarkable decision. The author of *Time and the Conways* and *Midnight on the Desert* continued to write plays and novels but each one during the period of the war, and immediately after, was deliberately set in the war situation.[1] The future was not eliminated from his new view of things but it was seen in a different way: the kind of future that the people of this country could reasonably expect to enjoy once the sacrifice and suffering were over.

It is useless to pretend that this wartime writing of JBP is among his best work. It isn't and it couldn't be, for the simple reason that it was essentially propaganda. But it was not unthinking, Establishment propaganda (though JBP wrote on behalf of the Government when he was persuaded of its rightness). The propaganda was always on behalf of the ordinary people, explaining that the plight they were in was the result of fearful social and economic and political muddle, but the best thing to do was to defeat the external enemy first and then make quite sure that they put their own house in order. It should also be pointed out the JBP himself did not make any high claims for the work of this period — in fact, in one case I think he has always undervalued the product. In the Introduction to Volume 3 of the *Collected Plays* he makes the point unequivocally. Writing of *Desert Highway*, 1943, he says it was never intended to be a contribution to the Theatre. 'It was specially written, as a gift to the Army, to be produced by the Army Bureau of Current Affairs.' Nevertheless it had a civilian production after the war which was apparently successful.

Most of his plays of this period seem to lack plausibility. That a tank should break down in the desert (as happens here) is acceptable, but that its inmates should start cataloguing themselves and their backgrounds (to assist the audience, of course) is not. It is the fault of so much political writing which attempts to put the 'common man' in the picture. Smith meets Brown, they sit over a pint, talk about their gardens and slowly the conversation turns to the best way of doing things, how the situation went wrong, what we ought to do now — and at the end Smith has converted Brown, who goes away feeling a glow of inner wellbeing and a determination to help bring in the New World. *Desert Highway* belongs to this species, with the tank crew replacing the 'common men' — they are, of course, 'common men' in uniform. When JBP tries to be profound about society he tends to lose his dramatic skill, which he does not always do when he attempts to be profound about time. The general message he is putting across here is that everyone is to blame for the mess we're in — so it follows that we must all work together to get out of it. Thus spake Donnington:

> It isn't just the chaps at the top — as you call them. What's wrong goes all through. Nobody learns anything and nobody wants to. We're all barmy somewhere inside. The Nazis and Fascists and Japs are worse than we are, but we're barmy too.

And later he concludes that 'we're all wandering about in a colossal lunatic asylum.' It is interesting to compare this sort of thing with Evelyn Waugh, who was reactionary, snobbish and didn't give a damn about the 'common people'. But whereas JBP can only tell us that society is rotten, Waugh exhibits its rottenness. Waugh can make a living character out of an upper-class man who refuses to take a commission, whereas JBP's Donnington is simply a type. When the play is over he dissolves. It seems likely that JBP's deep involvement in political matters damaged his work as a creative writer. A politician feels compelled to omit or gloss over certain unsatisfactory aspects of his characters.

How Are They At Home?, 1944, was called a Topical Wartime Comedy. It was written for E.N.S.A. (Entertainment National Service Association). Again we see JBP trying to be down-to-earth, common-man, presenting the new-found solidarity of English society, and if it existed, as so many people agreed it did, he was the man to feel it. But despite such happy auguries, it is patronising in tone. The mistake was fundamental — the heroine is a titled lady working in a factory, and no one is going to take her trials and tribulations on the one hand, and democratic bonhomie on the other, seriously. JBP singling out an aristocrat to fill the centre of a democratic comedy is like Lord Longford singling out a horror-murderer to show his concern for the prison population. Her Ladyship has just been made a charge hand, and there is a little celebration in the ancestral home, now sadly decayed. The theme was popular among playwrights and middle-class audiences at the time (and at the time all theatre audiences were middle-class, except the special, captive military ones). The theme was mucking-in-together, aristocrats are human beings after all — but what did the fellers think of it? Not much, I imagine. Although Lady Farfield works in a factory, her friends on the bench (Hilda and Eileen) still refer to her as Lady Farfield. There is a little, though mercifully not much, of the kind of propagandist talk which, even when they agree with it, makes English people writhe. And JBP, wily old bird, puts it in the mouth of an Austrian refugee: 'It does not matter so long as *they* — the Nazi cheats and murderers — and all the people like them — have gone — and all nice simple friendly people — in Yorkshire — in Austria — anywhere — everywhere — can get to know each other and understand each other . . .'

They Came to a City, 1944, which opened in Bradford and moved to a long run at the Globe, also in 1944, was an improvement. David Hughes calls it 'unquestionably Priestley's most successful attempt to contrive a drama in which the quite obvious element of debate was not resented by the audience.' The conflict between the stoker and the waitress 'produce one of the most gripping moments in all Priestley's plays. She needs the city — he knows he must return to the old world to spread the good news. The audience is saved from embarrassment by JBP's sincerity, for the ideal is neither stated nor implied but is presented in human terms.' It is symbolic drama where the other plays of the war period were realistic. Perhaps it was this distancing which saved it. Nevertheless, there are some very notable faults in it, and I will discuss them at some length because they are typical of JBP's drama.

'Nobody has seen it,' writes JBP in his Introduction to Volume 3 of *Collected Plays*, 'who did not see the original production,' and it is only fair to bear this in mind. A good production can remedy many of the faults which appear on the cold and naked page. JBP warns producers against turning it into a melodramatic production with too heavy a bias against the older characters. *Pace* David Hughes, who felt the play succeeded because it presented a problem in human terms, I do not think the characters come alive. It is difficult to imagine them with any extended life, going beyond the play. I am the more convinced of this when I think of some of the characters JBP has given us in plays such as *Time and the Conways, When We Are Married* and *The Linden Tree*. When he was below his best, and that included all the plays of the period we are considering, he gave us a gallery of types: the lively, life-loving young girl type, the steady, down-to-earth midde-aged man type, the fiery revolutionary type, the thoughtful professor type, the wastrel type. JBP has the trick of observing them closely, which first gives the impression of reality, but later one realises that the same types have been wheeled out for display and then put away into cold storage until wanted again.

This play is a fantasy, a mode in which JBP is very heavy-footed (his recognition of fantasy must not be confused with his per-formance), and it becomes all the more embarrassing when he insists on trying to dance. He sees the play as an exercise in 'symbolic action', which he explains is a term of his own coinage, and says he uses it frequently in his work. But he is so conscious of the symbolism that the necessary underlay of reality gets lost. It all comes down to the familar Priestleyan situation of the fortuitous group, only this time they are gathered together by magical agency. When Cudworth raps out, 'Who are we, anyhow? What are we doing here?' we feel inclined to answer, 'You are puppets put together by Mr J.B. Priestley and you're where you are because he wants to lecture us.' The wonderful city of human justice is first seen by the innocent eyes of youthful girlhood (Philippa and Alice) while Joe and Cudworth, who are older and more cynical, can at first only see the mist. The mist is the physical representation of JBP's 'muddle' (a state we will discuss in more detail later), and it recalls the mist encountered by Virginia Woolf's Orlando as she entered the nineteenth century. In JBP's work the social muddle is a nineteenth century legacy.

Class divisions are sharply sketched, as they had been in *People at Sea*. But loyalties and affinities cross class and sex lines — Alice with Philippa and (after a nervous beginning) with Joe. The dialogue is choppy, at times even childish. (This is almost certainly the result of trying to use a play for explicit preaching, and the enormous strain this imposes on the playwright's control.) Take this outburst from Joe: 'I can't believe in the Revolution because I've gone sour. I don't see people making anything good together. They always seem to be making something bad. When they do anything good they don't do it altogether but by themselves. But if the Revolution is to be any use, they're got to be able to make something good together.' This makes Revolution sound like something you get from a gents' outfitter. What a decline such nebulous talk is compared with the genuinely human constructiveness found in *The Good Companions*. Joe talks with the insensitivity of the Communist Party ranter, yet he is meant to be a sympathetic portrayal. At times he is incredible: 'Where you people made the mistake was in ganging up with these money boys. You ought to have ganged up with us — the crowd, the mob, the people without any money. I read a piece by Disraeli where he said that.'

With all due deference to a successful playwright, I should have thought this was exactly not the way to write a play: it is nearly all discussion, issuing from text-books, though roughened by colloquial language. The old, old rule which even the best can forget is that without characters that have their own inner life, drama doesn't work. This is merely propagandist work, and if you look carefully you will find this sort of thing attacked by Mr Priestley himself in *English Journey*, 1934, and *Bees on the Boat Deck*, 1936. Here is an example of it at its worst:

> *Joe.* Some of you pick up any bit of happiness as if it was a chicken — and then wring its neck.
> *Mrs Stritton (suddenly stormily).* Why do you keep on insulting me?
> *Joe (with equal sudden passion).* Because I'm trying to save your life.
> *Mrs Stritton.* My life isn't in danger.
> *Joe.* You've got a knife in its throat now.

One is reminded of Orwell's dictum: sloppy thinking leads to sloppy language.

On the whole JBP's wartime novels were superior to his wartime plays. There was not such an intense desire to preach and when it did occur it was diluted by the greater length of the novel. *Black-Out in Gretley*, 1942, is sub-titled *A Story of — and for — Wartime*. It is dominated by the darkness that enveloped the whole town and engenders an atmosphere such as that built up in a good creepy story. (In *Letter to a Returning Serviceman* JBP expresses his disgust with the black-out which he condemned 'as an ill-considered piece of panic legislation'.) The novel is in fact a spy thriller and JBP is much better at this kind of thing than he gets credit for. Once again he is the victim of his own versatility. Serious novelists were not supposed to write such things in the nineteen-forties. We owe it largely to Graham Greene that novelists such as Kingsley Amis can write adventure stories and not lose face, and as a consequence that Len Deighton and John Le Carré can now be taken more seriously than they would have been in a previous generation — or than JBP, who belongs to an earlier generation, is when he attempts the genre. This particular example is not terribly convincing but it is certainly lively: I would place it not far behind Buchan. The major weakness is that its hero, Humphrey Neyland, who does a first-class job of Nazi spy-catching, possesses powers of guessing at the truth on the most marginal of evidence that verges on the supernatural.

Being Priestley, there is a good deal of social comment. As was later apparent in *Daylight on Saturday*, 1943, the attitude towards victory in the war was ambivalent — by which I do not imply that JBP ever wanted Germany to win (that would have been the basest of libels) but that he was very doubtful about the propriety of a victory by British industrialists and landowners. Gretley was such a hideous place and who made it so? 'I go where the department tells me to go, and every time I catch a Nazi agent or anybody who sells out to one, then I'm delighted, for you don't have to tell me what sort of a world Hitler and Himmler would leave us with; but that doesn't mean I haven't my own ideas or that I don't know what I'd do to the idiotic old noodles who come to these places and ask people to fight and sweat for "our traditional way of life". Holy Moses!' JBP's hatred, anger, frustration, contempt for the ruling class is pronounced. An idiotic genteel tradition hung round the necks of people who believed it was still 1904. He admitted that Neyland's handling of his job was influenced by his 'impatience and utter bewilderment, fed too by my hatred of the cold wet dingy town.' And when the spy-ring is finally unmasked it is a fierce local patriot, Colonel Tarlington, who is found to be its leader and organiser, looking to the Nazis as the only possible defenders of the way of life he stood for.

Daylight on Saturday, which appeared in the following year, is a greatly undervalued novel. It is usually dismissed as part of JBP's war-work. It is sub-titled as a *Novel About an Aircraft Factory*, and it never leaves the factory. Both this factory and Gretley are excellent examples of Priestleyan symbols. To write it at all JBP had to emulate Zola but it lacks Zola's sexual intensity, which JBP never could manage. I don't want to make exaggerated claims for *Daylight on Saturday* but it is certainly superior to some novels which have attracted more attention. The class relationships, for example, which are so integral a part of nearly all modern English fiction, are dealt with very subtly. The fundamental differences are stressed. It is the psychological ones that do the damage, rather than the economic or even the functional. For it is what class distinction has done to the individual mind of the individual person, rather than what it has done to social organisation, that is important.

Elrick, who has worked his way up to one of the most important positions in the factory, loathes Blandford, who has a landed-gentry background. 'The trouble about Blandford is that although he's come into industry, he's also never left his country mansion and estate. You know what I mean? It doesn't matter if he hasn't got a country mansion and estate. He behaves as if he had, and it's the same thing . . . Blandford does think himself altogether superior, a different kind of man.' Blandford makes him 'feel sometimes like a bloke, floundering about in a muddy ditch and watching another bloke, all spick an' span, come strolling down the road an' take out his handkerchief to flick a bit of dust off his coat.' The feeling between the two men finally comes to a head and Elrick puts the situation bluntly. 'I don't like what you stand for and you don't like what I stand for.' In this novel JBP pinpoints something about the class situation which so many people fail to grasp, including the Communist Party member who can only think in terms of wages and output and those who are wearied by the whole subject and think it can be dismissed by refusing to acknowledge it. It's not the economic divisions or the classification into groups according to interest that corrodes English life, but the attachment of spiritual quality to these divisions so that they come, in some extreme cases, to take on an almost religious character.

Bob Elrick, the works superintendent, lacks self-control and is eventually removed. He is of working class origin and is a bitter enemy of those from a higher class. He is replaced by Angleby, a

young man with a similar background but educated and command-
ing the control Elrick lacks. (We will see more of his kind in the
later novels of C.P. Snow.) He has a love-hate relationship with a
rather superior secretary who is connected with the gentry. In the
end they agree to marry. He admits that she represents 'nearly
everything that I dislike in theory, and that in practice I'm
frightened of.' But JBP shows him overcoming his fear, originally
based on insecurity, and asserting a new confidence which allows
him to turn aside if she resorts to mild tantrums. The observation
is excellent and the symbolism is obvious. Not only do the classes
merge, but the new representative of the working class is getting
rid of his crudeness and prejudice. This merging happens period-
ically in British society, as when Henry VIII's new men entered
and took over the aristocracy and the nineteenth century brewers
and steelmasters entered the House of Lords. Many commentators
have remarked on the warm, co-operative and hopeful atmosphere
that pervaded our society during the worst years of the war. JBP
felt it too and believed that the agony of class division that eats like
a canker at English society would be cut out and cauterised by the
war. But he was mistaken.

Three Men in New Suits, 1945, was about the demobilisation
period and was greatly inferior to *Daylight on Saturday*. An intro-
ductory note tells us that it was written before the end of the war,
when JBP assumed that the demobbed men would be given
horrible 'utility suits'. They weren't, and he apologises to the
Services and the Ministry of Supply. But it sets things off on a
wrong footing, with an admission that this particular item in his
vision of the immediate future is at fault. In this novel JBP is
telling us what he expects the post-war world will be like. Three
men, of differing backgrounds but bound in a firm friendship
based on their shared wartime experiences, come back to a world
that doesn't want the changes that the servicemen consider
necessary. A lot of novels bearing this theme were appearing at
about this time. Mrs Kentford is surprised to hear that her son
Herbert had become friendly with Alan Strete from the Manor and
Eddie Mold, a quarryman. 'You'll find it different here,' she says,
'an' don't think you won't. Eddie Mold — Mr Strete — neither of
'em's your sort here. Never was, never will be.' As usual, JBP
hammers the point and will not leave it alone. Too many of those
who stayed at home have become wrapped in selfishness. Herbert

is appalled by this 'Fuck you, Jack, I'm all right' attitude. He tells his new girl friend how they sat round the table, carving up their little empire, 'all pleased that they'd got a good fat share and all so determined to stick to it whatever happened to everybody else — I felt terribly about it.' This characteristic lies like a toxic element in the heart of all JBP's later fiction, changing by the time of *Carfitt* to internal arrogance.

It is a thesis novel, well meaning like all JBP's social writing, but too naked to win a doubting reader. Herbert (again — he has moments of surprising articulateness), says, 'What I can't stand any longer, not after what we've been through, is all this old stupid greedy grabbing and screaming, like a lot of half-starved dogs round a lump of horse meat.' There is always a temptation for JBP to turn his novels into jeremiads, and here was an occasion he couldn't resist. In his own case, being faced by the question set before his characters: What are you going to do about it? he tried politics, and was a flop.

Chapter 12

A Changing Society

The change from metaphysician to politician was not as abrupt and complete as I may have suggested. As JBP has said, exaggeration is one of the tools of the writer's trade. In this chapter I intend to examine his growth of interest in social conditions, with especial reference to *English Journey*.

As a young man he had regarded himself a socialist and had written for Labour newspapers in Bradford, but this was not known to his new readers when he became an essayist based on London. And certainly there is very little evidence of his political sympathies — even of political interests of any kind — in this early work. But it peeps out here and there, and with the hindsight granted by his later career we may now note its significance. If you turn to his volume of essays entitled *Open House* which appeared in 1927 you will find one essay ('Having Covered the Card Table') which is quite different in tone from the others. It is the most serious contribution to this collection and it is the only one that completely transcends the relaxed, Sunday afternoon atmosphere of the Familiar Essay style. It is of great interest to the modern student of Priestley because it anticipates the judgements and criticisms to be encountered later in *English Journey*. JBP tells us how he has just fitted a new felt top to a card-table and found immense satisfaction in doing it. He reflects that a man who earns his living doing such jobs is 'in no bad case', a good example of English understatement. If a man in that situation grumbles, he is a 'churl'. But if he is bundled into a roaring great factory and has to do similar jobs, only much more restricted in scope, we can hardly blame him for feeling cheated. 'He thinks he is being cheated out of money, but whether he is or not, the fact remains that he is certainly being cheated out of something more important, namely, a decent and amusing job, that honest and engrossing work which is also great fun.' People turn to handicrafts for fun but he has yet to meet a person who spends his leisure taking part in mass production.

The language is old-fashioned but the awareness is modern. People inevitably grumble about pay but the major problem of our society lies in the deplorable quality of the work it offers its members. JBP has already told us that when he left the Army he shied away from communal work, but involvement in the theatre brought him back. I think it is possible to pin-point fairly accurately the moment when social and political topics returned to assume an important place in his mind. An essay in *Apes and Angels*, 1928, is quite unlike any of the others. It is simply entitled 'Servants': it is very serious, it is puzzled and hurt, it is even angry; not the normal essayist's mood at all. It should be borne in mind that the disappearance of the servant from the private home is one of the major marks of twentieth century social development. 'A girl came to us as a cook,' he writes, 'demanding the wages and privileges of a cook. Now this girl could not cook; she would not even try to learn how to cook; and at the least hint of criticism she either raged or sulked.' He tries to parallel her behaviour in his own profession: the editor asks him for essays of a certain length and he sends in fewer words copied at random out of a dictionary. He begins to puzzle this business out in social terms.

> Their mothers were frankly servile, and their daughters will probably be frankly independent, but this generation, as oddly placed as this generation of masters and mistresses, will neither abandon itself to servility nor cut itself loose from it.

Here is an admission that society is in a state of flux and that he, J.B. Priestley, is in the middle of it. It brings us straight to *English Journey*.

Published in 1934, it is not only one of his best-known books but also one of his best. It belongs to a tradition in which Daniel Defoe and William Cobbett had been his forebears. It is far more serious and progressive in tone than most books by popular writers. To get some idea of the general tone of such books the reader should turn to H.V. Morton, a contemporary who was always following In The Steps of Somebody-or-Other; others were In Search of Something-or-Other and inevitably finding slush, slop, charm, oodles of sentiment and absolutely no problems. Priestley encountered the English economic system.

He finds England a very mixed entity. Now it's all very well to say, This is good, or This is bad, but it's a great mistake to pick on *the* good and make everything else conform. This is the economist's method and it leads to something JBP deplores: soulless regimentation. He goes to the Cotswolds, sees a miniature seaport that some eccentric has built in a village, finds it charming, indulges in all the joys of a man who worships Charles Lamb — and then tugs himself back into the contemporary world. 'We need a rational economic system,' he writes, 'not altogether removed from austerity.¹ Without such a system we shall soon perish.' Then the other side tugs and he decides there must be room for eccentricity, for austerity without variety means the death of the spirit. Eccentrics are not dangerous. They don't lust for power or behave like bullies. They show the herd another way of life. 'We are glad to know such experiments are still being made . . . And I suspect that the system that rigidly excludes him (the eccentric) will prove to be too narrow for the good life, which would not be good if it banned the mild dreamer . . .' It is exactly this, the determined banning of the dreamer, which makes the collective societies of Eastern Europe such deplorable places to live in. (I lived in one for six years.) This is the point at which most social and economic reformers fail. The real advance will be made when someone manages to incorporate dreams into social justice. JBP has never gone back on this attitude.

There must be freedom, there must be scope for experiment and fancy, but below these things there must be a solid basis of social justice. JBP talks with a steward from one of the big liners in Southampton. He is very discontented. The ships have *Louis Quinze* drawing rooms, Tudor smoke-rooms, and wretched accommodation for the staff. 'It is not pleasant, to say the least of it, to remember that the poor devil who is waiting upon you may have been washed out of his quarters the night before and has not sat down to a decent square meal since the voyage began.' These sentiments are repeated later in *Bees on the Boat Deck*. Throughout the journey JBP shows his sympathy with the underdog, the victim of undeserved poverty and injustice; he also shows his impatience with inefficiency and sordidness, especially of the kind often found in small shops. While he tends to support the individual he does not do so merely because he is an individual. First of all he wants the individual to show he is superior to the bureaucrat. He can be attracted by size and glamour, but only if it works, as it did in the ocean-going liners and the new style factories, then sprouting at the

London end of the Great West Road. But size could be appalling, as he found in Swindon. Each street was exactly like the last, each house, built for Victorian artisans, was exactly like its neighbour. 'If a number of bees and ants cynically working in bricks and mortar, had been commissioned to build a human dormitory, they could not have worked with more desolating uniformity.' The symbolism of bees frequently recurred — that they should have been active on the boat deck was the most alarming thing of all.

He often strikes a fierce satirical note in his attacks on social injustice. There is a good example of this concerning the exploitation of women in the Bradford mills. A weaver who has worked for fifty years has proved herself a valuable servant and is naturally rewarded — with a pension of five shillings a week, 'five shillings to do what she likes with.' The State adds another ten and the lucky creature has a whole fifteen bob to squander — if only she didn't have an invalid sister to support.

> But perhaps it is as well that she cannot go splashing her fifteen shillings about, because if she could, although she is old and heavy and tired, she might arouse the indignation of those honest fiery Tory patriots who write articles for and letters to the newspapers, protesting against the treatment afforded this pampered class . . . She does not complain much, perhaps because she realises, like all the protesting gentlemen who lounge before large club fireplaces, that if, during and after her fifty years of toil, she had been treated with any more consideration it would have meant the ruin of a great country.

In Lancashire, when taken to working class homes, he made notes and reproduced them as they stood. 'Income here 29/3 a week, with rent about 8/6. All living in luxury according to the Ministry of Health, but do not seem to realise this, not having scientific and official minds.'

These minds are both the product and the cause of the contemporary impasse. The horrors and shortcomings of modern society do not come from any particular system but from industry itself. (This was stated in *Golden Fleece*, a post-war play; it had, of course, been at the heart of D.H. Lawrence's critique of society.) JBP's visit to Bournville brought up a large number of questions. Bournville was admirable, in many ways a success, but he was not convinced.

> If one of these paternal factories were taken over by the State tomorrow, only one weakness of the system would disappear, the fact that the

whole organisation is there for private profit; all the other weaknesses and dangers would remain, for the individual workmen would still be compelled to look in only one direction for all the benefits of his life, would run the same risk of losing his independence, could still believe that he was made for his factory and not his factory for him, could confuse and mislay all his values, even though the directors had now to report to a public ministry instead of to a body of shareholders.

The most fashionable and potent illusion of our time, shared by both Communists and Fascists, was the belief that somehow State ownership would bring a richer and more significant life to the ordinary man than any other form.

But one of the most important points for JBP, one he returns to again and again, in other books as well as this, is the question: Who is master, man or machine? Economic status has nothing to do with it. The more machinery is used and the more complex it becomes, the greater the gap between those who care about the enterprise and those who don't. 'I do not see that any change in the economic system will bridge (this gap). If the State ran the factory, the division would still be there.' And it still is in those countries where factories are huge State-holdings. This is something that communists, even sincere ones like Bob (whom he meets on Tyneside), cannot understand. Such ideologies are

the entrance into a Human Paradise and a new Golden Age, from which, by some mysterious means, all the selfish wickedness of the present world will be banished. Nobody could be more cynical than he is about elected persons and men in authority here and now, but he has no difficulty in persuading himself that in a communist England all elected persons and men in authority would acquire a new mystical virtue.

Such views as JBP here enunciates are widely accepted these days by thinking people, but not so widely in 1934.

English Journey has remained in print. It is a shameful indictment of a society that had little to recommend it. One year earlier JBP had brought out his novel, *Wonder Hero*, which made many of the same points and was probably based on much the same experience. It is now forgotten and is even usually omitted from a list of JBP's fiction. Yet this story of a young man who is taken up by a national newspaper for an act of heroism shines a spotlight on the class conflicts in our society more strongly than anywhere else in his work with the exception of *Daylight on Saturday* and perhaps *Three Men in New Suits*, although less successfully in the latter. In

London Charlie Habble meets the idle rich, the pompous and the powerful. It is a novel of protest and it contrasts the desperate yet morally superior provinces with the corruption of the capital. Charlie gets support from a chambermaid working in a luxury hotel, who would like to put some of the rich female guests to work and let some other women who had exhausted themselves with work come there and be waited on hand and foot for a change. There is also a good portrait of a cynical young newspaperman, who knows the truth Charlie is discovering but has no intention of doing anything about it.[2]

Charlie leaves London to see his sick aunt. It is a symbolic act. There is a general picture of waste, hopelessness and decay. 'Some of the towns in the Midlands had been knocked sideways by the depression, but this place had been knocked flat.' His aunt is ill simply because she has been starving herself, in an effort to provide for an unemployed husband and son. The daughter earns eighteen shillings a week working in a sweetshop, and more than half of this is deducted from the miserable amount they get from the dole. And all the time, fresh in Charlie's memory, are the idiotic and stupid luxuries of the West End cabaret and hotel. There is a tendency these days to forget the horrible suffering of the ordinary working people during the depression years. No writer described them more forcefully than JBP did here. It is honest, heartfelt reporting, as good as anything Orwell did, and much better than the professional 'proletarian novelists' ever managed. It might be worth re-issuing for this reason — it belongs to the 'Lest We Forget' school of experience which causes large numbers to go to the Cenotaph each year on 11 November and to watch programmes like *Holocaust*, whether they are good or not so good. The reason why this novel was not adopted by the Left Wing movement is simple, and can be found in the sentiments of Dr Inverurie (who unfortunately roars everything at the top of his voice in typical pell-mell Priestleyan style): 'If I thought it would get us out of this, I'd turn Bolshie tomorrow. And I don't like Bolshevism. I don't like Soviets, committees, fools who win elections, officials, half-witted comrades and damned interference with everything and everybody. I don't like public ownership of property. What the public owns, nobody owns; like something between a museum and a lost dog.'

English Journey was a landmark in JBP's development. Thereafter, despite his continued interest in Time and Dreams, the social muddle is never far from his thoughts. It naturally had a powerful effect on his creative works. David Hughes even says that *They Walk in the City*, which appeared two years later, can hardly be regarded as a novel at all; it is an 'object lesson, a lecture with plenty of lantern slides on the increasingly mechanical civilisation of the thirties, in which natural ordinary people could be lost for ever, to each other and to their own spirits, in the desert of brick, the cruel maelstrom of self-seeking.' The author's voice is too loud for the central characters, Rose and Edward. This is the first book, he says, in which JBP appears to have deliberately repressed his creative energy to allow the politician and social thinker to crowd the forefront of his mind and 'shout themselves hoarse'. First his English Journey and then the war seem to have roused his social conscience. The socialism of his youth was probably an intellectual exercise; now his nerve centres were involved. And the pessimistic view of society he adopted during these years has stayed with him and is brought to the reader's notice again and again, in book after book. Here, for instance, is a tirade from *Over the Long High Wall*, published in 1972:

> We are now living in a society that appears — outside its propaganda and advertising — to dislike itself just as much as I dislike it. We are house-guests of the Sorcerer's Apprentice, who has let loose what he can't begin to control. What was not quite so bad yesterday will be much worse tomorrow. The past (we assume) has gone. The present is dubious and mainly unrewarding. As for the future — well, I am now an old hand at this and could be eloquent and fairly terrifying on the nightmare agenda of the world population, vanishing natural resources, radio-active garbage, nuclear doomsday failing that, half-starved billions staring at endless vistas of concrete and cement — I could, but why should I? You know I know; I know you know; we have all been warned; and most people really *don't care*, and I think I know why . . .

Is it hopeless? There has been much talk of a Hippy Counter-Culture, but what is it? (Or, from our present vantage point — what was it? It seems to have disappeared.) It was devoted to pop music, an excellent example of the commercialism the Hippies denounced. 'Certain gimcrack values of our society may have been rejected by the Hippy movement, but then many of us, now considered to be too old to be worth a hearing, have been challenging such values for years and years, long before the first Hippy arrived on the scene.'

In the summer of 1977 JBP and his wife, Jacquetta Hawkes, revisited some of the places he had been to and described in his famous book. This formed the basis of a BBC television programme in three parts. Although he was restrained in his comment, he did not give the impression that there had been much, if any, change for the better. He noted that envy had increased in the modern world, and he repeated that all big towns are hell — for he had said this before on several occasions. Bradford had deteriorated. He had once worked there in an Italianate building that had style; why did anyone think its replacement was an improvement? It was all nonsense. At the end he quoted Wordsworth: 'men live by admiration, hope and love.' Many writers today have replaced these qualities with 'denigration, despair and hate' and are praised by critics who feel the same. But it won't do, we must return to an earlier mode, Wordsworth's mode. (Many modern writers seem to get great satisfaction out of calling Wordsworth dull!)

Priestley's thinking about society has not so much moved on two levels as jumped from one level to another — perhaps as one might jump from one Time dimension to another? In 1934 it was the economic structure leading to physical degradation and the most appalling poverty that concerned him. Later, as money and food and clothing became easier, it was the quality of a society dominated by the adman that angered him. In 1934 he seemed to have felt more venom for the banks than for the admen. Everywhere he went he saw their palaces, in depressed towns like Coventry, rearing high above the squalid houses of the workers.[3] When he was told the wool trade was recovering there were others who denied it. It was the banks that made the money, not the merchants. But the law of libel made it difficult to expose the conduct of the bankers. 'Until they are openly proved to be crooks, our own financial jugglers are regarded as distinguished if somewhat mysterious figures, so many benevolent wizards.' It was only the clumsy, like Hatry, who suffered. It was a sphere where you 'get away with' things in a manner denied to the carpenter, the engineer or the writer. These supermen work 'with one eye on Maidstone Gaol and the other on the House of Lords.' It is a world where metaphors and similes are actually drawn from medieval brigandage and the Wild West. There seems to be something 'anachronistic, crude, violent, barbaric' about that world and it is time it was brought into the twentieth century, cleaned up and civilised. One tends to forget what a master of polemic JBP can be when he is roused.

The financial system is a joke, but a cruel one. In *They Came to a City* Joe says he heard people laughing and wondered what the joke was. Malcolm Stritton, a City man, replies grimly that he was explaining the British financial system to the city-dwellers. The same feeling is expressed in *Bright Day*, one of JBP's best novels. Joe Ackworth, the woolbuyer, gives Gregory some advice about his future. It is to learn a trade.

> If a chap learns a trade, he won't do so much 'arm. What Ah don't like are these Clever Dicks that don't learn a trade but want to mak' money fast and easy, an' there's too many of 'em now an' there'll be a lot more afore we've finished. That's new London style — you know nowt abaht wool — you care nowt abaht it — but you see a chance o' gettin' quick profits aht o' wool — an' that's good enough — so it's wool today — an' summat else tomorrow.

Note that Joe is not giving advice on how to 'get on' or make a lot of money but to be useful and not do harm. Writing many years later Gregory comments that Joe was right. He had never met a man who had an expert knowledge of things who hadn't a decent core to his character, nor one who thought first of money and profits and cared nothing about the things he dealt in who was a satisfactory human being.

There is possibly a mellowing of JBP's attitude to the financier in *The Linden Tree*, 1948. Perhaps it was because he was beginning to transfer his critical gaze to the adman. Rex, the professor's son, has made a fortune on the Stock Exchange. The professor asks him how he did it. 'Well, I make money — by buying stocks and shares — and then selling them at a handsome profit — all for myself, not for other people. I'm not a broker.' Later he is a little more specific. He had been left some shares. 'I began playing about with 'em. Made money. Made more money. Got in the know. Paid no taxes, don't forget. Lived well, but still piled it up. Every time some bit of news made the fools in the City feel shaky, I bought. The minute they felt better again, I sold.' Although JBP doesn't actually approve of the system he suggests in this play that there is a place for the speculator, who may use his gains in creative ways which might not otherwise be followed.

As I have already said, it was the war, and the immense threat it embodied, both from outside and inside, that swung JBP heavily to a personal involvement with the social situation. From the beginning he regarded the Nazis as a force that had to be eliminated. This was not a case of blind patriotism — he is the last person to be blind about anything — but an example of the poet C. Day Lewis's view that men of goodwill had to support the bad against the worse. It didn't take the *News Chronicle* long to decide that JBP might be the spokesman of the tough and cheerful Britain that would defy the enemy. On 4 September, one day after Britain declared war on Germany, he contributed an article called 'Two-Ton Annie', subtitled: 'A Story from the New War'. He watched patients being evacuated from Portsmouth hospitals, among them a huge, triumphantly smiling woman who needed six men to carry her stretcher. 'Better than the biggest Dreadnought is a people who, when their whole world is turning upside down, can still show a merry face, swop jokes and laugh.' (But one gets tired of the journalist's trick of pretending that universal human traits, such as cheerfulness in the face of adversity or courage in the face of the enemy, are particularly British virtues.) A week later appeared 'The New Wartime', asserting that there was very little grumbling, the people were in a resolute mood and there were no cheap heroics. But he also urged the Government, which had swept away all forms of entertainment as a precaution against bombing, to bring some back in a modified form.

It was easy to be cheerful in the first few months and through the 'phoney war' period that ensued. It was not so easy when the bombing really started. This is when JBP really became a household name, even if *The Good Companions, English Journey* and the Time plays had not made him one before. There was a period during the early part of the last War when the British public seemed to be sustained by three radio offerings: Churchill's political speeches, Tommy Handley's ITMA and JBP's Sunday Evening *Postscripts*. These were what modern jargon would call micro-talks, about seven minutes long, and they followed the news each Sunday evening, from Sunday 9 June to Sunday 20 October 1940, with one week's break for a holiday. There had also been a preliminary talk, immediately after Dunkirk, on Wednesday 5 June. These talks were later published in book form (*Postscripts*, 1940) and in his Preface JBP reminds the reader that they appeared in this form in response to many requests. (In fact, most of his later shorter pieces, which have been published subsequently as books, originated in this way, he tells us.) They had not been altered and therefore should not be regarded as finished essays. In one of his talks he reverted to this, reminding correspondents that his job was to provide a seven-minute postscript to the news, not a four-hour lecture on political, social and economic developments.

In these talks he stressed the small things, family life and affection, the courage of unimportant people, even quoting Hardy's 'Only a man harrowing clods. . .' He made no attempt to disguise his scorn for those who wanted to restore the world to its pre-war state. 'We're not fighting to restore the past; it was the past that brought us to this heavy hour' (14 July), and 'I will tell you what we did for such young men and their young wives at the end of the last War. We did nothing — except let them take their chance in a world in which every gangster and trickster and stupid insensitive fool or rogue was let loose to do his damnedest' (28 July). Undoubtedly he made enemies for himself through his outspokenness. At times he even dismissed the whole business as a supreme folly, as when he referred to 'this vast lunatic puppet-show of armed men and machines' (25 August). This was too near the bone for many people who did not want JBP to use the air for the propagation of subversive views. Priestley stood for the Festival spirit and continued to uphold it after the war. Away with gloom, no matter how dreary life has become. Ignore the Dismal Desmonds, laugh at the Hush-Hush Harolds — and he referred with admiration to Two-Ton Annie, whose progress through the streets of Portsmouth we have already witnessed. People were being ordered about too much. Trust them — and they would respond. 'I'd stop making everything dreary and create as much fun, colour, romance as possible. I'd have bands playing everywhere, and as much swagger and glamour as the moment will stand.' The talks stopped abruptly. Perhaps JBP was tired; there is no evidence that his audience was tired of him; but a lot of influential people were angry.

JBP often bides his time, waiting for the right moment to hit back. A letter to *The Times* on 24 March 1942 was probably relevant to what had happened. In it he said there was a contradiction between the Government's complaint of too much criticism on the part of 'those who address the public' and the charge of too much public complacency in the public response to Government appeals. 'Surely we are not to understand that too much criticism, fault-finding and "croaking" leads to complacency?'

What worried JBP more and more as the war went on was that there would in fact be no social changes of any significance. To use a word that has become popular since those days, the public would be 'conned' again, just as it had been after the first War. When invited to introduce a series on post-war reconstruction which was to appear in *Horizon*, he took the opportunity to advocate serious planning. It didn't interfere with the war effort. He warned his readers not to trust those who said the outline of the new society could be left till later, who in other words were telling them to mind their own business — as in fact JBP was once admonished by Churchill! But JBP was not urging ordinary people to take the law into their own hands. Instead he was urging them to entrust the future to the right people. In parenthesis he wrote, 'If you are a writer, instead of being a banker or a brewer, it is not your business to meddle in politics.' But it is your business to act before 'the gangs' move in. People feel instinctively that when the time comes affairs should be handled by disinterested persons. Those who are interested in the quality of life, not in the acquisition of power, should guide the national destiny. 'The reason why some of us, who make no claim to have exceptional experience of or insight into public affairs, are read and listened to so eagerly and widely by the people is simply because the people feel that at least we are disinterested and not working any racket'. It is not leadership we should look for but cooperation.

These ideas were later developed into *Letter to a Returning Service-man*, a 32-page pamphlet published in 1945. It was part of a series of which Osbert Sitwell's *A Letter to My Son* was the outstanding contribution. This was in fact the Age of the Open Letter, often addressed to some prominent personage, and dealing with a topical matter usually in an apocalyptic tone. This one by JBP is a rather nebulous example, a plea not to be taken in by the Old Gang who had led the country to the brink of disaster and were now claiming support once again. It was a warning against apathy and might well be read in conjunction with *Three Men in New Suits* which appeared in the same year. It provides a hint of the direction in which the author was moving during the decade that lay ahead. 'Remember that even if you are not interested in politics, the fact remains that politics are interested in you . . .'

It was during the war period that JBP made his experiment, largely unsuccessful, in practical politics, and I shall have more to say about that aspect of his career in the next chapter. But there was one movement that occurred after the war, during the late fifties and early sixties in its most intense form, that attracted him above all others and into which he threw for a time his considerable energies. This was C.N.D. — the Campaign for Nuclear Disarmament. This was much more the kind of thing for which JBP (and any other creative writer, for that matter) was fitted than practical politics, with their deadening grind of action without positive and discernible result. C.N.D. was a crusade; it aimed at a definite target and you would know if and when you hit it. But to get JBP's feelings about nuclear war into perspective it is worth examining a statement of his made in *Horizon* in an article entitled 'The War — and After'. (This was the first issue of the magazine, appearing in January 1940, and creating a degree of interest quite exceptional in the literary world.) JBP's contribution was, in fact, a Statement on War. It seems fairly certain that the editors of *Horizon*, Cyril Connolly and Stephen Spender, agreed with the ideas expressed, and that these ideas were representative of the more progressive writers of the time. This is why I feel this article has more than usual importance.

That a stand must be made against the Nazis is his first point. It cannot be left to Stalin, as Shaw says. 'Well, Stalin may have made special arrangements to see that Shaw comes to no harm, but the rest of us in Western Europe do not feel quite sure of our fate, especially those of us who do not share Shaw's curious admiration for dictators.' The first war aim, then, must be the defeat of the Nazis. After that a new world order must be considered — we are ripe for change in international affairs, especially the young, who are bored with nationalism, with the strange exception of the Russians. Perhaps Drucker is right and we have come to the end of Economic Man.[4] Human beings most want security and freedom.

> Security comes first, for if you do not know when your children will have their next meal, you are not interested in the refinements of political theory. (This fact is apt to be overlooked by the democracies.) On the other hand, the point at which the demand for security changes into the desire for freedom is soon reached. (This fact is overlooked by the totalitarian states.)

Freedom does not mean anything transcendental, but the absence of a censor, the informer, propaganda-at-all-costs, forced labour and the paraphernalia of the police state. Ask the nearest refugee what he thinks. Finally, there is something in the modern world, whatever its system, 'that is bent on rapidly reducing the number of the healthy-minded, is addling the wits of man, is making it harder and harder to be easy, merry, affectionate and wise.' Perhaps the use of machinery does damage the imagination (for he had made this claim for several years now, going back at least to his English Journey), perhaps life in our 'huge cities poisons the psyche . . .' We are creating an atmosphere in which the spirit cannot flower freely.

In this short article JBP brought together a number of strands which together spotlighted man's contemporary dilemma. Security must come first — but with the end of the war, with the celebration of victory, what security could be felt with the shadow of the atom bomb darkening the landscape? It took some time for the Campaign for Nuclear Disarmament to get started, but when it did it found a ready supporter in JBP. But it wasn't merely the physical threat, which was real enough. What roused all his hostile instincts was the conviction that the atmosphere in which the spirit could not flower freely was being fortified by this new weapon and its effect on the general public. It was the kind of response one might expect from a creative writer.

On 16 June 1959 a public demonstration in London marked the beginning of the first European Congress of the Campaign. In his speech JBP claimed that nuclear armaments produced an 'enormous neurosis' in which every small difference between the nations becomes a crisis. 'Once you've accepted these weapons you can never think straight again.' In fact, most people refused to think at all about them but pushed them down somewhere into the subconscious and sat on the lid. And this of course affected their thinking on other matters. The British people used to be much more alert and politically minded before the Bomb neutralised their minds.

From that moment JBP was in the forefront of the new movement. It represented for him one of the more important defences against the catastrophe that was threatening our civilisation. In the following year he published his monumental *Literature and Western Man* in which he introduced his section on Modern

Literature with a gloomy picture of its background: violence, class-hatred, Sorel, the urge to destroy, rejection of the past, rebellion, massman, the death of God. The new bomb took on the appearance of a weapon of destiny, the one that would finally seal man's fate: his self-sought fate. In speech after speech and article after article JBP pleaded with his fellow-countrymen to act before it was too late. In an article entitled 'Unsound to the Summit' which appeared in the *New Statesman* on 7 May 1960 he explained his support for C.N.D. The powers were preparing for a Summit Conference. The nuclear deterrent, as it was now euphemistically called, represented the hostage system, declaring that millions should be punished in the most horrible fashion for the sake of a guilty few. The whole idea of the deterrent was wicked — *and everybody knew it!* It was no longer part of practical politics but had become a neurosis. There was a colossal vested interest, emotional as well as material, in 'the legend that passes for tough realism.' The Americans and Russians were not really playing the old game of power politics, they were moved at the deepest level by hysterical fear, not the desire of conquest. The ordinary citizen could not see himself as part of such a mad world, to say nothing of the impossible expense. The real enemy was 'a weakness in ourselves, in Modern Man, so clever and so foolish, and the expression of that weakness, perhaps deep down a hatred of life, in the unimaginable explosions and the creeping horror of radio-activity, only waiting for somebody to press a button.'

Almost exactly one year later, again in the *New Statesman*, he attacked politicians, experts and editors who were misrepresenting and abusing the Campaign ('The Fading Image', 19 May 1961). 'Deep down they want the Bomb, they love it.' The psychological effect of the deterrent on the young had been catastrophic. 'Ours is now a thoroughly corrupt society.' He had looked to the Labour Party but it had failed the nation badly — first in accepting the deterrent, then rejecting the protest. A new excitement and enthusiasm were flaming but they were being smothered by the professionals and time-servers. The 1945 election had been won by amateurs and now the machine was taking over.

Somewhere there is a frontier between the writer and the essayist giving his opinion about the behaviour and government of society ('sounding-off', as the practical politician would rudely call it) and active participation in this field. JBP had taken the plunge

September 1961

into political action during the war, with little success. Now he found himself once again in the political arena, not because he fancied a political career but because as a writer he was deeply concerned with a mass 'neurosis' which affected the nation at every point. You may not be interested in politics but politics are interested in you . . .

Chapter 13

The Political Frontier

JBP is in one way a familiar type among writers: he is intensely interested in society and its structure, he cannot resist giving us his views on them, he insists he is only a writer and not a politician, he cannot resist entering the political arena from time to time . . . And, like most writers of this type, he retires much bruised. This is not the place to trace his experience as an active politician but it is relevant to note what attitudes he has adopted to certain political situations.

People who have read his work, he says in *Outcries and Asides*, 1974, imagine him to be a man of action. Wrong: he is and always has been a writer. 'To a man of my temperament, vocation and profession, when I have written something I have done what is in me to do.' He does, however, believe he has certain valuable intuitive faculties which equip him to be a political commentator. He states this expressly in the Introduction to *Thoughts in the Wilderness*, 1957, a collection of polemical pieces, what he calls 'shouting in a drawing room', first published in the *New Statesman and Nation*. Unlike the essays of the twenties they are usually concerned with real topics of positive national concern (that is, not cosily personal), although sometimes they seem a little static. Like some of his novels they tend to start well and then get bogged down. On the whole, JBP is usually right about the matters he deals with (which means, of course, that I agree with him) but one is sometimes put off by the element of self-congratulation. It may be true that the hero has disappeared from modern writing but this doesn't worry JBP — he is his own hero. He says he has an intuitive insight into what English people in general are thinking and feeling. (This explains the success of his wartime broadcasts.) 'When it is working — and I think it worked in several of these pieces — it enables me to be a jump ahead of the politicians, leader-writers and assorted pundits.' Of course, the average politician cannot afford to think of tomorrow; he wants votes Now. Only the very few, those of the stature of Charles James Fox and

Aneurin Bevan, have the capacity to take such risks.

As a critic JBP's guiding light has been 'affection'. (More of this later.) When it comes to politics it is a similar quality, that is, an emotional one, compassion.

> My politics are based almost entirely on compassion. When the working classes faced long hours and low wages,I was always on their side . . . Now that the middle classes risk extermination, I am one of their loyal supporters. At the core of my political belief is the feeling that if we lose a reasonable liberty, we are lost indeed, turning into so many robots. (*Instead of the Trees*, 1977.)

But this is rushing things too much. The threat to the middle class has become pronounced during the last two decades. During his most active period as a writer JBP was mainly concerned with the poorer section of the population, those who have been exploited in the past, whom socialists call the 'working class' and whom JBP saw as the underdogs when he wrote *English Journey*. But compassion by itself will get these people nowhere. In fact, they have been bathing in crocodile tears for generations. It was fashionable during the thirties to treat personal compassion as a signpost to Marxism. JBP, who had been a democratic socialist as a young man, rejected this path but there still remained the problem of which one to take. I can best illustrate the way in which he wrestled with this problem by reference to two plays written before the War.

The first is *Bees on the Boat Deck*, 1936. Gridley and Patch are sailors and they are contemptuous of many civilian values. Patch says he was a mug to become a sailor, he ought to have 'learned to play the saxophone or to work the tote at greyhound races — something really useful.' Gridley says ironically it breaks his heart to think about how much the ship-owning Duke has to pay in super-tax. But when these men try to work out a way in which these anomalies could be corrected, it is not so easy. The automatic remedy in the twentieth century is socialism, but Gridley is suspicious of it because it seems to him to be unrealistic. He has already given his views on the ship-owners; the workers who made the ship don't really care much about anything except beer and football; and what political party could guarantee to change such attitudes? 'I don't care about capitalists and proletarians,' he says, 'masses and bosses, red shirts, black shirts, brown shirts, green shirts.' But he has nothing else to offer, save a demand for 'real men who know what sense is, and duty is, and order is.' This is as helpful as saying that the class struggle doesn't exist or that if only we could solve the problem of power . . . Gridley is a sympathetic portrait of a man who is bewildered by modern complexity.

The political attitudes are progressive and sincere but they are crudely put. They are expressed intellectually, not dramatically. Gridley's discussion with Lord Cottingley about ships becomes tiresome because it is all so predictable. Gridley tells Cottingley to look at the ship. All right, says his lordship, not looking at her. 'Yes, but you're not looking at her,' says Gridley. 'You never have looked at her properly. Sitting in offices, adding up figures, holding meetings, passing the cigars, that's not running ships.' This ought to be an example of JBP's 'symbolic action', but it is over-played. A quoted snippet may sound all right but in fairly large dollops it becomes wearisome, and is certainly not drama. Of course, it was a method favoured by many writers at the time: everything was spelt out, everything was very explicit. The categories were trotted out one by one and then dismissed — capitalist and communist, fascist and ordinary man. Gaster, the communist in this play, is a mere mouthpiece and is treated as such by Gridley, yet in the end he is allowed a certain amount of respect, for it was one of the shibboleths of the day that communists were mistaken but sincere. JBP says this is one of his favourite plays.

The other play I wish to use as illustration was *The Golden Fleece*, a comedy written just before the war but not copyrighted until 1948. It was performed by the Bradford Civic Playhouse and the Glasgow Citizens Theatre under the title *Bull Market* but did not achieve a London production. It is a Shavian-type denunciation of the financial system. JBP thinks it would have been more suc-cessful as a film. It is set in a hotel at Cheltingate Spa, with a large cast of idle rich. Dr Alec Rothbury is a vehement young man who denounces this class roundly. Referring to one of the guests he says, 'It wouldn't matter if there were just one of her, but there are thousands and thousands of her — like — like — stuffed old frogs — crocodiles — dinosaurs. This country's full of 'em. And there they are, doing no good to anybody, not even to themselves — and because they have the money, demanding services all day long from other people. That's what you see everywhere in this country

— the living waiting upon the half-dead.' Veronica comments that this is an odd thing for a doctor to say but he modifies it by stating he is not referring to the sick — he's talking about people who have 'money, appetites, prejudices and nothing else.'

William Lotless knows all about money for he is a speculator, but he once fell foul of the law and has served a prison sentence. He is something of a philosopher. Money should be pocket-money and nothing more; it shouldn't be used to force someone to do something this time next year, as if he had a pistol at his head. It shouldn't be able to grow by itself. Meanwhile, he takes advantage of the system although he knows it's wrong. It is a moral tale. Again and again we come back to the evils of money-grubbing, the corrupting influence of wealth. Alec says speculation is 'playing about with people's lives — the lives of thousands and thousands of people you've never even seen.' This impresses Molly, who has unexpectedly come into a fortune which has been enormously magnified by William's financial expertise. At times the tirade borders on the melodramatic, and therefore incredible, as when Lord Fleetfield, himself a financier, tells Molly that in time she could, without leaving the hotel, throw her shadow across the world. 'The fate of whole industries would have been in your hands. You could have controlled commodity markets and, if you wished, created famines. You could have dominated the political life of people at the other end of the world, etc. etc.' By giving the impression that this sort of power is available to anyone who has money, the argument becomes crude in the familiar Marxist way. Then what about State control? Lord Fleetfield has the short answer to that one. 'Do you suppose the government will manage these affairs any better than my friends and I would?' This is at least realistic and it avoided the prevalent naivety of contemporary Marxist propaganda. It also corresponded with JBP's views for he was no statist.

How important was this kind of writing? It's always useful for a writer to blow off steam about matters which are not his immediate concern. It does him good — does it do the nation any good? Those who can write eloquently about political matters (and JBP is certainly very persuasive at times) often implant a sense of crusade within the reader, but in practical terms it leads to very little. Politicians are irritated by discussions of personal freedom and government control in the weekly press, and not entirely because they are scoundrels. The politican faces difficulties which the writer barely understands, just as the writer faces difficulties which the academic barely understands. Susan Cooper, in her book on Priestley, said he is 'the kind of man whom professional politicians need: as both a bulwark and an irritant; a voice of conscience; a reminder of what politics and government are for.' True — but the voice of conscience is only enjoyed by prudes. Shelley saw himself as an 'unacknowledged legislator' but he got nothing on the statute books.

JBP's forays into practical politics involved membership of the 1941 Committee (a kind of Left wing ginger group — but note: in those days Left wing meant socialist, not quasi-Marxist), membership of Common Wealth (a new progressive party formed during the war as a reaction against the electoral standstill) and unsuccessful attempts to get into Parliament after the war had ended. I doubt if his heart was really in these activities, except perhaps the writing of pamphlets. He probably saw politics as a challenge which his wiser self advised him to leave unanswered but which his diurnal self, the one that can't resist a bit of nonsense, urged him to respond to. One certainly can't discover much consistency in his attitude. In *Out of the People*, 1941, which is a kind of political testament, he said that politics should never be regarded as a career. In a few exceptional cases, with those who have a genius for statesmanship, it should be a vocation.

> For the rest, it should be regarded as an ordinary civic duty. We are all living politics, whether we like it or not. Every hour we are making political statements, whether we are aware of it or not. We all adopt political attitudes, whether we know it or not.

Yes, yes, but all the same someone has to be responsible for action and set it in motion. No one should 'go in for' politics, he wrote, but a society needs something more than noble precepts if it is to satisfy its members.

The 1941 Committee was set up to prepare for the remoulding of society after the war. It was the practical counterpart of the ideas expressed in *Daylight on Saturday*, *Desert Highway* and *Letter to a Returning Serviceman*. Its main ideas were set out in *Out of the People* and an Appendix contained explicit reference to the Committee's aims. It ended by saying that though there was no desire to form a new political party in wartime there was good reason to meet, form groups and discuss matters which might lead to the formation of a new democratic party after the war. As a sample of its views, here are the proposals for a reform of Parliament.

> Parliament should be the apex of a pyramid of elected councils and should not, as it tends to do now, drain away all the political life of the country. As it is constituted now, it has many grave faults: it is too big and unwieldy; its procedure is cluttered up with too much fancy 'tradition'; it has often far too long a life, without any reference to public opinion; too many of its members do not genuinely represent their constituents but are in Westminster as the delegates of sectional interests. Much of the work now done in Parliament might be given with advantage to Regional Councils, with which Parliament should be linked. The electoral system should be made more flexible. Candidates should be personally known in their constituencies, and their elections should not be valid until they have received a certain proportion of the total possible votes of the electorate. About a fifth of the members should be compelled to seek re-election every year, so that public opinion can be tested. More use too should be made of impartial surveys of public opinion. The House of Lords is an anachronism and should be abolished, a genuine Second Chamber, a Senate, taking its place. This Senate, made up of men of real distinction, should not have the same legislative power as the House of Commons, but in some matters, chiefly cultural, it should take the lead. So long as the majority of the people, here and in the Dominions, approve of it as a symbol of executive power, as they certainly do now, the Crown should be preserved, though much of its feudal flummery could be abolished.

Towards the end of the war Common Wealth issued a series of pamphlets which they called the Popular Library. The first was by JBP and was entitled *Here Are Your Answers*. This was a common feature of the publishing scene in those days and this particular pamphlet adopted the familiar method of Question and Answer. A few examples will illustrate the tone adopted. (The Questions are Priestley's; the Answers are abbreviated.)

Q. *Why should a man risk his money if he can't be reasonably sure of a profit?*
A. This is not for him to answer, as he wishes to destroy capitalism. Today we are trying to work a system which simply will not work.

Q. *Where is all the money for public enterprise to come from?*
A. Money has no real value of its own. It has only a token value. We use it as a convenience. In our idiotic system we cannot distribute goods, even when available, if there is no gold behind them. Therefore money for public enterprise will be printed, as now, and it will come from public credit. Financiers say we will be poorer after the war, but this is a trick.

Q.   *What about Liberty, if there is to be a planned economy and public enterprise?*
A.   Liberty is often a disguised plea for economic chaos. There are two kinds of liberty: liberty from oppression, and economic liberty (which means a dog-fight, with all the advantages going to privilege, cunning and greed).

and here I will quote, for this is an aspect of political life which JBP has written about on several occasions.

> In short, we must take care to keep our individualism in the right place, where it does good and not harm. So with our liberty. We must all have a certain amount, but it must be in the right sphere, the one in which the more we are ourselves the more other people will enjoy us. It is the same with nationalism, which should not be rooted in the economic and political life, where it can do most harm, but in a people's cultural life, where it can do most good, if only by adding to the variety and oddity of existence.

Priestley's real strength as a social thinker lies where you would expect to find it, in his feeling about the nature of our society, a nebulous matter it would appear when compared with tax levels and the distribution of wealth and parliamentary procedure and yet basically the most important thing of all. It is the pervading atmosphere that shapes the detail. When George Orwell and J.B. Priestley and various other commentators, ranging from G.D.H. Cole on the one hand to Winston Churchill on the other, noticed the solidarity that seemed to weld the nation together during the Blitz, it was clear that something important had happened.[1] For a moment, really a very brief moment, England seemed to be a democracy. It certainly had not been one before and in fact JBP declared in *Rain Upon Godshill*, which appeared the year the war started, that she was further from being one than she had been twenty years earlier. One is always hoping in this country that the worst aspects of the past are about to be set aside, but they have a habit of clinging like limpets. The Englishman still seemed to regard privilege as a necessary part of the natural order. 'Hardly anybody thinks or feels like a democrat. If you begin to talk like one in public, there is a rumpus . . .' For example, there was a time when public men openly declared themselves republicans. How many dare do it now? he asked. In his view England was a plutocracy disguised as an aristocracy. All our government was done by the Right People.

One of the great dangers in political movements lies in the crude misunderstanding or half-understanding of an important need. For example, a crowd of rich wheelers and dealers control the government machine. Some of them are the heirs of privilege, others have assumed it. They have evolved a certain graceful way of life, which governs behaviour, food, speech, clothing and other matters which concern all of us. There is some kind of upheaval, these people are removed from power, and conscious efforts are made to reverse the social codes by which they lived. Put crudely, it is felt that somehow the transport caff and its ways are morally superior to the first-class restaurant. But this is dangerous — it's a classic example (for it has happened many times) of throwing out the baby with the bath-water. JBP referred to this danger in an article contributed to *Horizon* in June 1940 called 'Labour Leaders at the Ivy'. The Ivy was a first-class restaurant and he enjoyed dining there. Now and again he was glad to see some of the Labour leaders there, usually upstairs and away from the theatrical crowd that were its main patrons. He felt this was a good sign. He wouldn't like to be governed by men who had spent years in back kitchens eating bread and marge. If this sounds trivial I must hasten to urge the reader to regard it as a metaphor. What we are concerned with here is culture. Unfortunately the Labour movement had never shown any signs of cultural interest. The old William Morris visions seemed to have faded; the *Daily Herald* (normally regarded as spokesman for the Labour viewpoint) may have been excellent politically but it was a non-starter in intellectual and cultural matters. Culture, in fact, was left to a couple of Right wing Sunday papers. And this was dangerous, for Labour had a responsibility towards the arts; if you ignore them, and regard them as mere decoration, you starve the spirit; if you simply regard them as servants to be manipulated you produce a parody of socialism on the lines of the Soviet Union. There is no point in exchanging socialist robots for capitalist robots. We must create a truly urban civilisation. Perhaps the Labour men at the Ivy would start inviting some of their fellow guests, intellectuals and artists, to their table.

JBP was really trying, by an unorthodox route, to establish the need for a peaceful revolution. Talk of revolution is always in the air these days — in fact, the very idea has been grossly devalued by its frequency and triviality. The wise man will not be influenced by this. He will still acknowledge that injustice demands revolution, but it must be divested of all its old claptrap of barricades, uprisings, terror, bold yet meaningless manifestos and romantic attitudes. In fact, any revolution that is to have the required results must avoid the very methods that most modern revolutionists seem to consider necessary. Because the French and Russian Revolutions 'shook the world' they go on shaking people's intelligence. JBP put the point clearly in his play *The Linden Tree*, produced shortly after the war and long before Gangs and Fractions (or Factions — the press can never make up its mind) and Brigades decided that killing anyone who happens to get in their way was an essential part of making life better for the rest of us. Professor Linden's daughter Marion has married a French aristocrat and she deplores the drabness of the English scene in a way that would have satisfied Nancy Mitford. He tells her that this drabness is the price the country was paying in its attempt to create a better society. There had to be a price and not everyone wanted it to be paid in blood.

> For Heaven's sake recognise that we're trying to do something that is as extraordinary and wonderful as it's difficult — to have a revolution for once without the Terror, without looting mobs and secret police, sudden arrests, mass suicides and executions, without setting in motion that vast pendulum of violence which can decimate three generations before it comes to a standstill. We're fighting in the last ditch of our civilisation.

Orwell said the English contribution to political science was the ability to change things without killing people. It's a puzzle to know why so many people shy away from this idea (in practice) with horror.

Isms have proliferated like nettles in our time. JBP called one of the pieces in *The Movements*, 1966, 'Wrong Ism'. There are three Isms we should consider very carefully: regionalism, nationalism and internationalism. One of these, nationalism, is a major danger. The nation is a power structure and thinks in terms of power. What would benefit the life of the region, which is you and me in our ordinary capacities, is sacrificed for the power and prestige of the nation, which does no more for us than give a psychological lift at times when we can't think straight.

> Among the new nations of our time innumerable peasants and labourers must have found themselves being cut down from five square meals a week to three in order to provide unnecessary airlines, military forces that can only be used against them and nobody else, great conference halls and official yachts and the rest.

Meanwhile one of the noblest Isms, democratic socialism, is going wrong. The wrong people have got hold of it and magnified certain aspects to the detriment of others. Even a saint would be useless if someone changed the balance of his virtues and introduced other qualities that didn't belong. In *Bright Day* we hear Councillor Knott telling young Gregory that socialism is inevitable. (This book must have been written about the time of the 1945 Labour victory.) All the early pioneers, such as the ones JBP had known in Bradford, asked for was a decent chance and decent conditions for the folk that did most of the work, and that wasn't much to ask for. There could be no stopping it, said the Councillor, though some Tories would go any length to obstruct it. Gregory knew that Knott had a limited intelligence and a childish vanity and yet 'I think he had something I have rarely found in later and more important Labour politicians, who knew more than he did but also seemed to me to have forgotten some essential things that he always remembered.'

Chapter 14
Evil — or Muddle?

I am sometimes puzzled to know why JBP is held in such a low esteem by the critics and intelligentsia. He seems to have everything that is required by them: a progressive attitude towards society and politics, an experimental attitude towards the theatre (though many have forgotten this) and a serious metaphysical approach to Time, one of the major unknown factors in our existence. Three such distinguishing marks in a writer should be enough, one would suppose, to guarantee him a high position in the contemporary literary pantheon. But on the contrary, Priestley is a kind of forgotten man among writers. He himself believes it is because he has attempted too much and written in too many different fields. There might be something in this — it could rouse sentiments of mingled envy and disbelief — but a more probable reason is to be found in the tone of his writing. He is unashamedly, even aggressively, Anglo-Saxon in his approach to his craft. During the past fifty years, while he has been active, English intellectuals have tended to look to Germany and Central Europe, often via North America, for their stimuli. They have been impressed by, and in turn demanded, clear-cut codes of thinking and the exercise of the tragic sense. On the whole JBP has shown little interest in these qualities. In his best writing they are conspicuously absent.

JBP gives no convincing indications that he believes in the existence of positive evil. Man is responsible for his own follies and he creates them more because he hasn't always the intelligence to avoid them, or if he has is too lazy to use it, than because part of him deliberately seeks disaster and apocalyptic suffering. The nearest JBP ever came to this moral stance was during the war when he found it difficult to fit the Nazi explosion into a view of man that allowed for any comfort or optimism. In his personal writing he always accuses men of muddle, constantly repeated muddle. This was something he could come to terms with, some-

thing that extended hope. The only occasions on which he projected a sense of evil, with its concomitant of inevitable tragedy,
were in his fiction, and then almost exclusively in the early novels.
They are not convincing because they are simply the work of a
man whose fiction still tends to be based on a theatrical view of life
rather than an objective one. This method of looking to the theatre
for his effects, which worked so well in some instances, damaged
some of the earlier novels.

In *Benighted* Miss Femm is intended as a figure of evil. She is
incredible. If we saw her on the stage we would murmur inwardly,
'Melodrama!' and make the necessary adjustment. She is described
as 'malignant, corrupt, a witch.' Her spirit is said to pervade the
house, and in consequence Philip 'picked up the idea of an evil
desolation.' He experienced a 'density of evil.' But JBP had set
himself an impossible task. He knocked the reader's head constantly against a wall of evil which turned out to be made of india-
rubber. You cannot evoke evil and at the same time insist on the
theatricality of the life you describe.

He makes another attempt in *The Doomsday Men*. But even here,
where three men plan to destroy the world (it can only be
deliberate, this is no muddle working its way out) there is no convincing aura of evil. The plotters are simpletons. (Evil spirits are
always intellectually brilliant.) Malcolm refers to 'a kind of evil
madness' but in fact it is not transmitted and the destructive
element has as much conviction as the 'horrors' of a boy's
adventure story. This novel appeared in 1938 when the Nazis were
in full cry, and it could be seen as a conscious attempt by JBP to
accept the active existence of evil and to show it at work. He is
driven to clichés, copied from the glossary of evil and not felt,
such as the 'unseeing amber gaze' of Father John or the 'gigantic
conceit, amounting to megalomania' of the mad scientist, Paul, or
'the heavy-jowled brooding face, like that of some ancient and
incredible despot' of the millionaire, Henry.

Black-Out in Gretley, 1942, written during the war, is slightly more
successful because the hopeless environment of a Midland town in
the black-out supplies all the atmosphere that is required, without
straining to invent it. Humphrey Neyland, a counter-espionage
agent, goes to Gretley in the Midlands to investigate leaks of
military intelligence. He is depressed by the almost unrelieved
darkness in which he has to operate. 'Somebody inside me — not

Humphrey Neyland afraid of his skin, nor one of the British tribe doubtful about his possessions — shook and screamed, seeing in front of him a great and ever-widening black pit into which men, women, houses, whole cities, went slithering. It was a vision of Evil triumphant. It was the idea of Hell let loose.' The Nazis hadn't started it but they were ready to push you into the pit. 'All Gretley was on the edge of it. And a few of its citizens — and that fellow I bumped into at the corner might have been one of them — were working hard to push all over the brink. Here, behind the dark curtain of the black-out, was deeper evil within evil.'

JBP hated the black-out and considered it unnecessary; 'panic legislation', he called it. It seemed to him the best image to hand in the evocation of evil, a state of deliberate opposition to enlighten-ment. But it is too obvious and too stark to stand on its own. The reinforcement of the idea of evil was taken not from observation, where the evil would present itself to the senses, but from some imaginary world of supernatural horror, vague and uncertain in outline. This is the inevitable recourse of the writer who is fascinated by the idea of evil (though in JBP's case the fascination was temporary) but is not personally convinced of its action. Here lies the difference between the horror story, which is merely an exercise, however serious it may be in its expression, and those rare evocations of evil, which combine hard objectivity with the necessary sense of mystery, such as *The Turn of the Screw*. JBP tries to chill our blood just a little in a story called 'The Grey Ones' (*The Other Place*, 1953) by suggesting that we are being taken over by beings with ant-like minds, whom he calls the Grey Ones. The Evil Principle wishes to make mankind go the way of the social insects, 'to turn us into automatic creatures, mass beings without individuality, soulless machines of flesh and blood.' There are two ways of doing it — by remote control, 'a sort of continuous radio programme' which never leaves our minds alone, and direct control, which amounts to a sort of Evil Fifth Column, working among us, here and now. In fact, although this has the trappings of a horror story it is really an extension of JBP's social interests, for it is an explanation of how Admass has come into existence. And he is by no means averse to the idea of a Super-Mind, but prefers to think of it as a beneficent entity with which we are at times in contact.

He doesn't really believe in this Evil principle. Perhaps he is

sometimes driven to recognising it as a result of irritation at mankind's continuing folly. What he really believes in is muddle. We
simply are not clever enough to find our way through the maze we
have created. Perhaps we could manage if we really set our minds
to it, but this rarely happens. He even likes to call himself a
'muddler' and on two or three occasions he has declared his faith in
the despised 'woolly-minded.' He loves to describe muddle in
public affairs.[1] The common man senses the muddle though he
doesn't understand it. We see this as early as *The Good Companions*,
when Mr Oakroyd knows there's something wrong but who is
responsible is beyond him.

> I nivver knaw who they are. Other fowk allus knaws, though. It's allus
> either capitalists or t'working men, or it's this Parlyment or t'last, or it's
> landowners and employers or it's Bolshies. I can nivver mak' nowt out
> on it mysen, can't tell whose fault it is, but then I'm not one o' t'clever
> sort. It's allus all a right muddle to me.

It was naturally in *English Journey* that JBP developed his Theory
of Muddle most comprehensively. In Birmingham, for example, he
found a 'parade of mean dinginess'. For half an hour on top of a
tram he saw nothing to raise a man's spirits. 'Possibly what I was
seeing was not Birmingham but our urban and industrial civilisation. The fact remains that it was beastly. It was so many miles of
ugliness, squalor and the wrong kind of vulgarity, the decayed
anaemic kind.' His most powerful arraignment of the system (but
there was no system) came after visiting West Bromwich. It was an
environment that naturally bred violence. He would not blame the
kids if they smashed every pane of glass in the district. 'Nobody
can blame them if they grow up to smash everything that can be
smashed.' And then his tirade on 'the political and financial and
industrial gentlemen', congratulating each other, begins. It is
ridiculous to congratulate ourselves on anything while such places
remained. 'They make the whole pomp of government here a
miserable farce. The Crown, Lords and Commons are the Crown,
Lords and Commons of Rusty Lane, West Bromwich. In the heart
of the great empire on which the sun never sets, in the land of hope
and glory, Mother of the Free, is Rusty Lane, West Bromwich.' It
is not a great plot or conspiracy, it is sheer muddle. On Tees side
the women talked quietly to him about wages and conditions and
made him feel like a fat rich man. 'And I object to feeling like a fat
rich man. That is yet another reason why we must clean up this

horrible dingy muddle of life.'

He even found Muddle in Stalin's Russia, as reported in *Russian Journey*, 1946. I am not suggesting that muddle does not exist there but JBP's point was that much of what passed outside Russia for sinister Machiavellian policy was really no more than the result of ordinary bureaucratic stupidity, timidity or inefficiency, which are the ingredients of muddle, and this would have been recognised if anybody else but the Russians had been concerned. The Muddle Theory, of course, is in direct opposition to the Conspiracy Theory, which attracts capitalists and communists alike. JBP drew attention to this clash of interpretation in his play, *Home is Tomorrow*, 1948. Sir Edward Fortrose, director of the UNUTO scheme on the island of Corabana, says he doesn't believe in a world of deliberate conspiracies. 'I wish I did, because they would make life much simpler. But we don't live in a world of neat plots, but in a foggy atmosphere of prejudices and cross-prejudices, silly rumours, tragic blunders.' The implication is that if the conspiracy theories were true, faults could be corrected simply by knowing a code. You know Marxism, you can check Stalin. You know National Socialism, you can check Hitler. You know Mad Idealism, you can check Doomsday. But you can't know Muddle, so how are you going to check human degradation?

There is a theory, popular today, that Evil is the product of the unconscious. This won't really do for JBP because he has another role for the unconscious, which he described in detail in *Literature and Western Man*. The unconscious is the source of a therapeutic agency which expresses itself in literature as the irrational wisdom of the race, the counterbalance to errors inevitable in a logic based on incomplete knowledge. The unconscious may also be the home of certain aggressive forces but aggression in itself is not evil. It seems probable JBP's thinking self would concede the existence of evil but it has only the most shadowy existence in his creative self. The modern critic, in his bewilderment, cries out for evil in the material he works upon, for this alone will neatly and undeniably explain for him the tragedy he sees around him; if he cannot find this strain of evil he dismisses the author as having no message for our times. The idea of muddle will not satisfy him because even Jess Oakroyd was aware of muddle.

Chapter 15

The Machine Menace

Many of JBP's comments on and criticisms of society are now regulation material and are likely to be encountered in any discussion of the social scene. But it should be remembered that when he first expressed these views they were not so familiar. In fact, he has played an important role in opinion-forming. As in the case of D.H. Lawrence, a writer of vastly different character, much of what he has written is now accepted by millions who have never read either. And if Lawrence and Priestley differed in most things they were at one in their view of what machinery and mechanistic methods did to people.

His journey through England was the eye-opener. For one thing, it showed him, a man who had been brought up in the shadow of modern industry, the difference between the factory worker (or hand, as he was significantly called) and the craftsman. JBP had far too much common sense to be overcome by sentiment, as is all too common among city-bred writers who have achieved their cottage in the country. Like any honest person he was compelled to admire the craftsman, his dignity, his long tradition, the superiority of his adjustment over that of the alienated modern worker. But his attitude was ambivalent. He didn't want to to be trapped into arty-medievalism. He could see the virtues of the modern proletarian, especially his liveliness and mental alertness in certain areas of thought and behaviour. It was a puzzling situation. It was also quite obvious that there were two types of decline and decay. With one of them he was familiar, for he had grown up with it: the industrial. But the other had a much longer history yet was new to him: it was rural and he found it in the Cotswolds.

This seemed to illustrate one aspect of the topsy-turvyness he scented in modern life. It was to be found in the enormous seriousness with which people in what appear to be frivolous occupations take themselves and their work. The barman who spends an evening expounding the arts of cocktail-shaking; saxophonists who talk as though the world's future depended on their notes; the professional dancing partner who could not have been more impressed with his own importance if he had been Foreign Secretary; the dirty lyric writer who discusses his 'work' as if it were on a par with Beethoven; and today the examples increase all around us — the salesman who drools about the 'creative' aspect of his foolery, the TV personality who has no ability but enormous self-admiration. Who are these people? Are they craftsmen *manqués*? They are the throw-outs of the industrial system, which has no use for them. They have this urgent need to feel their work is important, and so they act as if it is even when it demonstrably isn't.

This is perhaps an unusual angle from which to approach the machine. But JBP is consistent in this, for what he has insisted all along is that it is nonsense to blame the machine for the plight we find ourselves in, for the machine is our slave. Some people show a determination not to allow this relationship to be reversed. The real villain is 'the shoddy, greedy, profit-grabbing joint-stock company industrial system' which we permit to dominate us. It is the acting out of the Frankenstein myth which explains so much in our civilisation. And behind it all lies the greed which drives our social and financial system and for which JBP reserves his most severe vituperation.

One basic thing to remember when considering the Man-Machine relationship is that Man is far more complex than the Machine. 'If only life were an internal combustion engine,' he writes, 'for we have shown ourselves remarkably clever in producing it!' He doubted if the children of the Coventry workers were looked after as carefully as the cylinders, pistons and gears they worked on. Secondly, machinery has enslaved some people but liberated others. There is in fact a small class of men who find fulfilment through the machine, although the mass employees are involved in monotonous routine work. Bonus and welfare schemes can never bridge the gap between these two groups. Although the use of machinery has its dangers it is human greed that remains the true enemy to a satisfying life for all. His visit to Tyneside supplied him with evidence of past greed 'now satiated here and ravening elsewhere, and present indifference and neglect.' The desire for profits raged across the land and, in a touching passage arising from his reflections on a re-union battalion dinner, he considers the effects of this commercial greed in the past.

> I have had playmates, I have had companions, but all, all are gone; and
> they were killed by greed and muddle and monstrous cross-purposes, by
> old men gobbling and roaring in clubs, by diplomats working under-
> ground like monocled moles, by journalists wanting a good story, by
> hysterical women waving flags, by grumbling debenture-holders, by
> strong silent be-ribboned asses, by fear or apathy or downright lack of
> imagination.

Eden End was first produced in the same year as *English Journey*
was published and, as usual with Priestley (but not only Priestley
— many other writers, such as Aldous Huxley, have been subject
to this effect) ideas spilled over from the book into the play. *English
Journey* was concerned with society, people in the mass, and behind
it lies a vision of large numbers of anonymous people working on
and with large numbers of identical machines. But a play is concerned with people as individuals. This one is set in a doctor's
house in the North of England in 1912. Sarah, the old servant,
thoroughly distrusts machinery. She has never been subjected to it
and one can imagine that her ancestors had been farm workers or
even servants like herself. The telephone rings. 'That wants
answering now,' grumbles Sarah. 'Daft thing. Got to wait on a
machine, that's what we're coming to. It'll never get me waiting on
it, and it can ring its head off.' (Her imagery is still human.) She
concedes that it might be useful for the doctor, but no good will
come of other people using it. 'If it's worth saying, it's worth
saying properly, instead of gabbling into a daft machine.' The
doctor himself has a tendency in the same direction for, after all, he
is a craftsman. Talking of the gramophone, which belongs to his
son, he says, 'I've got to listen to too many patients to want to hear
mechanical music — if it is music.' This is quite irrational and yet
accurately observed.

The machine was having particularly deleterious results in an
area greatly loved by JBP: the popular theatre and Music Hall.
Outwardly it was summed up in the success of the cinema, so well
observed by Lawrence in *The Lost Girl* (it is fascinating to find how
often these two extremely unlike writers seem to work in harness!),
but the damage to the human element ran much deeper. *Let the
People Sing*, 1939, was one of those novels which have a special
appeal for JBP — modern picaresque, traditional man trying to
make a traditional living in an increasingly unsympathetic world.

The mechanical invasion was changing, if not destroying, the old genius of the nation. Timmy Tiverton, the old style Music Hall comic, is one of its victims. At the beginning no one will give him work. 'Not that there was anything wrong with his act; he was as good now as he had been when they had paid him a hundred a week; but people weren't the same and the world wasn't the same, that was the trouble. All machines now. Films — fun out of a tin. Wireless — more machines. And now these Hitlers and Mussolinis with *their* machines.'

The Czech professor, who is collaborating with Timmy, agrees although he puts it in a different way. They have arrived at a transport cafe, where the customers are playing the automatic machines. 'They come here driving machines,' says the professor, 'and soon they will go away driving those machines. But now that they are having a little rest they must play with these machines. Why is it they cannot feel either useful or happy without a machine?' And when Hope says she longs for a little sports car of her own, the professor starts a lecture. It is the symbolic utterance of her generation. She wants a machine not to come to terms with reality but to escape it. Although JBP is not always very tolerant of the academic profession he tends to develop the anti-machine theme using scholars as spokesmen. The professor in *The Linden Tree*, 1948, is not happy at Burmanley University and now he has reached retiring age an attempt is being made to force him out. He does not conform, he is a teacher and not a new-style 'educationalist'. What, then, is an 'educationalist'? He possesses a machine-mentality. 'It's not so much men — as machines — that we have to beat. The new educational machine here, for instance. And generally — the capital-industrial machine — and now the Trade Union machine and the Civil Service machine.'

In his later work JBP has not relented. In fact, he seems to feel that a corroding spirit ('machine' is merely a convenient metaphor which the alert reader will freely interpret) is taking the spring and flexibility out of the English mind. In *Margin Released*, 1962, one of his personal books, he remembers a type of workman who seems to have disappeared from English life. They could hardly survive as they were not the material from which steady production growth is made. JBP was a clerk in a woolman's office, and he used to encounter sorters on piece-work, men who came and went as they pleased, skilled men who didn't give a damn, preferring a week or

so of hard work followed by a few days' lolling and boozing to
regular hours. (Counterparts of Hardy's itinerant labourers?) JBP
comments: 'This irregular rhythm of effort and relaxation, I
believe, is what most of us English really like; we are not happy as
a people with the machine tempo of modern industrialism, often
going on strike to prove we are not yet robots.' Is there something
wrong, mentally wrong, with the human race, that it should create
an environment and then kow-tow to it? In *Man and Time*, 1964, he
looks at the Maya civilisation and is impressed by its ingenuity but
reflects that there must have been a severe lack of balance. And
will some future JBP feel the same about us?

> It is just possible that some future age, discovering our passion for
> science and technology, our willingness to follow wherever they might
> lead, might see us in the same light as we see this Maya priesthood —
> earnest, devoted, clever people but perhaps not quite right in the head.

It is significant that in the later stages of his career, having
established reputations as a playwright, novelist and Time-
philosopher, JBP turned to history — but history of a very special
sort, social history, the study of how people thought and organised
themselves in communities. His interest lay mainly in the recent
past, a period just preceding, even overlapping to some extent, his
own lifetime, a period before the full weight of the machine and
mechanistic ideas had begun to crush the organic spirit out of
people. *The Prince of Pleasure and his Regency*, 1969, is one of these
books, and is concerned with the earliest period in time. There was
one group of people in this period who naturally engaged JBP's
interest and sympathies: the Luddites. He does not dismiss them as
entirely stupid. 'Perhaps because I grew up in their region I cannot
dismiss them so easily.' The home weavers were miserably paid
but at least they could take the afternoon off if they wanted it.
'They worked to their own needs, their own rhythms, their own
moods. They were not dominated by and geared by machines.'
Something of their protest has lingered to our own times, he
writes. Strikes occur in the same industries, where hours are
reasonable and wages high, but men have to adapt themselves to
the rhythm and unceasing demands of machines. If only men were
more articulate, would they not realise that their enemy was
neither the boss nor a cramped market, but the machine?

Chapter 16

The End of the Civilised World

This phrase does not mean, in relation to Priestley, a holocaust in which man and his works are wiped out, although his concern with the nuclear weapon (known as the 'deterrent') left him with no illusions on the possibility of such an event. A madman's finger on the button might start the process and make Doomsday a reality, and there seemed to be no lack of madmen in high places. But this is not what he meant when he stated, as he often did, that the civilised world came to an end in 1914. What he meant was a world of civilised behaviour, a world without anxiety.

Although many critics disagree with me, I believe that some of the most significant statements and opinions are to be found in the lesser works of writers. The great work of art is often consciously shaped and by no means does it reflect the total personality of the author. Whereas when he is in unbuttoned mood, not much caring whether what he is writing is regarded as 'important' or 'significant' or not, he will often disclose his innermost self to an exceptional degree. In this chapter I am going to quote several statements by JBP that indicate he believes there has been a steep decline in civilised values and conduct over the past sixty years, but I would like to start with reference to a little-known work and certainly not an important one with which he was only peripherally associated. It was a 'Pictorial Survey' entitled *The Beauty of Britain* and it was published in 1935 with an Introduction by JBP. 'Pictorial Survey' does not mean what it would mean today, i.e. a wealth of pictures with minimal text. It is a complete book with nearly 250 pages of text by many contributors, of whom A.G. Street was the best known. The choice of JBP to write the Introduction does homage to his versatility. He has in his time edited or introduced books on the countryside, English tradition, cricket, collections of essays, humour and poetry, and also classical and picaresque novels.

This book, published over forty years ago, seems weighted down with a sense of doom. Rural England is a lost cause. Most of the contributors refer to the deleterious effect of modern inventions, particularly the motor car, garish ribbon development and the indiscriminate use of red brick. The photographs show the farm horse still in possession. It was published the year after *English Journey*, which might have suggested JBP as the natural person to launch it. It was already twenty-five years, in his view, after civilisation had reached its peak.

The approach of the Second World War (only politicians and newspaper proprietors failed to see it coming) probably started JBP reflecting on the world that was broken by the First. In 1938, in the play *Music at Night*, Bendrex, a Cabinet Minister (and certainly one of the aware ones), says the era of good sense ended in July 1914. That was the last time he had been able to make any sense of the world: 'since then I have not been able to make head nor tail of anything that happened three miles from Westminster' — and that last phrase acts as a corrective if we are tempted to think too highly of Bendrex. He repeats this view later in the play, saying that since 1914 'we've all existed in a series of vast mad-houses, shrieking with hate and violence, stinking of death.'

The Linden Tree is a superior play — it is one of his best, largely because the people are more important in themselves than their pronouncements. It was performed in 1948, that is to say, after the second explosion had rocked Europe. There are now more things to complain about and different people seize on different *bêtes noires*. Mrs Linden, who has had just as much as she can bear of modern austerity, says everything's getting worse and worse, and it's time they stopped pretending it wasn't. She wasn't just thinking of rations and queues. 'But when we were young — up to 1914 — the world was sensible and safe and kind — and even if people didn't have much money, they had most of the things they wanted. — They could be happy in a simple easy way — because life seemed good.' But the professor, who is more determined to win through the contemporary difficulties, has more faith in a future, yet even he agrees about the attractive past. He feels it is expressed in Elgar's Cello Concerto, especially the first movement. 'An elderly man remembers his world before the war of 1914, some of it years and years before perhaps — being a boy at Worcester — or Germany in the 'nineties — long days on the Malvern Hills — smiling Edwardian afternoons — MacLaren and Ranji batting at Lords, then Richter or Nikisch at the Queen's Hall — all gone,

gone, lost forever — and so he distils his tenderness and regret, drop by drop, and seals the sweet melancholy in a Concerto for Cello.' But the professor is too realistic to believe that this is the whole truth. He qualifies his pessimism by saying that things will be better for his youngest daughter, Dinah. The sun will shine on her as it once shone on Mrs Linden.

Professor Linden looking back is Priestley looking back. Worcester is a substitute for Bradford. They were still batting at Lords and the young JBP was entranced by Nikisch and Richter. In *Margin Released* he tells us admiringly of his youth in Bradford, not the dirty industrial slag-heaps of Southern imagination but a city where music and poetry flourished only a stone's throw from the bracing air of the Moors. He writes of a rich culture, thriving theatres, music, discussions in pubs and cafés, walks over the Moors — and wonders how they found time for it all. 'Perhaps the very hours began shrinking during the murderous imbecility of the First World War. I will swear that afternoons were never the same again, shrinking to a pallid, characterless interval between lunch and tea: all the great golden afternoons, when a man might plan an epic and even begin it, came to an end in August 1914.' In nearly all his later books, even the novels, there is something along these lines. In *London End* (Volume 2 of *The Image Men*) Tuby says, 'If you take the whole period 1901 to 1914 as Edwardian — and I always do — then you can say that English genius and talent were ablaze in the Indian summer of its Empire.' Stretch a king and the Golden Age appears. There is nostalgia here, of course, but perhaps there is something else. There may be truth. Can we be objective?

A book called *The Edwardians*, published in 1970, seemed the place to make the attempt. Here he had to justify the claims he had been making for the Golden Age. He wrote: 'I have long believed that the decade, say 1904-13, was more richly creative than any decade since then, far more representative of essentially English talent and genius.' This kind of statement is often made but usually by people from a privileged background. JBP's wasn't, and he stresses that ordinary lower and working class people were able to get fulfilment out of their lives in a way that has become less common. The Great War destroyed the mood of hopeful debate and liberating eagerness that marks the period for him. If there had been no war 'we might have saved ourselves and the world.' He suggests that there were promptings from the unconscious that the era was coming to an end. The Balkans were like an exposed powder keg, there was frequent talk of war, but the major signs of coming disaster were to be found in mysterious promptings and premonitions in the dark recesses of the mind. (He had been especially eloquent on this point in discussing the literature of the period in *Literature and Western Man*, 1960, a few years earlier.) The unconscious may have a different time scale from the conscious, he said — and this of course provided a link with one of his main interests. Events such as the sinking of the Titanic, the siege of Sidney Street, the Crippen murder and the assassination of Jaurès, the ravings of Marinetti, they were like warnings that all was not well beneath the placid surface. In 1913 Isadora Duncan's two children and their governess were drowned when their car drove into the Seine: 'It was that kind of year: unlikely accidents, duels, various types of *crime passionel*, being all too common.' It is clear that this pattern of events made a deep impression on Priestley. The pattern could merely be one self-created within his own mind, but he suspects that there is a design to life which we can sometimes glimpse.

It is easy to make fun of this sort of thing. No scientific positivist could be expected to do anything else. But it is a feature of the creative mind that it believes in the existence of a pattern; that art is an attempt to discover the pattern, to reduce apparent disorder to order. As a result you get statements of the kind he appended as 'Some Afterthoughts' to *The Happy Dream*, which was included in *Instead of the Trees*, 1977: 'I have sometimes thought that round-about 1910 something peculiar — perhaps rather sinister — happened in the inner world of youngish men of talent, even genius.' Doesn't this ring a bell? Didn't Virginia Woolf assert that human nature changed at about this time and, like JBP, gave a date for it? Without enquiring any further into this aspect of the case, we can note that he is convinced that there has been some kind of human deterioration since those days. 'Taken as a whole were the people of — let us say — 1912 better than people as they are today? And I say they were. There can be regress as well as progress, and it is a kind of sentimentality to deny this.' Also heresy, of course, for the self-described progressive. A world without social welfare, the National Health Service, the female suffrage, forty-five universities, powerful trade unions — such a world to be better than our own? The man must be a reactionary. Priestley, who has shown far more awareness of the reality of modern society than most, who has never been in danger of being mistaken for a Tory, asks: 'Would I like to go back to 1912? Certainly, without hesitation.' He shares with Gregory Dawson of *Bright Day* 'a deep-seated nostalgia for that golden haze of youth before the First War . . . ' And if we ask how much of this is merely nostalgia and how much is truth, there can be no answer. But it is very hard to love and admire the world around us in 1981.

There is one symbol which represents for JBP the full horror of the contemporary world, and that is the huge and bloated city. Today, when the city appears to be breaking up, when anyone who can gets out, and those who can't often live in fear of the streets and take their neuroses to a Health Service that cannot cope with them, it is easy to agree with him. It is not so much the size of the city that appals him as the quality of its life. After all, *Angel Pavement* did not project any hatred of London, at that time the greatest city in the world. In fact, the London of the 1920s could still be viewed as a collection of overgrown villages, with their own corporate lives going on side by side and not being dwarfed by metropolis. But if he managed to keep this view of the city under control in the novel he was already giving it an airing in his essays. In one of the essays in the *Apes and Angels* collection, 1928, simply entitled 'Too Many People', he says he finds he no longer enjoys visits to London. He goes to Olympia to see the circus but he cannot get in because all the seats are sold. It is the same with the theatres and restaurants. His vision of Hell would be a very long Oxford Street with no side-roads at all. 'As year follows year there seem to be more and more people walking the streets, waiting at shop counters, jumping on buses and tube trains, filling the theatres and hotels and restaurants and tea-shops.'

Either the modern city is an ant-heap of meaningless activity (guided by who knows what sinister influences?) or it is a collection of dark satanic mills, as we saw in Gretley. Hatred of the city lay beneath the slightly hysterical note to be found in *The Doomsday Men*. Three madmen are out to destroy civilisation, and they must be prevented, but there is a tiny part of JBP's mind, the part that created them in the first place perhaps, that murmurs its sympathy. Andrea takes Malcolm to a little platform on a spur which commands a tremendous view of the landscape spread out beneath them. As they admire it, she says it is because it's itself, just sun, air, rock and sand, with no people to spoil it. He asks her if she really thinks people spoil the world. She replies:

> Of course they do. Look at this, and then think of the places where people are, millions of them, your London, and New York, and Los Angeles, all crowded together, screaming and squabbling and thinking dirty little thoughts and all getting ready to murder each other again. And the more there are of them, the worse it is.

If the big city is the prime symbol of modern horror, New York City is its most infamous expression. 'New York is a city I can do nothing with,' he wrote in *Delight*. (Much of this volume should be titled *Undelight*!) When he is there he longs to get away, where 'there will be no more telephone calls, urgent messages, interviews, noisy parties . . .' He invites us to think of Athens, Florence, Elizabethan London and Weimar, and he asks, 'What has come out of Megalopolis but rubbish and hysteria.' In *Trumpets Over the Sea* he recalls how W.H. Auden told him that New York is the only city in the world which is not provincial, which presumably means that he, JBP, is incurably provincial, but it is an argument he cannot accept. He has noted a change in New York City over the years. In the thirties he was afraid of it (see the account in *Faraway*, 1932) but he felt its power, boldness and glamour. But now, thirty-odd years later, it has become increasingly dirty and sour.

> No other big city offers you fewer people of genuine talent, simply because such people now prefer to live and work somewhere else. Over tall highballs that merely freeze the stomach and never illuminate the mind, the fifth-rate yap and yap about the recent doings of the third-rate. You are still asked if you can stand the bustle and pace when in fact you are increasingly appalled by the slowness of everybody and everything.

Again, it could stand for a symbol. Today, when everything is done in such a rush and hurry, it takes longer to send a letter, to conclude a business deal, to get a book published or to cash a cheque than it did fifty years ago, and very often longer to buy a loaf of bread or five gallons of petrol, according to the political situation.

It is easy and at times tempting to assume that we are all Going Downhill. It can give a sense of personal superiority. In judging the accuracy of such a charge we must always bear in mind that adaptation becomes increasingly difficult as we grow older. This factor certainly operates in JBP's case, but on the other hand he does give a considerable amount of chapter and verse illustration of deterioration over the years. The general tone is summed up in *Faraway*, a novel which is basically about the retreat of its main characters from the modern world of mobs and machines to a romantic quest for an unspoilt Pacific island — but the intention behind the quest lies in the search for pitchblende, which modern industry demands and will pay a high price for. The quest is poisoned at birth. They decide to make for Tahiti, which William says is supposed to be a sort of human paradise. The Commander says it was, but 'it may be spoiled now. Most places are.' It is a casual remark, but it sums up JBP's feeling about what man has done to his environment.[1]

Chapter 17

The Monster Admass

How should we regard people? The answer is obvious to anyone who is not a power-maniac or who is not engaged in dealing with people in large numbers. They are individuals and they have individual desires, feelings and ambitions. 'I wouldn't raise a finger for the "masses". Men, women and children — but not masses,' he writes in *English Journey*. Gridley was to say the same later in *Bees on the Boat Deck*. The distinction lies at the heart of the major political struggle of our time — the attempt of the pristine social democratic ethos to withstand the Marxist perversion. There is such a thing as society, but it consists of individuals. Any other conception is nonsense and false mysticism.

JBP's quarrel with the communists was reflected in *English Journey*. He admired many of them as sincere, hard-working people. He gives an attractive portrait of one on Tyneside. Bob was realistic enough in most things, but experienced a blind spot in his belief in the theoretical existence of people as 'the proletariat'. JBP disagreed with his diagnosis because whereas he saw muddle everywhere Bob put everything down to conspiracy. He thought people were poor because a few were rich. He was aware of the weaknesses of the men around him, but as soon as he argued politics they became 'the workers', bright, beautiful, unselfish, industrious and incorruptible. On the other hand, men of the employing or managing classes were always sneering, cunning tyrants, to whom the poverty and suffering of others were sources of deep satisfaction. JBP ends his account: 'I shall not join Bob's party yet; but I wish I had a party fit for him to join.'

Democracy is not a high-falutin thing that needs learned books to expound it. It used to be apparent in the Northern towns, when men and master were all on christian name terms. 'Nothing illustrates the genuine and deep-seated democracy of Lancashire better than this practice of using Christian names. It is, I think, a sounder democracy than those that insist upon "citizen" or "comrade".' These titles are imposed, anyway (they are less sincere than 'mate'), just as the renewed modern practice of using Christian names often seems a bit self-conscious or forced. JBP wanted to see people making their own decisions and thinking their own way through life's problems. For this reason he opposed both state action and private paternalism on the Bournville pattern.

> I . . . would infinitely prefer to see workers combining to provide these benefits, or a reasonable proportion of them, to see them using their leisure, and demanding its increase, not as favoured employees but as citizens, free men and women.

It seemed at times, however, that he was trying to move against the stream. For every individual who desired to make his own decisions there were five or ten who just couldn't be bothered, who were only too ready to have everything done for them. Perhaps these individuals, in their millions, were longing for the day when they could become masses. Perhaps the Marxists realised that this longing existed and were only too ready to give the push that would make it reality. In *Brave New World* Huxley had already shown how much simpler it would be to control people by making life easy for them than by making it harder. In JBP's excellent novel about an aircraft factory, *Daylight on Saturday*, Blandford expresses his opinion of the new masses. They sound like fodder for Marx or Huxley's new world.

> Most of them are fixed at the mental age of twelve. They're all being paid twice as much as they're worth. Very few of them care a rap about the war. They've got to be coddled and cared for like babies. They haven't an idea in their heads. They know less about the technique of living than any Southern European peasant or, for that matter, an East African negro. They've lost the medieval virtues and haven't yet acquired any modern ones. They don't *know* anything and they don't care.

Although Blandford is an engineer he comes from the landed gentry. It is not enough to argue that he speaks like one. What is more to the point is whether he is speaking the truth.

JBP's irritation with 'the masses' can be seen taking shape in his *Letter to a Returning Serviceman*. Giant organisations are beginning to control the national destiny and genuine power will lie in a few hands if nothing is done to extend political democracy. 'Gigantic state machinery could soon be erected to compel the masses — and I use the term deliberately, for soon the rootless, powerless and doped folk could rightly be described as "masses" . . . ,' he warns. The denigration of political democracy by 'advanced' and 'progressive' politicians and journalists has made it that much easier to pull the wool over the individual eye. Non-stop TV, bawling in picket lines and carrying placards with mis-spelt slogans to Trafalgar Square are valuable training exercises for those who control society, whether in a collective or a private capacity.

In *Margin Released* JBP tells us how in his adolescence he wrote a story called 'Poor Old George'. It was not a good story, but on looking back one point about it astonishes him now — it foresaw the modern advertiser, or rather, celebrated his arrival much earlier than one normally envisages him. And the advertising copywriter is a kind of Scriptwriter Laureate to the new Merovingian. Its name (not his, for the crowd has no sex) is Admass.

During the next century amateur companies may cease to put on *When We Are Married* or *Laburnum Grove; I Have Been Here Before* may seem no more than a rather quaint approach to a problem that has been solved; *The Good Companions* may be taught in the universities as the last exercise of the picaresque pen; *Angel Pavement* and *Lost Empires* may still be read by connoisseurs of the novel as today *Gryll Grange* and *The Ordeal of Richard Feverel* are read — that is to say, not often; but perhaps the name of Priestley may survive through none of these and yet be remembered as the originator of the term Admass. For Admass is that great formless mob of our time that is corrupted by advertising and propaganda and whose only aim in life seems to be thoughtless comfort. It was defined, with its many derivatives, most comprehensively in *Journey Down a Rainbow*, 1955, which JBP wrote with his wife Jacquetta Hawkes.

This splendid piece of sustained invective is to be found in a section entitled 'New Names'. *Admass* comes first: 'This is my name for the whole system of an increasing productivity, plus inflation, plus a rising standard of material living, plus high-pressure advertising and salesmanship, plus mass communications, plus cultural democracy and the creation of the mass mind, the mass man.' *Propmass* is its equivalent behind the Iron Curtain. *Nomadmass* is the land of the new nomads, dominated by the internal combustion engine. *Hashadmass* describes the situation where everything is turned into one tasteless hash. Most of the money earned in this area is spent in *Luxad*, the domain of

Gracious Living. Throughout this book JBP makes use of these terms in a furious assault on our society and its values. Steak Worship is part of the Admass culture. 'If a good *Admass* man does not order a steak, either he is not hungry or he cannot afford the price . . . *Admass* types who have spent the whole day in an arm-chair, merely lifting a telephone, will then order steaks that would daunt a six-foot navvy.' The huge Breast (particularly on girls with boyish figures and no pelvis to speak of) is another symbol. *Admass* is unhealthily dominated by the masculine principle. There is no true feeling for Woman herself; these creatures do not lure man to bed but make him leap in his cradle. Action is frowned upon, except as a spectacle.[1] The ideal is to be supine. 'In *Admass* the crowd is no longer asked to make some effort, to get out of its armchairs and try to climb a little; it stays where it is, yawning and twiddling its thumbs, and everybody and everything that might have brought it richer experience, new life, are delivered to it down on that level.' Elsewhere in this book JBP's description of the opening of a new hotel in Houston (a cultural event in Admass!) is superb. The hotel is the symbol of Admassian wealth and power, the ceremony is an expression of the shocking muddle at the heart of things. It showed *Admass* 'fully flowering in a single gorgeous night.' A night of stupendous vulgarity, vapidity and chromium-plated boredom and confusion.

Priestley has a genius for inventing apt names to describe social phenomena. The appeals in *Times* advertising to Top People stimulated him to write *Topside, or The Future of England*, a Dialogue which appeared in 1958. Top People are remarkable for neither thought, vision nor action but simply for being Top. They control society, not as a class but as a power structure. Around and beyond them are the Takers, the governed, those who meekly and unthinkingly accept whatever the Topsiders give them. The creative part of society, a thin band lying between Topsiders and Takers, are being squeezed out. Hypocrisy and self-deception leave no space for the creative mind. And, to do him justice, JBP fore-cast in this book the increasingly hopeless, directionless society we live in now.

I have already referred to JBP's participation in the Campaign for Nuclear Disarmament. Apart from its intrinsic importance it represented a great opportunity for the British people to assert themselves, to compel their political leaders to follow instructions rather than to issue them with the certainty of meek obedience. They might show they still cared, still held dear certain public values. If they had been cozened unthinkingly into an acceptance of Admass, here was their chance to reject it. Nothing of the kind happened. In *Man and Time* JBP sadly acknowledged the truth. He was shocked by people's indifference to this issue of stupendous significance for the human race. Propaganda had not made them accept the Bomb but equally the protesters had not made them reject it. 'They remain profoundly, astonishingly, shockingly *indifferent*. They are indifferent, I can only conclude, because in their heart of hearts they no longer care what happens.' He calls this an 'inner nihilism'. Only two matters, sex and family life, seem to move most people to action. They alone seem to retain value where so much value and meaningfulness have vanished. The advertisers have been quick to take advantage of this situation.

The writer suffers more than most from the conditions imposed by Admass. In 1955 JBP gave the Hermon Ould Memorial Lecture for P.E.N. which was first published as a pamphlet under the title *The Writer in a Changing Society* and then incorporated in *Thoughts in the Wilderness*, 1957. First of all, production goes up and up because high-pressure advertising and salesmanship constantly create new needs that must be satisfied: 'a consumers' race with donkeys chasing an electric carrot. This enables you to build up and enjoy a civilisation in which innumerable men with anxiety neuroses sit cursing in new and larger cars that cannot move, just because innumerable other men, with stomach ulcers, are also out in their new and larger cars. In *Admass* you press on with your particular swindle in order to have more money to spend on other men's swindles.' The net result of all this is the enthronement of triviality. The writer, who is concerned with values, falls to the bottom of the pile. This is particularly noticeable in film-making — and in *Faraway* JBP had already described a film unit engaged on a script that was so idiotic and syrupy that it was absolutely tailored for Admass consumption. Safe men are employed at every stage of production. JBP is fond of 'symbolic scenes' and often introduces them into his writing, both fiction and non-fiction. One of these is the gala film première. Waiting in the drizzle and the outer darkness is the huge, faceless, nameless mob. The privileged guests, arriving in huge cars surrounded by police, are the aristocracy of the new order — Cabinet Ministers, high officials, wealthy industrialists, newspaper magnates and the glamorous darlings of the watching crowd, the film stars, the TV personalities, the gossip columnists. The writer, who is the essential creator, might be on the edge of the guests, his place in the hierarchy being 'a little above that of the chief make-up man but below the camera-man.' And among the crowd will be a few thousand pretty girls and clever young men who are watching, with despair or deter-mination, the summit of achievement.[2]

Priestley has always been a great admirer of the funny men, clowns and comics. He tends to be retrospective in his admiration but he did recognise the genius and the significance of Tony Hancock. He was a figure born out of Admass and TV was his natural medium. His pretensions (in his TV character) were absurd, and we all laughed at him — 'yet this was somebody close to mass man of today, coming out of the faceless crowd, hopeful, near to glory, for some minutes, before the lid comes on again, before he shrugs his way back into the dark.' It is always noticeable how every period produces its own heroes effortlessly and unthink-ingly. Society takes on a certain colouring and produces its man. At the other extreme from Hancock was the darling of the in-tellectuals, McLuhan, who prophesies the end of the printed word and, wrote JBP in *A Visit to New Zealand*, was winning. He had no admiration for McLuhan's 'sweeping generalisations' but that was exactly what his public wanted. For Admass must have its own fringe with its own jargon.

Admass was born in America and for years JBP has been warning against undue Americanisation. It would be quite wrong to accuse JBP of anti-Americanism.[3] He has a great admiration for certain aspects of American life, he feels particularly at home in the mid-West and he has many American friends. But he has criticised certain elements of American life and has been severely chastised by journalists who are quite content to distort the truth to get a good story. But it is the worst side of American life that Europeans often imitate and Americans cannot be blamed for this. In his early work he often drew attention to the immense influence Hollywood had on the English young. In every town there were cinemas, serving as outposts of Hollywood, 'where you may see its tough guys, who knock fellows down so readily and easily, and its young women with their egg faces and voices like seagulls,' as he writes in *Let the People Sing*, 1939. Nearly all the girls in the shops tried to look like these glamorous beings 'with the result that there is hardly a whole young feminine eyebrow left in this part of Dunbury.' In this novel Fern Mitterly was so busy trying to emulate one of those exotic and enigmatic creatures who are always seen at the beginning of their films sitting alone in very fashionable restaurants or standing alone on the promenade decks of liners, that she herself didn't appear in the least mysterious and exotic but simply not very well and strange in her manner. What was even more insidious was the fact that the biggest employer in Dunbury was United Plastics, with its HQ in New Jersey. This company was trying to import American industrial and commercial methods into the Dunbury factory, where Fern worked. While eager to accept the cosmetic side of American life, Fern was not so keen on functional innovations and finally triggered off a strike against the introduction of new 'time-and-motion' measures, which increased production and shoved the workers a little further down the Admass road. Daisy, an old trouper, had been in America for a short time. 'What the Yanks did last year we'll do next year,' she tells Timmy. The reason was that there must be a leader in fashion. It used to be us, now it's them. 'Every new thing you see here nowadays is only a copy of something they've had for years in America.' This explained the success of her roadhouse.

JBP felt so strongly about this that he introduced the idea into his political campaign during the later stages of the war. He gave a warning to a teen-age audience in a speech later published as a pamphlet under the title *The New Citizen*, 1944. Although the world is becoming interdependent, he said, there are some areas where the differences should be stressed.

> I see already a danger that we English will soon not be as English as possible, for I think we are tending to become Americanised, and though it is a good thing for the Americans to be very American, it is not a good thing for us English to be semi-American, and I hope that you young people will attend to that.

It was not only distaste for the idea of becoming a mere imitation but also grief at the disappearance of many things that he felt had been valuable in themselves. Often very trivial things, except that it is not always easy to know whether a thing is trivial or not. In *English Journey* he had detected three co-existent Englands: Old England, with its roots very deep in the past; Nineteenth Century England, which, on the face of it, appeared to be a kind of

Dickensian Wonderland; and New England — and here lay the main danger, even shame, for it was in fact American England. Many aspects of Old and Nineteenth Century England had disappeared, or were fast disappearing, and being replaced by something quite alien. *Delight* had been full of nostalgic complaints. Let us take one example and follow it through JBP's later writing. When he was a young man every small town had at least one good tobacconist, a shop where the proprietor understood tobacco and could distinguish between the varieties. There are very few left. When he went to Daytona Beach with the London Symphony Orchestra he found the packaging of pipe tobacco was always much superior to the contents. It was the admen and the salesmen, not the tobacco blenders, who were directing the enterprise. 'And I mention this because it is a good example of what has gone wrong — and is going wronger — in American life, and of what is now being widely imitated in Britain and most of Western Europe. It is a bad trend enthusiastically adopted by the "trendy". We are increasingly bamboozled by the outside of the package.' Is this trivial? The wrapper can hide a multitude of sins.

It crops up everywhere in his writing. When he went to New Zealand he crossed America. He enjoyed Santa Monica with its traffic-less shopping centre: 'This seemed to us progress as against American *prog-ress*, the deepening nightmare.' Certainly not everything has gone wrong — much has gone right — but America does export the worst and not the best of its ideas, habits and styles of living. (It might be more accurate to say we import them.) He concedes that America had the enormous task of turning masses of Central and East European peasants into responsible citizens. One result has been the blurring of language with a consequent lack of definition: any kind of disagreement becomes a 'fight', any insect a 'bug', petrol becomes 'gas'. This is the language of Admass, and examples could be multiplied indefinitely.

Is there a way out of Admass? No doubt there are many possibilities but JBP does not suggest them. His job has always been exhortation and if Admassians will not listen, the responsibility is theirs, not his. But in his *Visit to New Zealand* he did make a remarkable statement which indicates one way, though not a very hopeful one, out of the dilemma. For him New Zealand is the hope of an embattled world. The modern American virus has not yet established itself there. The population still consists of individuals rather than a kind of half-set social jelly. (There is more than a hint that JBP supports genetic theory in his view of social development.) The New Zealanders resist the attractions of Americanisation because they are the people they are, or descendants of a special kind of people, namely, people who chose to go there of their own free will and not by force of law or circumstance.

Chapter 18

Time in the Novel

The purpose of putting this chapter here is to demonstrate that despite JBP's increased interest in social and political matters, which became evident during the war and has remained with him ever since, his concern with Time has not correspondingly lessened. Time became a major preoccupation towards the end of the 1930's, in what we now call the Time plays and also a couple of autobiographical books, *Midnight on the Desert* and *Rain Upon Godshill*. There had been a suggestion of this interest, but without any clarification, in his first play, *Dangerous Corner*, and there had been one or two other hints. This chapter will be concerned with the treatment of Time in his fiction.

There is only one of his novels which makes a primary concern of Time and this novel is, to me, a mystery in itself. It is called *Jenny Villiers*, is sub-titled *A Story of the Theatre*, and was published in 1947. The mystery is entirely extrinsic, and is simply this: that although it is a novel (short, it is true, and perhaps more accurately called a novella) and is undeniably by J.B. Priestley, I have never seen it referred to or discussed in any treatment of his work. David Hughes, who wrote his informal study in 1958, and Susan Cooper, who published her portrait in 1970, both ignore it. This seems extraordinary to me, considering its subject, and suggests that it is not only a ghost story but also a story-ghost. If it were by any other writer it would be dubbed, without any more ado, a ghost story. But as it is by Priestley we are aware of how Cheveril living in our time was able to watch and encounter Jenny Villiers and some of her colleagues in the 1840's. He or they have momentarily strayed out of their normal time-dimensions. Cheveril, an aging and embittered playwright, who saw the Theatre as inevitably rushing towards its own extinction, recovers his faith through his encounters with two hopeful young actresses, one whom he meets in the flesh and the other whom he meets through a vagary in the time-scheme. This novel, which is so far removed from his normal fictional work (and has therefore, I assume, puzzled his admirers), does not demand detailed credibility in the way that *Angel Pavement* or *Bright Day* do. We read it as we would read a ghost story (JBP's theory certainly allows for the poltergeist phenomenon) and it doesn't matter at all whether we accept the theory or not. It is not credibility that is required by faith, and it is not faith in metaphysics but in theatre. JBP manages to bring together all those strands which I have mentioned earlier that make, for him, the wonder of the Theatre: an almost unearthly combination of human effort and magic.

For the rest of his fiction, it is largely a matter of catching the various Time references when they occur. Before he became established as a Time philosopher (to use a convenient shorthand) it would have been a very astute reader indeed who would have caught the references and realised their significance. But now, looking back, we can see that the nature of Time had been lying quietly at the back of his mind for some years. To us now they appear to be a series of rather shy signals. We can see how this operated in *Faraway*, published in 1932, the very year that *Dangerous Corner* was first produced. Talking to the Commander and Ramsbottom about their proposed trip to the South Seas, William suddenly feels he has done this before. He wonders if he had dreamt it. Then follows this very significant passage.

> Perhaps he had talked to the Commander and listened to Mr Ramsbottom many a time before. And the island itself, was that really new? Had there not been an island before, nothing solidly geographical, of course, not a place you could recognise perhaps, only a shadow on a veil and seas breaking in an inland night, yet an island? Had they all been there already?

And then, in italics: '*The three of them sitting on a rock, very hard, hot, jagged, talking earnestly.*' It all comes true, although we are not reminded of this premonition when it does.

Later in the novel there are a few more very delicate references to this effect. There is a moment on board ship when William wonders if he has 'wandered into a new sort of time.' He had the same feeling while watching some brightly coloured fish and 'for years afterwards, at odd moments, there would come a sudden sheen of unearthly blue, brighter than the flash of a kingfisher, and then the little fishes would go swimming through his mind, and he would be back in the lagoon, puzzling over their magic.' This is not

mere association in the Proustian manner, for there is no obvious
triggering agent. But the most remarkable example came from the
extremely prosaic Ramsbottom who met an old man on one of the
islands and was put by him into some kind of a trance. In it he met
an old sweetheart. It sounded like nothing more remarkable than a
dream but even Ramsbottom felt it was too real for that — as
though either he or Maggie had been removed from one time
dimension into another. Of course, such an idea was far too
revolutionary and fanciful for Ramsbottom who could only mutter
about its queerness, but obviously some such notion passed
through William's mind and, even more certainly, through his
creator's. 'Then all of a sudden,' Ramsbottom recounts, 'and Ah
remember it as plain as plain can be — Ah gave a sort of shiver.
No waking up or anything like that, just a sort o' little shiver . . .'
and it is all over.

It is the 'shiver' that fascinates. It is mentioned by JBP on several
other occasions — just as though everything is so delicately poised
(perhaps the consciousness for one moment peering across a
boundary?) that a mere shiver, a tiny breath of air, will upset the
balance. The first time we encounter this metaphor is in an essay
with the suggestive title of 'Dissolution in Haymarket' which
appeared in the collection *Open House*, 1927. He tells us that the
Haymarket is one of his favourite thoroughfares with its gentle-
manly air and suggestion of the eighteenth century. 'It would be
hard to find a London street less morbid, less gloomy, more likely
to augment rather than diminish one's zest for life.' And then, as he
goes along it on a bus, there is a sudden change of mood. 'The
whole cheerful pageant of the street immediately crumpled and
collapsed, with all its wavering pattern of light and shade, its
heartening sights and sounds, its warm humanity, its suggestion of
permanence, and I was left shivering in the middle of a tragedy.'
What had happened? A change of mood? Certainly, but what
caused the change of mood? Normally we dismiss it as a psychological event (which explains nothing) but could it perhaps be the
consequence of a temporal event? Even if we keep the term
'psychological', it is his awareness of such upheavals that always
distinguish JBP from the run-of-the-mill popular writer — and he
is a popular writer, and proud of it. At the back of his mind he is
always alert to other moods, other potentials; and then, even before
he had read Dunne, it occurred to him that these effects might not

be private possessions of the ego but something external, action across dimensions. (It must be understood that he was thinking in terms much subtler than those used by Wells in *The Time Machine*. He did, in fact, enter this territory once in a story called 'Mr Strenberry's Tale' which appeared in *Four-in-Hand* in 1934, in which a man arrives from the future, fleeing from the destruction of his world.)

But we can trace the time-and-dream interest to an even earlier date. In *Margin Released* he makes the fascinating conjecture that just as dreams may give a glimpse of the future, so might myths and legends. This idea occurs to him as he recalls some of his juvenile verse, especially a very bad piece (his own words) called *Evensong to Atlantis*. He was once haunted by the idea of Atlantis, and a little of the fascination still lingers, despite the derision of his archaeologist wife. What caused this fascination? It was not the mere fact of a cataclysm itself that held him but the idea that Atlantis had destroyed itself. Was this feeling based in his unconscious and did it look forward rather than back? Maybe, he thought, we are rushing towards Atlantis, not away from it? The original notion in all this is that the unconscious is actually concerned with the future, and not with the past as had always been assumed. But if this were true it required a complete re-assessment of the nature of Time. The idea began to expand and take possession of him. He even felt he might have foreseen the War — the First War, which very few foresaw, not the Second, which nearly everyone did. During the first part of 1914 he crammed as much experience into his days as he could, as if he knew what was coming. Consciously he was unaware: 'but deep in the unconscious, which has its own time and a wider *now* than consciousness knows, already the war was on, a world ending.'

For the remainder of his writing career, which still continues, JBP has managed to work in references to his Time theory, usually fairly slender ones along the lines of those we have noted in *Faraway* but now likely to be picked up by the attentive reader. In *Let the People Sing*, 1939, Candover, a rather weak-minded old man, has extremely detailed dreams which he can remember without effort. He only has to close his eyes and he sees them. They appear to be both precognitive and retrocognitive — in other words, he moves with great facility in a time dimension. The professor asserts that one of his dreams must be the sack of Bagdad by the Mongols under Hulagu. He believes that Candover's unconscious dreaming mind reflects the universal mind or world memory. So far, so Jungian. But later he is taken to court and tells the magistrate he had dreamt the whole occasion before, just as it happened. He is dismissed as half crazy. One is left not quite clear as to whether Candover's experiences are Jungian or Dunnian.

Bright Day, 1946 adopts a more recognisably Priestleyan tone with a brief reference to the recurrent theme. 'If the universe is not simply an idiotic machine, grinding out nothingness, then in some queer but cosy dimension of it my Aunt Hilda is still trotting round to the Miss Singletons to secure the last brown loaf and the remaining six Eccles cakes.' The logic of this is certainly obscure, for there seems no reason to hold that Aunt Hilda on a perpetual trot is less idiotic than Aunt Hilda on a single trot. But JBP was not always in positive mood about the time-dream-magical moment effect. Sometimes it was merely sufficient to resort to the 'as if' approach, as he did in the play, *Summer Day's Dream*, 1949, when Rosalie says, 'There was a moment tonight, when Christopher was playing, when it was as if we had all broken through into a larger and different sort of time, like that of a clear happy dream . . .' In the same year he even managed to work in a Time reference in *The Olympians*, an opera for which Arthur Bliss composed the music. Hector, the romantic poet is in love with Madeleine, the miser's daughter. Time is referred to in traditional style as an agent that can aid or hinder human beings, but when the author is J.B. Priestley one suspects rather more than normal significance.

Hector. Time that ran to bring me to your side,
       Now runs no more, but stays to cherish our love.
Madel. Silent and still as the silver fields of the moon,
       Time waits for us, because my love is here at last.
Hector. Time has halted
       The pulse of the night,
       And this hour only knows
       The beat of my heart
       Crying, 'I love you.'

This is something more than specious, psychological time conflicting with mechanical clock time. The lovers are in fact moving from one time dimension to another, not in a poetic conceit, but in reality.

The Old Man of the Mountain in *Saturn Over the Water*, 1961, knows how to catch glimpses of the future, but it's not a fixed future. There are possibilities, and you have a choice (cf. *I Have Been Here Before*). 'It is what could and may happen, not yet what will happen. So it is a vision of a vision — out of any order of time yet — among possibilities.' Incidentally, the Man of the Mountain character bears strong resemblance to the Wild Man character in *Faraway* — not in his view of life, for we know nothing of the latter's, but in his way of life, his closeness to and rejection of the civilised world.

Uncle Nick in *Lost Empires*, 1965, is an illusionist. He is much more than a run-of-the-mill magician, the kind that fascinates the children's party by mastering sleight-of-hand and keeping close to the textbook. Uncle Nick *uses* time. He claims that he owes his success to his manipulation of different times. While he operates in one dimension, the audience operates in another. He says he has read every book he can find on the subject but 'not one of them sees the importance of this slow time in the audience's mind when you're working fast on the stage.' His nephew Richard, who takes part in the act and tells the story, can appreciate different kinds of time. He falls in love with one of the artistes, whom he eventually marries, after many misunderstandings and emotional ups and downs. As soon as he saw her he felt excited, but this was because their relationship already existed in some larger time, and made itself felt to him in his immediate narrower time. Thus the 'future' was influencing the 'present'. In this excellent novel Uncle Nick's theory of stage-music serves to reinforce JBP's broader theory of Time.

It will be recalled that *Man and Time*, JBP's most serious and extended treatment of the subject, was written in the sixties, so it is no surprise to find that the novels of this period intensify the time-association. This is particularly noticeable in *It's an Old Country*, 1967. Again, the apparent vagaries of time in the lover's consciousness become the centre of interest. Helga is an extremely beautiful but entirely vacuous person, whom Tom Adamson falls for when he has only her looks to go by. When he found her out and realised he had made a fool of himself, he tried to puzzle the affair out in terms of time. 'When he really wished to know what he'd done, thought, felt, while in pursuit of Helga, the time refused to be sorted out into days in which certain things happened: it remained a blur of a mish-mash. He had spent longer than a week but less than a fortnight trying, it might be said, to juggle with large coloured jellyfish.' This novel is also concerned with the contrasting richness and poverty of different moments in time. As Tom is engaged in conversation with a County Conservative Women's group, he is depressed by the emptiness and meaninglessness of the occasion. What time is it? someone asks and then follows the re-iteration: Yes, indeed — what time was it? This is a cry of despair from the author, for time is an element we cannot afford to waste, but which we 'kill' remorselessly.

JBP's characters can be divided into those who honour time and those who don't. Hilda Neckerson (in the same novel) can feel behind the minutes that tick by so relentlessly, and sense that below 'the obvious outward pattern — what people who are so sure about everything call the *facts* — there's an underlying hidden pattern, no real facts anywhere, that we occasionally catch a glimpse of — and say it's a feeling we have.' From this point of view, facts are congealed time, and are only encountered in one dimension of time. The feelings come from another dimension. JBP makes use of this concept of different varieties of time in one area where it is surely justified. *Snoggle*, 1971, written for intelligent youngsters with an interest in extra-terrestrial possi-bilities, is about a strange creature that arrives on Earth by space-ship. There is some suspicion that he might have a degree of prevision, perhaps because his present time, his *Now*, is much wider than ours. Peg and Robin think their way on to the space-ship. (They find it impossible to exchange thought pictures with the aliens.) Peg even had a vision of their planet but couldn't take much in: 'it was all too quick, and I got the idea that his time and mine weren't the same, that they could slow up time or make it speed up just as they pleased.' Perhaps this can happen *to* us but we are not yet able to manipulate it.

Chapter 19

Art and the Public

Priestley has always taken a lively interest in the relationship between the artist, especially the writer and dramatist, and his public. He himself is far more than a professional in those fields. He is also an amateur painter with a very pronounced feeling for music, although his appreciation of music is probably contained within a narrower band of interest than his involvement with the other arts.

One of his convictions is that the English people have a considerable artistic potential. He is not misled by English 'reserve' or 'conservatism' for he knows that artistic ability has no positive correlation with either emotionalism or exhibitionism. He expresses this point of view in some of his discursive writings but nowhere more effectively than in the novel *Let the People Sing*. Here he uses a favourite device, a character who tends to lecture his companions at the drop of a hat. In this case it is a comic foreign professor, which gives an additional dimension to the views expressed. It is probable that many readers of this novel skipped the professor's extended lectures but with others the occasional seed may have germinated. He is baffled by the English but admires their basic qualities.

> The official tradition in England is hostile to art, and so I think is the social tradition based upon the prejudices of a ruling landed class, the feudal England. But a great many of the English, because they are dominated by what lies in the unconscious, are genuine if only half-developed artists. In this they are the opposite of the French, who are controlled by their conscious minds, and appear to be more deeply artistic than they really are.

If England were to lose its wealth and power, the English would soon become famous throughout the world as poets, painters and actors. Since JBP expressed these ideas, the circumstances he described have arisen; England has lost her power and some of her comparative wealth. It is too early to decide whether the prophecy has been fulfilled but there can be little doubt that the international

J.B. Priestley in 1970

standing of British dramatists, musicians, painters and sculptors has risen.

The professor enumerated the great traditions of England. They are the liberty of the individual, toleration, voluntary public service, a very deep love of their own country and the English way of life, and a high degree of humour, irony and sentiment. The professor was a refugee from a regime that cared for none of these qualities. The time was 1939 and the war was imminent. In the same year JBP edited a volume called *Our Nation's Heritage*, a book about the qualities that were being threatened. His editing of this book paralleled the earlier editing of *The Beauty of Britain*, which I have already mentioned. In his Introduction he linked two of his abiding interests: the English watercolour school (Girtin, Turner, Cotman, Crome and Cox) and dreams. The former exploit the humid atmosphere of the English countryside where forms melt into one another, 'almost like the strange places we see in dreams.' That he should have been asked to make this anthology is an indication that his love of his own country was already widely acknowledged. The title is, of course, a cliché and puts us on our guard. Too many hungry writers have rifled other people's writings to make half-books of their own, and the results are usually bitty and often dreary. But most of these pieces seem to have been chosen with affection, which is of first importance for JBP. It is with the poems that he fails, not because they are insincere but because they are banal. But poetry was never his strong point. On the other hand, his feeling for the English water-colourists is. He always writes sensitively of them and it is clear from reproductions that he has included in some of his books that he has built up his own small private collection with superb taste.

The general effect of this volume is one of nostalgia and regret for a warm if sometimes harsh civilisation that has gone forever, and which has been replaced by something uglier which in turn is under threat of something even worse. Can it truly be called a heritage, one wonders. JBP is perfectly aware of this and he ends with an Epilogue called 'Britain is in Danger', which is a warning against the spoliation of the countryside. This must have been an early shot in a campaign that is now familiar to all of us. Today JBP is a Vice-President of the Conservation Society.

With the war there came, as we have seen, a tremendous surge of concern on JBP's part for the future of our country. He hoped there would be social gains, less injustice, less greed, less muddle. Socialism was apparently coming and there was an excellent opportunity to do something for the arts — action that the British ruling class in the past had sternly avoided, as the comic professor had told his passive audience on more than one occasion. Just after the war had ended JBP gave a lecture to the Fabian Society which was later published as a pamphlet under the title, *The Arts Under Socialism*, 1947, with a postscript on 'What the Government Should Do for the Arts Here and Now.' It was dedicated to Harold Laski, who took the chair, with a typically tart note to the effect that he had added some notes 'I should like to think for the benefit of some colleagues of yours.'

He told his audience that art is not icing on the cake, as most politicians suppose. It is the leaven in the dough. Some artists are afraid of socialism, believing they will be called upon to make too great sacrifices. The State sould provide conditions favourable to art and make sure that artists are not exploited. But here he entered a warning against making artists paid employees of the State. The artist should retain his copyright. His work should not be controlled by committees.

> It is dangerous for the State to maintain its artists, instead of merely doing its best, which it is there to do, to ensure the conditions that will enable the artists to proceed with their tasks and to keep themselves. For, I repeat, the price is too high.

No committee can understand, or help, the original genius. He believed the growing public of art-lovers would be able to help the genius — surely an example of excessive optimism! Priestley was entering upon ground that we, with the benefit of hindsight, know to be exceptionally tricky. His fear was that the Arts Council, when established, might ignore the revolutionary and experimental artist. In fact, one complaint against the Arts Council has been that it encourages the freakish and the sloppy on the grounds that they might be anticipating the taste of the future. But that the artist works from inside and does not need external direction is an undeniable principle in any consideration of the relationship between him and his public. 'The State can only clear the ground and build a wall against the cold wind: it cannot pull out of the dark soil the flower of art; only the artist can do that.'

In some additional Notes he urged the calling of an Aid to the Arts conference which would deal with such practical matters as grants to galleries, licences for new buildings, including concert halls and theatres, musicians' pensions, the improvement of Civil List pensions, the creation of a National Theatre Authority to take over the theatrical duties of the Arts Council, and so on. It should be remembered that all these proposals were made against a background of wartime restrictions which had not yet been lifted. 'Why feed education and starve the arts?' he asked, and went on: 'What is the use of spending hundreds of thousands of pounds every year teaching children that Shakespeare is a great dramatist, if every playhouse accessible to those children and their parents is completely controlled by men who are determined to present nothing but leg shows and stupid faces?'[1]

This was a matter that JBP refused to let drop. It is one of the more admirable facets of his character that he has not allowed his own success to blind him to the fact that many other writers find it difficult to make a living, which is a trite enough phrase, but means in fact that they do not enjoy the psychological atmosphere that enables a writer to apply himself properly to his work — as, say, a bank manager or a librarian or a director of education can do. Over a decade later he was reviewing a couple of pamphlets on the arts in England in a piece entitled 'The Party Line on Leisure' (*New Statesman*, 5 September 1959). These pamphlets were issued by the two main political parties. The Tory one he called 'a dead mouse arriving on a silver tray.' It was not only the actual situation of the arts he deplored but also the whole approach of the politician, which was still as obtuse as it had ever been. He detested the 'use of leisure' concept, as though the arts were a set of spanners which could be applied to a knotty problem in wood or metal work — it 'always suggests to me a lot of tame, passive, half-dead people creeping home from their machines and ledgers to do a bit of fretwork or stare at their stamp albums.' The amount of Government money (after all, national money) set aside for culture (after all, the nation's way of life) was scandalous and horribly mean. The Civil List pensions were a damnable disgrace (he has often protested against their inadequacy). 'We writers were better off under George IV than we have been since the war under either the Labour or Tory governments.' He listed the things that were making England a place to avoid and escape from: shrinking green acres, atomic power stations, roads jammed with new cars, packed prisons, inadequate hospitals, desperate teachers and all the couldn't-care-less types.

As he has grown older JBP has also developed psychologically, a process that is not always found among successful writers. When he defined the three stages of the artist in *Particular Pleasures*, 1975, he demonstrated that he had learnt some important lessons along the way. When we are young (the first stage) we think genius or great talent is everything. We even suspect we have it. Then we realise that character has a good deal to do with the success or failure of an artist, quite apart from his talent. And finally, when we are really old, we see how much depends on luck. This is a brave statement for a successful author, who might well be tempted to say: Look, I've done it — there's no reason why you shouldn't too! The growing demand from writers and artists that the public, who enjoy and use their works, should make conditions more amenable for them, is really a suggestion that some attempt should be made to even out the luck. One of the things that has to be attended to is the public's idea of the artist. A great deal has already been done to change the image from that of a rather cissyish young man living on a private income to that of a rather rough customer (often too rough, the result of over-compensation) who drinks a lot of bitter in the local pub. Gregory, in *Bright Day*, has to make this very adaptation. He gets to know Mervin who is a rough, apparently uncultured Yorkshireman speaking in a strong local accent, and yet he is a fine artist, who is endeavouring to get the spirit of the Moors on to his canvas in colour, and is fully aware of when he succeeds and when he fails. Young Gregory is shocked. 'He was not at all my idea of an artist and, in my ignorance, I found it hard to associate this odd rough-spoken chap with those watercolours, at once so delicate and precise.' But this is the English convention, that an artist is something smooth and fancy, and it is one that JBP revolted against, especially after he moved South. It also partly explains his antagonism to many of his younger contemporaries, who were essentially from 'polite' middle-class backgrounds and were more at home in a drawing room than out on the Moors, as though they had actually been created by the convention.

It is always difficult to speak in general terms about artistic experiment. Priestley has been one of the major theatrical experimenters of our time and he has always admitted the importance of it in artistic development. But it is very easy for experiment to slip over its defining edge into mere silliness, exhibitionism or clueless obscurity. We have seen quite a lot of this recently. One might expect JBP to satirise this tendency at some time in his career and sure enough, it occurs in the novel *Sir Michael and Sir George*, 1964. We find Sir Michael dozing over 'one of the new French novels full of furniture and objects and nothing happening.' JBP would not have put it in this way if he hadn't felt the same. One of the main characters, Tim Kemp, himself not unlikeable and at least possessed of a certain vitality, is more in sympathy with the modern movement, one feels. He is going to contact a woman who wants to turn a mansion into a Creative Arts Centre. This is how he describes it to the philistine Sir George Drake. 'It will be a place where advanced young artists of all kinds can live and work — the novelists writing anti-novels, the playwrights anti-plays, the painters and sculptors creating anti-art.' (Then why isn't it called a Discreative Anti-arts Periphery?) Sir Michael is told a play is a fascinating experiment. Wearily he says, 'I don't want a fascinating experiment, but just — for once — a little intelligent entertainment.' He goes to the play, which is a bore — it was set in New York (the huge anti-city), a young man shouted, a young woman whispered, and all the other characters were dummies. 'Once again . . . the avant-garde had been trapped into trying to make a full-length play out of an idea for a ten-minute sketch in a highbrow revue.'

Another aspect of the artist-public relationship is illustrated by the BBC. On the whole, JBP feels a wonderful chance of creating a vital relationship has been muffed by broadcasting. During its fifty-odd years the BBC has created a considerable amount of respect but has failed to please the more discerning listener. JBP's views have been most clearly expressed in his play, *Goodnight Children*, 1942, which he called a Comedy of Broadcasting. It is very light, even to the point of triviality, but one feels it is the froth on a vein of potentially serious criticism. It is set in a regional studio. There is an air of discontent as most of the broadcasters feel they have been banished. They had started their careers full of idealistic faith in what broadcasting could do for the people. Martin Bradburn, a producer, put it like this:

> Some of us were very excited, at first, by the possibilities of broad-casting as a medium. I know I thought that with such a vast audience we ought to be able to provide some fine stuff on a grand scale. I really

believed the air could be used as a sort of huge People's Theatre.

It is noteworthy that this play was written during the war, when the need to create and maintain a vital relationship between authority and people was uppermost in JBP's mind. But that's not the way it happened. Martin had been a theatre producer, but he made enemies and soon had no work. He'd 'never bothered about broadcasting, hardly ever listened in — and thought radio drama just third-rate footling stuff.' The idealism and the contempt, existing side by side, were hardly likely to produce anything of value. But Martin was not alone. Paula Leeds, another producer, agreed with him. The theatre was alive but radio wasn't. 'It's a nice, easy-going, kind and considerate machine — but it's still a machine. And after a time it quietly takes something vital and essential out of you.' Sometimes it can be life-giving, moving, even beautiful. But the organisation is at fault. 'It doesn't care — and the people who run it don't care — for that precious vital impulse which makes the artist an artist.' So the impulse fades away and people sit around making wisecracks. Behind this situation lies the immensely important fact that radio was a monopoly, and still is largely, despite the existence of a few local stations with little finance and a tiny area of coverage. No drama that is anything more than a textbook exercise is likely to arise out of this situation.

Among his hopes and ideas for the artistic future of this nation music had its place. JBP is an artistic polymath. His personal writing, from the earliest days, gives continual evidence of his intense love of a musical era stretching roughly from Mozart to Elgar. It was a taste formed during his adolescent days in Bradford. In *Particular Pleasures*, 1975, he shows us exactly what music means to him and how he approaches it. His descriptions are programmatic and are usually related to an imagined physical environment. He wants music to tug at the emotions and feels that writing about music should do likewise. On the one hand this is the Cardus approach, on the other it is the popular one. When he wants more concert halls to be available for the ordinary people at ordinary prices, it is because he believes that through music they will be undergoing a quasi-dramatic experience. This is how he writes about Sibelius:

> Some genuine pleasure, even some life-enhancing moments, lifts of the spirit, have also come that way, across the frozen lakes; but let us admit that too often it can be chillingly bleak, bare, altogether far removed

from the firelight or candlelight and the faces of our fellow creatures. It is then we hear the strings turning into whiplash gales, the woodwind moaning through leafless trees, and the trombones and the tuba blasting their way out of the frozen earth.

He says he is a literary listener, 'with no stake in the musical with-it game. Music worthy of the name is not written by counter-pointing and harmonic computers but by men and women, hopeless or joyless, joyous or suffering human beings.' One can sympathise with his distaste for the intellectualisation of music but at the same time his approach barely veils a defeat, the effort to discover how music occurs, how the hopeful and the hopeless produce it. We are a long way from Pratt's proposition, that the auditory characters are not emotions at all, that they merely *sound* the way moods feel . . . or Stravinsky's idea that music is powerless to express anything at all . . . or Virgil Thomson's intriguing suggestion that no one can know the communicative power of any work while it is still young.

In his writing about music JBP exhibits the dangers of adopting the common-man attitude: the welcome admiration of and feeling for Mozart and Beethoven and Brahms accompanied by identical emotions about Percy Grainger and Ketelby and Addinsell. However, one cannot doubt his enthusiasm. 'What took J.B. Priestley to a "horrid little honkey-tonk like Daytona Beach", Florida, for a whole month last July when the humidity was 100?' asked the *Times* Diary on 10 June 1968 and supplied the answer: the same incorrigible curiosity as showed itself in *The Good Companions* and his love of music and admiration for the London Symphony Orchestra.

Chapter 20

The Popular Entertainer

It was not only the tide of civilisation that receded in 1914 but also one of its livelier manifestations: the Music Hall. 'Something had gone for good,' he wrote in *English Humour*, 1972. 'Looking back now, I feel more strongly than ever that the years before the Great War belonged to an entirely different era, in which gusto and popular humour came out of a confidence afterwards shakened and darkened by those black casualty lists.'

Priestley would rather think of himself as a playwright than a novelist. At the heart of the theatre is the funny man, or clown. So far as I know JBP has not written for revues or pantomime but there is no doubt that his talent had a strong inclination in that direction. On the many occasions when he introduced theatre people into his novels they were always artistes appearing in variety shows (comedians, singers, dancers, illusionists and so on) and never straight actors.[1] For him the theatre has a huge area of operation — it includes concert parties and circuses and fairgrounds as well as the more orthodox comedies and tragedies which some people amusingly call legitimate. All these forms are bound together by a single aim, that of popular entertainment, and JBP never forgets this. His theatrical references are constant, as we have seen, and whenever he writes of the theatre he immediately becomes professional, far more professional than when he writes of books. One has only to read through *English Journey* to discover the shrewdness of his comment on public entertainment — although 'shrewd' is a word he disavows about himself.

He distinguishes between the humorist and the 'funny man'. The latter has a relentless quality about him, he sets out deliberately to be funny (which of course is his job) but the deliberation is too evident. The clown is the abode of humour, he cannot help being funny — that is, if he is a true clown. He makes the same distinction in literature. P.G. Wodehouse, about whom JBP is less than enthusiastic, is a funny man; W.W. Jacobs is a true humorist.

The TV comic is the funny man *par excellence*. He has to be. He is compelled to be a kind of joke-factory (or at least, joke-wholesaler, with a busy team supplying the jokes by conveyor-belt) and once the joke has left him it has gone for good. He will never be able to polish his joke, to expend loving care on it, to guide it in its first faltering steps through a cynical world. And in addition to the mass-production aspect there is a new kind of audience. 'Their audiences are attacked, to be shaken into big belly-laughs, by humour that is aggressive, coarse in grain, predominantly masculine. (Women join in the laughs because women are great joiners-in, especially if taken out for the evening.) This humour does not ask for heart and imagination. Little thought and not much feeling are required from its audience.' But the great comedians of his youth, Little Tich[2] and Harry Tate and the rest, depended on thought and feeling. He adds that he does not attack the modern TV comic programmes in themselves — they have to adapt to changed circumstances and we have already noted his admiration of Hancock — but the type of humour they provide is very different from what he was accustomed to.[3]

Perhaps because in this book JBP was primarily concerned with humour, and was therefore careful to be impartial and fair-minded, his criticism of the modern comedian was mild. It was quite a different story in his novel, *It's an Old Country*, 1967. Here he mounts a full-scale attack on the degeneracy of modern popular entertainment. Tom Adamson visits a provincial cabaret and is appalled by the main act, Dally and Dolly. They were rapturously received and they couldn't go wrong with that particular audience. But Tom hated them.

> To begin with, they had no real talent, unless their knowledge of what would please their audience amounted to a talent. They had between them not even a suggestion of genuine wit or humour. Tom couldn't imagine them indulging in the tiniest bit of clowning when they were away from an audience. They were as far removed from gaiety, high spirits, authentic drollery, as a pair of moneylenders. They had learnt a lot of gags, some silly, some very dirty, and bashed and banged away with them to keep the Club roaring, yelling, screaming, applauding. The world out of which these gags came, the world it helped to create in the Club room, was a kind of hell of automatic and dreary lechery, of cheating husbands and suspicious wives, of sneering and sniggering and cheap cynicism, a grey and chilly hell without warmth and light or any real values of heart or mind.

And this, Tom thought, is apparently what the new English wanted.

Hugh Walpole said JBP had 'a gorgeous sense of humour.' When publishers wanted books on humour or an editor for a humorous selection, the chances were that they would turn to JBP. *The English Comic Characters* appeared in 1925, *English Humour* in 1929. The book with the same title, which I have already quoted from, was published in 1972; the text had been revised to such an extent that it was virtually a new book, and it was also liberally illustrated. In 1928 JBP edited a series of essays entitled *These Diversions*; each essay appeared as a monograph under separate covers; one of them was *Laughing*, by Martin Armstrong. Priestley also edited a selection from Leacock, one of his favourite humorists, with an introduction by himself. And in *English Journey* he tells us that he considers himself a comic writer. At a re-union battalion dinner they toasted the memory of the dead, and a pianist played the regimental march — but it sounded 'like a polka badly played.' He tried to keep a straight face. 'That little episode was just like life; and I suppose that is why I am at heart a comic writer.' For at the centre of life is this constant incongruity which the true novelist and dramatist seizes on and reproduces. For example, the admission that one is not really so clever as one would like to be. It is part of the stock-in-trade of the essayist and also the humorist, as any casual perusal of Thurber or Leacock or Perelman soon shows. Read Priestley's description of his attempts to throw a perfect Priestley bowl or vase on his visit to the Potteries, and you will see that a natural humorist is buried not very far beneath the skin of the social commentator. Whenever he tries anything new he always cherishes the wild hope that he will immediately perform like a master, be it tennis or billiards or the violin, or as an orator or singer. This is the truly human element he catches and which we recognise. But this is not enough to make a comic writer, otherwise most of us would qualify. To it must be added a facility with words and there have been few writers in our time who have been more successful with the short, sharp phrase that expresses the essence of a scene or a situation. Here, for instance, on a visit to the docks in Liverpool: 'We reached the docks, put out our pipes and entered their precincts, where a vast amount of gloom and emptiness and decay was being carefully guarded.' Of course, it is the guarding of the gloom and emptiness and decay that is funny, but it is the solemn putting out of the pipes that causes it to cling to the memory.

In *The Balconinny* there are one or two essays which show JBP's humour at the peak of his civilised expression. It is the quiet subtlety and the balance with a more serious intent that create the effect. It doesn't always come off — there are some pretty sorry failures. But to take an example, 'At the Verdun Film' is a very amusing essay combined with excellent sense — the reader is first seduced by the humour and then left at the mercy of the sound sense that follows. It is a neglected essay which I have never seen in an anthology, but which justifies the form, if anything does.

His humour is situational rather than verbal but when it is verbal it possesses a charm rare in his work. Take this first paragraph in the essay 'The Balconinny' in the collection of that name.

> One of my ambitions has been realised at last. For the past two months we have been living at the very edge of the sea and — this is the point — are the temporary owners of what the youngest member of this family, a neologist of something like genius, calls a 'Balconinny'. If you saw it you would see at once that it is a balconinny rather than a balcony, being just large enough to hold three comfortably seated people. You could have tea on it — at a pinch — but not lunch or dinner. There is only room for one bed. If this is not a balconinny, then what is it?

The formation is not his but he recognises it immediately. It aligns him with Carroll and Lear, only momentarily it is true, as a writer who still has sufficient of the child left in his adult self to enter that world of innocence and fancy that are the clue to creative writing. It even puts him, for a moment, in the neighbourhood of James Joyce, but only for the briefest of moments, for that is not his world. Now JBP has written a couple of books on English humour and although they are valuable in so far as they recall certain wonderful moments and may even introduce us to others for the first time, he does not get very far in the business of analysis. Nor should we want him to, of course. But whenever we discuss humour we come up against the simple yet intractable question: what is it? I have just said JBP's humour is largely situational, and so is most humour. In fact, television has lifted such humour to a new level of dominance and bestowed on it the title of Sit-Com. But the fully equipped humorist must have the words too.

In the first *English Humour*, which was part of the English Heritage series, JBP in his comparatively youthful innocence tries to face the problem and comes away with one of the most frequently repeated truisms of all time. 'What is funny to one man is funereal to another, and for that there is no help. Yet we have all laughed in concert before now, and there has always been a stout majority ready to declare that Falstaff is an infinitely greater droll than Captain Bobadill.' It didn't take him long to discover that it was pointless discussing humour but often quite rewarding to discuss the humourist. The scientists, in their early twentieth century confidence, made their onslaughts on humour as they did on poetry, and succeeded in proving how utterly ineffective they and their method were. Koestler's only unreadable book was an attempt to tame the joke. Freud made an inroad but only breached the outer works.

Humour is like ESP, another subject that fascinates JBP. You can't really focus on it, you can only walk round it and describe its effect on the environment. Priestley has very little respect for academics, especially literary historians and critics. In *Literature and Western Man* he told us that they are too often 'by temperament and outlook incapable of appreciating humour, as distinct from wit and satire, or the character, outlook and method of the essential humorist.' Most criticism — and all bad criticism — is based on certain rules and principles and axioms which dominate the critic, so that finally it is not a living sensibility that is reacting to the text but a set of instructions. Humour overthrows these. It is a dangerous companion. If you aim your arrow-rules at a target which is invisible you are not likely to hit it. You are even likely to make a fool of yourself.

And so it is the environment you must describe if you are determined to describe something. For example, the fact that different people laugh at different things and in different ways. In his Introduction to the *Bodley Head Leacock*, 1957, JBP mentions 'the amiable nonsense of characteristic English humour' (he suggests Wodehouse, despite his lack of enthusiasm, and I fancy today he might include Monty Python) and he contrasts it with 'the hard cutting wit and almost vindictive satire of much American humour.' (The *much* was a saving grace, when we think of Thurber.) Leacock comes somewhere between, being neither savage nor amiable. The amiability of English humour derives from the quality of affection, which JBP regards as an essential ingredient of the best creative writing. Those whose only response to humour is to analyse it (tear it to bits) are likely to find themselves in the company of the pompous, the empire-builders, the after-dinner speakers, the critics who call themselves New because their only standard is the clock. Such people have done enough harm to the quality of living. In the 1929 *English Humour* JBP wrote in his last paragraph: 'It would be better for us to be once more a small, outlandish people and yet be renowned for this spirit (humour rising out of affection) than to bestride the earth and lose our laughter in gloom, suspicion and hate.' This may sound familiar now, but remember it did not become a familiar point of view until the fifties.

Chapter 21

The Later Novels

'Wise, moving and optimistic, the book must be regarded as his deepest and most mature contribution to the experimental science of living.' This is how David Hughes sums up *Bright Day*, which appeared in 1946. One year after the war ended, following immediately on the unsatisfactory *Three Men in New Suits*, it reveals JBP at his best. Once again he is writing from within himself, from within his wisdom as Hughes might have said, rather than from a margin of noble ideals and social concern. In a way that is not very obvious it grows out of JBP's convictions about Time. It illustrates the way that (to quote Hughes again) 'in a man's life reference to the past can cure the present and provide the future with energy, simply because only the present can give a lucid and dispassionate view of the past.'[1] But this is a lesson the Conways never learnt.

It is the story of a Lost Paradise but one that is not lost irrevocably. There is a sense of personal loss against a background of post-war drabness and despair. Gregory Dawson, now a hard-bitten old film scriptwriter, idealises his boyhood, especially the part he experienced with the Alingtons. It was just before 1914 and as the war approached, so the clouds darkened the sky of the boy who is entering manhood. Christmas in those days, to take a single example, was genuinely more a festival of joy than it has ever been since. 'The gaiety, at Christmas Eve or any other time, has always seemed forced and feverish since then.' But it was not only festival time; everything, the whole quality of life in every aspect, was better then. He praises a little local train and adds in parenthesis: 'There don't seem to be any trains like that any more, empty and leisurely and chummy. All transport now seems to be fuss, crowds, rain and anger.' Interpellations of this kind are frequent throughout the novel.

It sounds dreary and well it might be, considering the background against which it was written. Yet this novel is a powerful declaration of faith. On the one hand there was the dreariness, known at the time as Austerity, and a degree of decadence that JBP attacks with extreme bitterness: 'London looked horrible, like the shabbier side of some third-rate American city. What were once decent shops were now bogus wine stores, fun fairs and places selling shoddy knick-knacks and pornographic drivel. Half the women looked like cheap tarts and the men like Black Market touts. There was neither dignity nor genuine high spirits, etc., etc.' It was a sad decline from the solidity of *Angel Pavement*'s London. And yet this distasteful picture was mitigated and enlivened by Dawson's paradisal memories, his Bright Day of Youth. It was something to look back on, to balance the picture. But it was more than that, for the Bright Day was still as real and living as the Gloomy Night that seemed to have superseded it. And then again, returning to the level of mere clock time, even if war (or two wars) had ruined everything, at least there was no doubt in Dawson's mind that the second one at least had to be fought.

When he meets one of his childhood goddesses thirty years later he gets another shock. Her vitality has drained away, she is nothing but a mother fighting to win her offspring a place in the sun. 'I felt that the flame and fire I remembered had burnt out long ago and had left behind some toughened metallic deposit.' So was age the enemy? Did memories have no more validity than ghosts? But then comes another twist and with it a final promise. The bitter old writer, hating the dream factory that had nurtured him, again finds purpose in the company of young men and women with no resources but immense enthusiasm and a good deal of skill, who want to make real films about real people in real situations. Life is after all a see-saw — no sooner is it revealed as a cheat and a delusion than something solid turns up. The seeds of degeneration are always present — and so are the seeds of rejuvenation.

Bright Day was an investigation into the private psyche. It was followed by *Festival at Farbridge*, 1951, a tremendous enterprise, on the epic scale — there is even a list of characters, in Russian style, with page references to first appearance. This inflation, however, adds to the irritation, for there is a tremendous falsity at the heart of the novel. There is considerable similarity between it and the less ambitious *Let the People Sing*, which is in fact more successful. The similarity extends to plot, characters and handling of dialogue. There is in fact no real characterisation in either of these novels, only types: Major Bulfoss and several others in *Festival* reproduce

the prejudiced, spluttering county types of *Sing*. Even Ernest
Saxon, the irritating Left-winger, presents the professor of the
earlier novel in a new guise; he is always ready to lecture but is
bereft of the professor's charm. There is a recurrence of imagery,
as if JBP was pulling it out of a stock bag. In Farbridge stood the
Elite cinema, ' as if a hundred feet of Los Angeles had been
dropped there.' It had done the same in *Sing*, with the substitution
of Hollywood for LA.

A group of people in each novel set out to rejuvenate the listless
English. Some of them come from outside the national boundaries
— a Czech professor in *Sing*, Jenks in *Farbridge* from Indonesia,
and eventually Laura's father from Central America. The
Commodore has spent his whole life globe-trotting. Not only are
the natives exhausted but they care about the wrong things. In
each case rejuvenation must come through entertainment. (It is
interesting to compare this with *Bright Day* where rejuvenation was
sought through the inner life.) JBP gives the impression (a familiar
one with him) of not being prepared to round out his characters.
The effect is as a staccato rushing about and jerking like puppets on
a string. New characters, sometimes strangers, nearly always burst
into a room unannounced; people notable for their mental sluggish-
ness (activity is physiological rather than psychological) are
astonishingly capable of remarkable intuitive insights; there are
romantic misunderstandings by the score, followed by unnecessary
flights; a woman who never finishes her sentences is an old
Priestleyan standby; and there is the character who fizzes or burps
between every second word, which takes us back to the world of
The Good Companions. Many of the people speak like telegrams. The
net effect of this is the suspicion that JBP is not facing up to real
observation. (But he is still capable of splendid imagery as when we
are told that Major Bulfoss takes his partners at the ball round the
room 'as if they were mobile petrol pumps.')

Another trick-character is the one who laughs frequently for no
obvious reason but we are meant to infer that they are quite right
to laugh, that there is a laugh at the heart of things. ('Getting the
giggles' is the vernacular phrase.) The choppiness of speech
becomes very irritating because of its lack of variety. It also
suggests that JBP has not really listened to the way people talk for
a very long time. The social intercourse (e.g., the talk of business
men with each other) is dreadfully unreal. Contempt destroys the

author's good sense; the only time there is a remission of contempt is when the character is portrayed as a lovable old bumbler. There's precious little in between. Take this description of the mayor.

> He had a powerful clanging voice, admirable for public speaking, but he suffered from two defects: some peculiar relation between his breathing, his bushy moustache, his dentures, compelled him to make a sound somewhere between a buzz and a hiss, a sort of loud *Pzzzz*; and like many other public men who are mainly self-educated, who talk a great deal but are always anxious not to commit themselves, he had much trouble with his syntax, often entangling himself beyond help in relative clauses.

This sort of thing is good observation if used sparingly, but in fact the mayor is nothing more than a creature of *Pzzzzes* and relative pronouns and has no existence beyond them. It seems quite clear that JBP had ceased to listen to the actual conversation of ordinary people some time before, though he may well have resumed the practice later. In its place we get theatre; people speak as if there is another audience beyond the apparent one. JBP has frequently pointed out the theatricality of much of ordinary life but here he seems to be creating the theatrical aspect himself.[2]

In *Farbridge* (and again, there had been signs of this in *Let the People Sing*) the younger characters have the unreal habit of approaching each other with utterly naked statements, such as 'I think you're really smashing' or 'Somebody told me you were something, and he was right' — and this at first contact! The odd person certainly does this, for life contains infinite variety, but it never has been a constant of social behaviour. Sometimes even the older characters join in. It presumably represents JBP's view of youthful directness (permissiveness had not yet arrived) but in fact it's part of his failure to see things as they are. Another trick is, despite this outwardness, for the young to fall in love gloomily because it is never reciprocated.

The enormous weakness of this novel is its imprecision. It sounds as if JBP had taken on such a huge task that its organisation absorbs all his energies, leaving none for the finer effects of taste or selection. Here is a young man finally achieving his object, the love of the girl he adores, after the usual delays and frustrations: 'He made some daft noise, moved, blindly clutched, and there she was, where she ought to have been weeks ago, in his huge enraptured

arms. And several more years, crammed with rockets, champagne
fountains, moons, bursting stars and a salty flavour of wet cheeks,
appeared to pass.' This is not what it's like; it's the clowns, JBP's
beloved Music Hall, taking over.

Low Notes on a High Level, 1954, is sub-titled a Frolic. But something goes wrong with JBP's frolics. There's a sourness that will
insist on breaking in and defeating the jovial purpose of a frolic.
The talk between his journalists and radio men is quite incredible.
Of course, a frolic might well be intentionally incredible but JBP
gives the impression he is describing things as they are. He seems
to seize on an isolated piece of nonsense or banter and make it the
norm. This doesn't matter with a writer like Wodehouse because
he intends farce and nothing else. But JBP's frolics are punctuated
by very serious criticisms, so one gets the effect of humour being
turned on and shut off at the author's whim. The result is only
partially frolicsome and this leaves a sense of dissatisfaction. To be
fair, there are moments of genuine comedy, expressed through the
medium of infuriated officials and the obduracy of young geniuses
. . . On the whole, JBP is funny in this book when he uses
language to get his effect. The situations are handled less skilfully,
which is neither expected nor normal in his case.

The Magicians appeared in the same year and is a novel once
more, and not a frolic or a romp. (They were getting wearisome.)
It also has a cunningly devised plot, despite some gaucherie in
characterisation. Taking his writing as a whole, it is clear that JBP
had been edging, a little warily, towards an apocalyptic view of
life. Now it is given full expression for the first time in a novel.
Although not so ambitious as the play, *Johnson Over Jordan*, it
moves on a similar wavelength. We are back with the theme of
recurrence and man's ability, if he only knew how, to make
changes for the better in his life cycle. There is no actual talk of
recurrence, as there had been in *I Have Been Here Before*, but there
is a strongly felt instinct that it might be possible. Ravenstreet
recalls an occasion when he behaved badly. He appears to be
remembering it but there is a sense in which it is something more
real than mere recall, and 'he felt certain there existed some power,
which he couldn't discover how to use, that could break this evil
spell of recurrence, a strength he couldn't find that would lift the
heavy hour out of this groove.' He also has the sense of two selves,
but they are not conventional two parts of the one divided self, for

one of them seems to be directed from outside. He was conscious of his own consciousness as it was then. Was it the adult mind working together with the earlier mind? Or another self, long in hiding, come forward to take control? Long before this JBP had expressed bewilderment at the idea that the self could be conscious of its self.

The Magicians knew that he had re-entered a past that was still going on. They called it 'time alive' or 'time as it is', in contrast with 'tick-tock' time. It certainly wasn't memory, traces in the brain of what was over and done with. In a second experience Ravenstreet felt his adult self had re-entered his childhood, and the result was full childlike perception and response yet tinged with adult knowledge. This is certainly the main theme of the novel. Technically it is not always very convincing. His treatment of business men never seems real and the collapse of Karney is hard to accept. He always manages difficult psychological crises better in his plays. His treatment of authority and officialdom is spoiled by a vindictive current which arouses little sympathy in the reader. His satire would be more effective if it were a little more good-natured. It is fiercer than Waugh's but much heavier. His method of describing people by flinging images at the reader is counter-effective. Done sparingly, it can work. But when it is overdone it gives the effect of hit-or-miss, even the sense (and it's one we've encountered before) that JBP can't really be bothered to examine his characters carefully. Here is Sepman, for example: 'He suggested a world of sulphuric acid works, dingy labs, packed and reeking canteens, crowded trams on wet nights, snarling political meetings held in Victorian Infant Schools, frayed collars sawing away at the neck . . . ' and so on and so on for ten lines. It's the kind of approach that irritated Virginia Woolf and which she attacked in her famous essay on Mrs Brown. Graham Greene would take just one image of this type and make it work.

The *Times* review of *The Thirty-First of June*, 1961, begins: 'Dull would he be of soul and ungenerous of mind who was not always willing gratefully to acknowledge his debt to Mr J.B. Priestley's writing.' But, the reviewer feels, this is a private joke that doesn't quite come off. It is a Romp set in a typically Priestleyan world of timelessness, or rather of various inter-locking time scales. It is cheerfully satirical as the first paragraph immediately makes clear:

Lunaday, the 31st of June, brought to Peradore the kind of summer morning we all remember from years ago but seem to have missed ever since. The tiny kingdom, one of several owing allegiance to the high king Arthur at Camelot, came yawning to life in the smoky gold of that morning. Owing to the deplorable lack of progress in Arthurian England, it was all very peaceful: no old buildings were being knocked down to make room for office blocks, no take-over bids were being made, no traffic problems were giving the subjects of King Meliot ulcers or nervous breakdowns, etc., etc.

And when we transfer from Peradore to our own world of the present we find progress is very rapid, with the sound of pneumatic drills coming in through both windows.

It is sheer fun and in places very funny. Here we see JBP as the comic writer he tries to be, not always successfully, in his novels about contemporary life. His *forte* is impishness rather than comedy and it was probably impishness that helped start him on this: the delight of giving one in the eye to those bores, themselves only capable of activity in one very limited area, who accuse JBP of spreading his interests too widely. Apart from the eccentric setting, it makes use of many of his favourite devices and preoccupations. He accepts magic as a means of describing the unusual, the un-expected, the irrational, the heartening and, most of all, the trans-forming. In this novel he goes the whole hog and gives us the very stuff of magic. He brings in well-worn jokes, such as the *Bah!* joke ('I've often read it but never heard it') and the 'speaking as a house-wife' joke (i.e., not as a space engineer or professional footballer). One old man goes *he-he-he* all the time, and is recognised by it — he must have been a flatter character than even E.M. Forster ever encountered. A doctor keeps going *um-um* and would be recognised by it if he played a larger part in the story. JBP even introduces the theoretical side of his Time beliefs. If the reader thinks this is a lot of make-believe, he can think again because Malgrim, the en-chanter, explained that there are six dimensions in our universe: 'The first three are length, breadth and thickness. The next three might be called — first, the sphere of attention and material action; second, the sphere of memory; third, the sphere of imagination.'

In the same year *Saturn Over the Water* appeared. It was a return to the intellectual-thriller and can therefore be classed with *The Doomsday Men* and *Blackout in Gretley*. It purports to be a manu-script written by Tim Bedford, a painter, and prepared for the press by a friend. Bedford writes exactly like JBP, with all his

familiar tricks of style, which is a pity, because Henry Sulgrave
goes to some pains, in his Prologue, to explain that it is not only
Bedford's work but remains virtually untouched. The theme is a
serious one, and had been treated before by JBP: the possibility of
a world-wide conspiracy to destroy our civilisation and rebuild it
again in a way more to the taste of the conspirators. It is wildly
improbable, which doesn't matter. Sulgrave quotes from J.C.
Powys: 'He combined scepticism of everything with credulity
about everything; and I am convinced that this is the true
Shakespearean way wherewith to take life.' This has impressed
JBP deeply for he has quoted it at least three times in the course of
his *oeuvre*. But it is unfortunate that he took very little care with
either his writing or the characterisation — far less, for example,
than Graham Greene takes with novels of a similar kind. Here is
just one small example: he adopts the *Greenmantle* device of strange
names on a sheet of paper representing the basic clues in an investigation, but does not trouble to exploit it with even Buchan's
degree of subtlety.

In the following year there appeared another adventure story,
The Shapes of Sleep, this time with a moral. In a way it is reminiscent
of Greene's Entertainments of the 'thirties; — the hero is a seedy
failure who lives on his pessimism — but it lacks the obsessiveness
of Greene's mood and characterisation. It is a pot-boiler from the
head, not the gut. It carries with it a quality to be found in all
JBP's fiction except the best, an air of not really caring. Many of
the details are not very plausible. The test of the good mystery
writer is that he should be able to finish without resorting to pages
of explanation at the end. This JBP fails to do. It simply isn't his
territory. One marked difference between him and his younger
contemporaries in this field is that he does not resort to violence to
maintain interest. The characters are either gentlemen or frustrated
thugs. (Their thuggishness is restrained.) Susan Cooper pointed
out in her book how JBP has managed to adapt himself to the new
permissive strain (she illustrates from *Sir Michael and Sir George*). He
admits it here, although in fact Sterndale's lust remains baffled
until the last page. Sterndale has his hand on Janet's breast and
wonders why 'did that nipple refuse to play.' This is a long way
from *The Good Companions*. The tone in this book most strongly
expressed is disgust with fashionable urban life — Greene again,
but both the roots and the remedies are different. This side of it

had its precursor in *Wonder Hero*, thirty years earlier. It is a far-fetched story which tries to justify its far-fetchedness through the sickness of our society.

Lost Empires, 1965, is a different matter altogether. This is writing from the inner man. Stylistically it avoids the jerkiness that spoilt, for example, *Festival at Farbridge*. One feels it has an organic life of its own and is not simply an artefact. In *The Happy Dream* JBP wrote that this novel is apparently crammed with symbolism — he cannot see it himself, but others tell him. This is significant for as symbols come from the unconscious it is quite true that the author is often unaware of them. When they are stuck on, as happens very often in modern fiction, they are a sign that there is something bogus about the writing. And this certainly cannot be said about *Lost Empires*.

The Empires are the old Variety and Music Hall theatres. Following in the steps of *The Good Companions*, *Let the People Sing* and *Festival at Farbridge* we accompany stage people on tour. It is astonishing how many times JBP has used this setting for a novel, all the more so when we consider that although he is a man of the theatre it is not *this* theatre. It is a *tour de force* arising out of some inner compulsion, and it is the most sincere tribute he can pay to a group of performers whom he has praised repeatedly in his essays and memoirs. I believe this novel stands along with *The Good Companions*, *Angel Pavement* and *Bright Day* as his best fictions. (I simply cannot rate *The Image Men* so highly although JBP thinks it is his masterpiece.[3]) These four are all good in the same way — they concentrate on people and they don't try to work in anything else, whether it be a theory of behaviour or a significant atmosphere. The only obvious fault I can find is that throughout the novel JBP (or his narrator) hints at coming trouble. We wait and we wait until in the end it comes — but we have been waiting so long that a slight sense of impatience mars the effect. It is an artistic fault of imbalance.

The main difference in technique between this and, say, *The Good Companions* lies in the much freer treatment of sex in the later novel. It illustrates the ground that has been covered between 1929 and 1965. JBP has told us elsewhere that sexual desire and conduct have changed little, but the recording of them has. The sex relationships between Dick Herncastle and the various women he meets are treated explicitly. Early in the novel he writes: 'Her sex came over the footlights like a sharp challenge,' which simply could not have been (or was not) put so baldly in the earlier novels. And this is followed by descriptions of torrid sex acts, sex talk and sex obscenities, even a bout of sadism, attempted (if vicarious) rape and a couple of voyeurs. It is real but not pornographic. 'Sex not friendship was the lure,' he says of one liaison. This is all gain, not only artistically but also socially. 'I was a fairly normal youth then, neither particularly prudish nor lecherous, but the atmosphere was such — and I think now it was a suffocating and unhealthy atmosphere — that I spent half my mental life prowling uneasily on the edge of sexual discovery and revelation.' I may be wrong, but I feel JBP has not always found it easy to make the adjustment. His heroes, including Dick, have been prone to find reasons for not going to bed with girls, which I suggest is puritanical rather than natural. It has to be love, or there's nothing doing. The evidence of the novels suggests that JBP only approves of sex if it is sanctioned or blessed, not necessarily by marriage vows but by love, although he wraps up the distaste in various kinds of moral delicacy. When there is a resort to bed (as in *The Image Men*) it's usually done in a ritualistic way. One would say that ecstasy is declared, not experienced. But Dick's and Julie's (in *Lost Empires*) is the fiercest and most natural we have from his pen.

When Dick at one stage meets some straight actors and actresses he doesn't care much for them. Some of the very old actresses and some of the very young ones were all right, 'but the rest, especially the better-known actors, seemed to me the hollowest, pasted-together, false-faced creatures I'd ever met, and I'd nothing to say to them and didn't want to listen to them.' Is this JBP speaking? I think it is, especially as he also says he preferred the Variety artistes — which figures, as the Americans say. He has managed to make the latter more real and living than at any time since *The Good Companions*. JBP is a great believer in the central importance of characterisation in a novel. One reason why this novel is so much better than *Let the People Sing* is that we do get the impression that the comedian, Tommy Beamish, is funny (even though he is also mad), which is something he never managed with Timmy Tiverton in the earlier novel. But one thing remains constant — JBP's skill in finding the telling phrase. 'I'm not going to mince words,' Alfred says, and the narrator's comment is, 'He said this as if he were refusing to make shepherd's pie out of a dictionary.'

It's an Old Country, 1967, is a search-novel (a son looking for a long-lost father), a well-tried device which can be guaranteed to maintain interest. JBP tries to bring in some of his main pre-occupations and the chief agent for this is one of his irritating Wise Old Men (they date back to *Faraway*), in this case, Dr Firmius. He is quizzical, smug and uncomfortably bright and appears to be writing JBP's own *Man and Time*, which had appeared three years earlier. The weakness of this method is that instead of situations being resolved by normal, unregenerate people, cosy little wonder-workers are employed instead. The method is Huxleyan, but JBP has not Huxley's vast range of knowledge. On the other hand, although JBP is anxious to connect his novel organically with his theory of Time, Life and Dream, it's not particularly intrusive. There's just a suggestion that mysterious forces have helped in the unravelling process. Dr Firmius can talk obliquely and mysterious-ly but nothing can really be attributed to him with any certainty. On one occasion we are told that Tom Adamson has a brief sensation that his whole life is being experienced simultaneously, but this is no more than a piece of decoration, at most a reminder to the observant Priestley reader. No casual reader would pick up the reference. And the novel ends with a mysterious telegram that is beyond the understanding of any positivist. On the more familiar level, JBP's major weakness as a novelist is again apparent: his lack of psychological nuance, which so often suggests impatience. And when he does try to inject nuance he describes it rather than presents it in action.

And now we come to *The Image Men*, published in two parts: *Out of Town*, 1968, and *London End*, 1969. This is certainly JBP's own favourite. He has been greatly disappointed by the unfavourable reception of the reviewers, and has stated two or three times in print (and again in a private letter to me) that it is a novel of which he is justifiably proud. It is large in scale and has a strong socio-cultural point. It starts very well indeed. Two elderly academics, who have spent most of their lives abroad, team up with a widow who has been left a fortune, to found the Institute of Social Imagistics. Saltana and Tuby appear to be a pleasant mixture of con-men and social avengers. The writing is at first taut and business-like, with very few of the irritating mannerisms that marred the earlier wide-scope novels. The minor exception is that people still start laughing for no apparent reason — it is implied

that reasons are deeply felt and not to be paraded. Also the women
still giggle a lot and increasingly as the novel proceeds. In the first
volume Saltana and Tuby try to install themselves in a provincial
university. Unlike C.P. Snow's universities, there are students as
well as staff, although they are more docile and easily manageable
than real students. On the whole JBP has a great distrust of the
young, but it's a generalised distrust. When he comes to individuals, he's won over. He likes to present a character unfavourably and then show that appearances belie. The first impression of
Primrose East, an ex-model, is conventional and unfavourable, yet
she turns out to be a pretty admirable person. We are told that
Mike Mickley ought to be in a pop group (no praise) but he turns
out to be friendly and co-operative with his seniors, though unsatisfactory in other ways. Tuby probably resembles JBP (in this,
as in many other ways) when he says, 'I tend to dislike everybody I
don't know, just as I tend to like everybody I *do* know.'

JBP's powers of observation and awareness (which he possesses
but doesn't always use, particularly when prejudice obscures his
vision) are illustrated again and again, usually in casual asides such
as this, of a rather flamboyant young man: 'He seemed to be a
careful driver, like several dashing types Tuby had known, the
opposite of those timid conforming little men who turn into
demons behind the wheel of a car.' (This observation is similar to
one made by Koestler, to the effect that the real artist rarely shows
off, either in dress or behaviour.) A character named O.V. Mere,
shrewd enough but dreary in his normal routines, drives an old
open-air Bentley. 'That's the point about England,' says Elfreda,
'other people think it's full of dull men wearing bowlers and
carrying rolled umbrellas. But really it specialises in odd and
surprising individuals who wouldn't exist anywhere else, certainly
not in America, which thinks it's exciting — and isn't, not in my
opinion.'

Unfortunately, the high standard of the opening is not maintained. Almost as if she's a warning signal there appears a woman
who punctures her conversation with *Ger-huh* — that is, until JBP
forgets or gets bored with it. Some of the familiar faults begin to
emerge. Everyone is so damned knowing and keeps telling one
another the truth about themselves. On their first meeting
Primrose makes a remark about herself and is contradicted by Eden
Mere, who speaks straight out of the cathedral though she had

never been there. The characters become progressively less human
and more Priestleyan, that is to say, they are abnormally naked in
relation to each other. They shed their coats of reserve, suspicion,
fear, all those emotions that stand between people (partly for their
own protection) and forever copulate in a state of extreme
emotional nudity. Two-thirds of the way through, what starts as a
good novel (the first volume) becomes flat and tedious and continues so throughout volume two. Characters cease to be individuals but are merely bags of tricks. The story becomes bitty and
the sense of flow practically ceases. It is like a river that breaks into
a many-limbed delta as it approaches what should be its moment of
consummation. The lack of tension makes tiresome reading; instead
of being strung like a bead on the string of narrative (and this
should happen unless the novel aims at a completely different
effect), the reader feels glued up.

   As a result, the *Farbridge* faults are revived. There is more
fatuous conversation with business men, who talk like their own
ads, which in life they never do.[4] Their wives indulge in strident
amorousness, as if prompted by a Sunday columnist. Figures are
set up to be knocked down. We wonder why we are taken through
all these boring negotiations with a string of conceited nonentities.
(JBP knows they're nonentities, of course, but nevertheless
indulges in overkill.) Saltana's triumphs are too easy; people are
not nearly as idiotic as they are represented; and in consequence
the reader is liable to develop a hearty dislike for Saltana. JBP once
admitted that he's not a congenital novelist. His personality is far
too intrusive. He always wants to explain why people say things,
not being content to let them say it and leave it to the reader to
guess why. Tuby appeals to Saltana, for instance, and we are told:
'Tuby gave Saltana this opportunity because he suddenly felt that
Saltana was about to change his manner, as well he might after
Meldy's obvious resentment.' Again, Elfreda asks Lois a question:
'This was deliberate because Elfreda felt Lois oughtn't to be left
out any longer.' This is not possible in plays, which helps to
explain why JBP is a better playwright than novelist. Blanket
antagonisms, especially with anything related to showbiz, weaken his
judgments. We are told of an auditorium 'now being rapidly filled
with pretty women and important-looking men and astonishing
hairdo's and sun-lamp tans and beautiful white ties, with almost
everything except talent.' The last phrase sinks this particular ship

and reveals the blunt truth that JBP dislikes the contemporary world because he is utterly out of touch with it. The affection that he considers so essential for the best creative work is noticeably lacking.

It is unjust to criticise a novel because the characters are unattractive, but there is some justification when the novelist makes it clear he approves of them. As JBP cannot keep his personality out of a single sentence he writes, one is faced by a bombardment of tiresome authorial prejudice. This is not to deny his mastery of phrase which he has not lost ('The club was one of those huge and solemn institutions where the food seemed all the more horrible because of the pomp that surrounded it, portions of shepherds' pie being served as if they were wild duck brought by helicopters') but no amount of this can neutralise the underlying pomposity of the main characters! And this is mingled with coyness to such an extent that increasingly the reader has that here-we-go-again feeling: 'You're a wicked man, Professor Saltana, and I like you — as I thought I would — and it's probably a very good thing you're going to be married soon. Tell me about her.'

At the end of the second volume, *London End*, a semblance of plot is restored and with it an attempt to inject a little tension. The discovery that Mere is working for both sides hints at revival, and is followed by *dénouement*, but we have waited far too long. It is too late, after what we have been through, to be entranced by a shapely foot or an elegant bottom. It is like reaching the boundary of an apparently endless estate, worn out. This novel has a message. It's a fake world, with fake values, and fake men rigging fake expertise. All these fakes can be played at their own game and overcome — but what a time it takes to say it! By the time we reach home base we have in all likelihood surrendered to the enemy.

It attempted so much and failed so heavily, that for anyone who admires Priestley it is a disappointment. But there is nothing new or even alarming when a favoured writer disappoints. Didn't something of the same kind happen to Dickens when he wrote *Our Mutual Friend* and didn't JBP himself draw attention to it? This is what he wrote in an Introduction to that novel in 1957:

> The uproarious comic writer of the early novels, on which superb drollery is is lavished without stint, was no longer to be discovered in this harassed, secretly embittered, rapidly ageing Dickens who worked so slowly, so laboriously, on *Our Mutual Friend*.

Dickens was ageing. When Priestley wrote *The Image Men* he was in his mid-seventies. Now I am not suggesting that this novel gives signs of 'ageing' for it does nothing of the kind; it is a remarkably vigorous piece of work. But creative writing is a mysterious process and is subject to influences and mutations that defy analysis. All that can be said is that observations made by Priestley on the later Dickens can equally well be applied to himself, and there is no shame attached. This, for instance, from the same Introduction:

> Where once there was a feast, here there are only scraps. There is something mechanical about these later funny men; we hear wires creaking, seem to catch a smothered sigh from the weary puppet master.[5]

The volume entitled *The Carfitt Crisis*, 1975, also contained the story 'Underground' and a novella, 'The Pavilion of Masks', as well as the title story. In a dedicatory letter to Charles Pick of Heinemann, JBP says these three, which were originally cast in dramatic form (this is very obvious in the case of 'Pavilion' while 'Carfitt' has been performed on BBC radio), provide an experiment in his manner of narration, in that they avoid all but the barest description and refuse to offer 'the usual accounts, with which so many novels are over-loaded, of what my characters are thinking and feeling.' This is puzzling, because the change indicated was introduced by English and American novelists roughly fifty years before this book was published, and is fairly common form these days. The writing in these stories is by no means as spare as JBP suggests, although there is a slight tautening of style in 'Carfitt', which is enriched to some extent by unknown possibilities. But the change is not a marked one. It is still recognisably Priestley and as far as ever from Compton-Burnett or Firbank.

Engram, the mysterious magician-type who guides the characters through their crisis, says he is trying to keep awake, meaning to be fully conscious. He wants to stay away from factories and offices and the gross national product, and has decided to acquire some useful skills, such as carpentering, gardening and cooking. His personality either captivates or enrages people, according to how fast they are stuck in trivia. In most people he finds an overbearing conceit, sometimes a timidity which leads to over-compensation in the form of bullying and shouting. Personality disappears and is replaced by role-playing. Deep inner unhappiness is the norm. 'Too many warring different selves and no central controlling self,' as one character puts it. Carfitt and his friend Roke are 'completely and ruinously irresponsible,' but they can't help it because they identify with every foolish thought and every gust of feeling that come to their minds. They're not integrated persons but a 'football crowd'. JBP works in his Time remedy, showing that the goodness that was once in a person is still there, somewhere. But it's beginning to sound like a lost cause. 'Pavilion' is a romantic trifle set in a German principality in 1847. It tries to put forward familiar ideas but cannot carry the burden. There is another magician-type here, this time masquerading as an astrologer. JBP's tendency to treat females as sybils leads to a good deal of pomposity, hinting at mysterious truths.

If one should try to set up a single characteristic as JBP's major target in his recent fiction, I think it could well be self-importance, which he sees as the modern disease. Our values are warped and we place emphasis on the wrong things. He illustrates this in a striking passage in *Man and Time*, which is central to his life's thinking. 'You have been elected, let us say, chairman of the company, which is what you always wanted to be. The company is important, now you are important, and you can hardly resist swelling and strutting . . .' Then an emaciated Indian appears in your office and points out that a single daytime of Brahma lasts 4,320,000,000 of our years. You resist such an idea but slowly your own eminence seems to evaporate, everything you know and understand shrinks, becomes a bubble and vanishes. This could almost be regarded as a text for JBP's work and it expresses the unity of writing that has continued unbroken for half a century. In a sense he is one of the major disciples of Gurdjieff and Ouspensky who tried to free men from a waking sleep or being mere machines, to urge them to become fully conscious, to rid themselves of wasteful and stupid emotions, to make 'essence' grow at the expense of false 'personality'. As a novelist and playwright it is the false personality that JBP pinpoints. It is his main aim in *The Carfitt Crisis*, where the emptiness and falsity of so much modern life is illuminated by a man who is aware of the true nature of Time.

Or we can regard this pathetic self-importance as a reversion to that state of childishness which has not yet discovered that the individual is a member of a community. The people under crisis in 'Carfitt' are closely related to others in the play, *The Glass Cage*, 1957. There is nothing magical or mysterious about Dr Gratton, yet his personal solidity acts as a kind of balance to the various inanities that plague human nature. (The manipulation of characters as diverse as Engram and Gratton to point to the truth is JBP's method of asserting that in his father's house there are many mansions.) We feel that Gratton speaks for Priestley when he rebukes Angus, who is parading his self-pity. 'You're a grown man, not a child. If you can't get over once wanting a pair of skates and not having them, you'd better start blaming yourself, not other people.'

Chapter 22

The Craft of Fiction

The *New Scientist* once printed an article by Joe Cooper and Alan Smithers showing the statistical relation between people's occupations and the time of year they were born. It appears that JBP, along with H.G. Wells, Agatha Christie and D.H. Lawrence, was favoured in this respect, being born in late summer.

Considering the variety of forms he has written in he has been fairly prolific as a novelist. He started late, as we have seen, but has continued to produce prose fiction for the remainder of his career. On the whole, these can be divided into three groups. First there is a small group which, in one way or another, may be considered as of lasting worth: they include *The Good Companions, Angel Pavement, Bright Day* and *Lost Empires*. They show a real concern for humanity and for the quality of life. A second group may be called romantic-adventure tales, and include *Adam in Moonshine, Faraway, The Doomsday Men, The Magicians* and *Shapes of Sleep*. The main concern in these is with the struggle between the human individual and the mechanistic establishment of technology and bureaucracy. The third group are topical novels of social concern and include *Wonder Hero, They Walk in the City, Low Notes on a High Level* and *Sir Michael and Sir George*. A wartime novel like the underrated *Daylight on Saturday* also belongs here. There is, of course, a good deal of overlapping between these groups.

If JBP has never produced a novel of the highest calibre, which can be compared with the best work of D.H. Lawrence or Graham Greene, it is probably because he seems unwilling to take the final step of complete involvement that is necessary for the best creative work. Even at his best, even when he is protesting most loudly his intention, he gives the impression of wanting to get it over and done with as quickly as possible. Laurence Kitchen once wrote that 'J.B. Priestley is such a good dramatist that the problem of criticism is finding out why he is not even better.' These wise words apply equally to his fiction.

It is easier to make these judgments on JBP because he seems to agree with them himself to a certain extent. At least, he admits he is not a born novelist. In *Margin Released* he tells us why he turned to fiction at a time when he had plenty of work for which he was being well paid. 'I turned to fiction . . . because I had a lot of ideas that would not leave me in peace and because I could not resist the challenge.' It is difficult to know how seriously to take this, especially as his first novel, *Adam in Moonshine*, which presumably resulted from the pressure of ideas, is nearly his weakest and seems particularly bereft of challenging ideas. He has never written anything of any length or serious intention on the craft of fiction but he has scattered useful comments throughout his personal memoirs. The most interesting of these is *Midnight on the Desert*, 1937, where he again makes no great claim for himself as a novelist although he believes there is more skill involved than most reviewers realise. One thing which has irritated him throughout the latter part of his life is his being labelled a jolly, hearty, popular novelist because of the enormous success of *The Good Companions*. 'I do not think I have met or corresponded with five-and-twenty persons who have not blamed me, either for having written this particular novel, or for not having written a lot of other novels like it. One party denounces me as a hearty insensitive lowbrow. The other party asks what the devil I mean by turning myself into a gloomy highbrow.'

He says he has a restless nature, is easily bored and flits from one kind of work to another. One sees signs of this in his fiction — I have already referred to the impression he gives of being too impatient to round his characters out fully. This could explain why he is more at home with drama, and in fact prefers writing it, as it is necessarily restricted in the time dimension. Incidentally, it is not lack of interest in his characters that is responsible, for JBP has always insisted that the novel must centre round character. It is impatience. He says he begins writing a novel slowly, hesitantly and badly, but gathers confidence and speed and ends with a fine flourish. This is odd, for his work gives an impression of the exact opposite: they seem to get off to a flying start and then develop some kind of engine trouble midway round the course. But there is one department — a minor one, perhaps, but an effective one — where he is a master. He can usually be depended upon to provide a vivid and telling phrase to clinch a description. In this particular book (not a novel, of course) he tells us that the Colorado River has poured itself into the Boulder basin 'to form a strange inland sea, younger than most police sergeants.'

His style has naturally changed over fifty years but there is an inner core that remains fairly constant. I would like to illustrate the essential Priestley style by quoting from *The Good Companions*. It is a description of Leonard and his friend Albert.

> They lived for dress and girls, above all — not having the opportunities of a Brummell — for girls. They ogled and pursued and embraced girls at the Bruddersford dances and socials, in all the local parks and woods, picture theatres and music halls; they followed them on the Bridlington sands, along the Morecambe piers, into the Blackpool ballrooms, and even went as far as Douglas, I.o.M., to treat them to eighteen-penny glasses of champagne and other notorious aphrodisiacs; they knew, and frequently discussed among themselves, the precise difference between the factory girls of Bruddersford and the factory girls of Bradford or Huddersfield, between the tailoresses of Leeds and the shop-girls of Manchester . . .

The main characteristics of this piece of writing are as follows:

(a) It is vigorous and pure. No tricks are imported for effect.

(b) There is exact observation. This was also to be found in another and later Yorkshire writer from the same area: John Braine.

(c) It has a humorous tone without straining to be funny.

(d) It moves at a fine pace, here excellently controlled. In some later novels, such as *Festival at Farbridge*, it degenerates into a pell-mell effect.

These were the strengths. There were other characteristics, not always so happy, though by no means repulsive, such as gravely pretending that impersonal objects have a personality: 'She insisted upon returning, as she had planned, by the 5.35, and said so a good many times, for somehow it sounded like a train that a strong-minded woman would catch.' Then there is mock profundity, now as dead as the villanelle: 'All three gentlemen exchanged glances, and they were glances of a deep philosophical significance, such as may be exchanged among members of a sex not entirely devoid of reason, not wholly given over to whims and fancies and irrational outbursts.' (JBP held traditional views on sexual psychology and behaviour.) At times he can treat a metaphor with too much respect: 'In Victoria Street the wind welcomed him boisterously as an old playmate, but his only

response was to demand that it should first be damned and afterwards blasted.' There is also a good deal of imagery which now
seems to us Georgian, that is, ultra-fanciful — we will come across
more of this when we consider JBP as a critic, especially in early
works such as *Figures in Modern Literature*. From *The Good
Companions* we can take this: 'Her legs were really beautiful. It was
as if she were being carried about by two fine sonnets.' But none of
these are literary crimes. The real literary crime is to be dull and
uninteresting, as many of JBP's contemporaries, some of them
highly regarded, have often been. It can rarely be said of him.

Tracing influences is a literary game with little value unless it is
so powerful that it cannot be ignored. Of his older contemporaries
I imagine that Arnold Bennett was in this sense the most
important. JBP admired him sufficiently to write about him in
Figures in Modern Literature. In fact, the opening of *The Good
Companions* is sheer Bennett, a geography lesson in the manner of
The Old Wives' Tale. He was not afraid to address the reader in
confidential style (I shall say more about this later), as he does in
this passage: 'And it may be admitted, here and now, that there
was talk of that monstrous bouquet for weeks afterwards in the
ladies' dressing-room, that we ourselves have perhaps not heard the
last of it, that the Unknown Admirer may turn up again.' But this
sort of thing is not to be confused with the imparting of straight
information, direct from author to reader, as when we are told that
in Bruddersford you should always be on the look-out for swelled
heads. The mock-serious, would-be humorous effect is another of
Bennett's tricks adopted by JBP. 'We have never heard that the
Royal Standard in Rawsley is famous for its dinners . . .' This palls
very quickly. Again, introducing known characters as if they were
unknown. There is an excellent example in the final stages of *The
Old Wives' Tale*. Priestley gives us this. The waitress in Ye Jollie
Dutche Cafe recognises two customers and reports to the others
downstairs, whereupon the author adds: 'And we recognise them
too. Miss Susie Dean and Mr Inigo Jollifant.'

JBP has often said that it is character that makes the novel, and
he repeats it in his major critical work, *Literature and Western Man*,
1960. He also adds that society itself has become more and more
important to the serious novelist and 'indeed turns into a character
itself, perhaps the chief character.' But character must be handled
discreetly. Too many of JBP's are not real characters but hurriedly

drawn types. It is also possible for characterisation to swamp the rest of the novel. The best example of this in JBP's *oeuvre* is *Faraway*, 1932. Here his love of creating characters seems to run away with him. Many characters are described at great length, but they are not part of the main theme, nor do they set in action a sub-plot, and thus the novel gains nothing from their introduction. This is most obvious in the section dealing with the voyage to Tahiti. Most of the people there described will not be seen again. They are responsible for the inordinate length of the novel, which would benefit greatly by cutting. If it were published today as a new novel at least one hundred pages would be cut, and it would be greatly improved, for basically it is a good novel. *The Good Companions* was equally long but in it every sentence was properly related to the whole. But it is only fair to state that the one story told by a character in *Faraway* in the style of the old picaresque novel is a success.

Of course, in an *oeuvre* as long as JBP's there are bound to be characters who reappear under different guises. One of the most familiar is the mousy little woman who turns out to be a Brick. She is the Slow Starter, who wins in the end. It is always stressed, on first meeting her, how dull she is and she is usually compared with a much more flamboyant female. In *Faraway* William cannot work up any interest in Margery at first. Then he discovers she is 'much less dim and mouse-like when bathing.' The Commander extols her virtues: 'a good type of woman. The real sort. Good English blood.' Then William feels ashamed of himself 'because he had once thought her a mousy and faded creature of no particular interest.' In the end he marries her. She is summed up thus: 'One of those people — and they are usually women — who do not seem to have much imagination, who have a sense of fun but little humour and no wit, who appear to be completely cut off from the stimulation and graces and ecstasies of the arts, who have never entertained an idea in their heads and have no notion of what is happening in the world, and yet in some mysterious fashion give the impression of being ripe personalities who live full rich lives.' Miss Trant in *The Good Companions* bears some relation to this type, though she is a fully rounded personality. After her, the character degenerates into a type like Margery. In the end, the character becomes a trick, an extended one, of course, but on the same artistic level as the Forgetting-the-Name trick (also used here) and a host of others.

As JBP has pronounced likes and dislikes among people he tends to resort to satire when his passions are aroused. It is his portraits of business men that suffer most in this way — one feels at times that he must have been frightened by a business man at a very tender age. The venom destroys the reality of the character. When he can stand away from his creation, and particularly when he is appraising that of other writers, he knows that this can be fatal to artistic truth. In his book on Anton Chekhov, 1970, he wrote: 'With the exception of a few pages there is in the stories written in his maturity no trace of that venom found in many satirists, who arrive snarling to revenge themselves.'

But I feel there is a more important weakness in his fiction which detracts from the sense of reality which one looks for. This is a tendency to over-explicitness, which again I think can be attributed to his impatience, his desire to get things over and done with. It is found throughout his lesser work but particularly in a novel like *Benighted*. His people are too outright, they say things that in life would be left to the understanding. This of course may be partly an effect of writing for the theatre, where the playwright sometimes causes things to be spoken because there simply isn't time to establish them in any other way. In fact, this illustrates the divide between the two crafts and is evidence of JBP's rare skill in being able to write successfully in both forms. We cannot be surprised at the result; he prefers writing drama to fiction and he is self-confessedly and demonstrably an impatient man. The novel, as every critic is compelled to state at some time or other, is a magic box that contains practically any kind of writing you can think of. JBP is at the opposite extreme from Henry James, who wrapped every spoken idea up so completely that the meaning frequently became smothered. He took immense pains. JBP doesn't take enough. He is so anxious to tell us what people think he often can't be bothered to show us how they actually express the thought. Again, one could illustrate this from most of the novels but here is a good example from *Wonder Hero*. Charlie meets a man at a party who without preamble says, 'I'm wrecking my evening. By quarter past seven, at the latest, I'll be three parts tight, reeking of gin, sticky with vermouth, no appetite left, and with the rest of the hellish evening to fill in.' This is no doubt what he thinks, and there is the odd character who does explode like this, but there are far too many in JBP's work. It is in fact what he, the author, is thinking but he resorts to this trick of putting all his own thoughts into the mouths of characters. The result is a nakedness of speech which produces a sense of falsity in what is otherwise a realistic novel.

But it would be wrong to dwell on these faults when there is so much to praise. *Wonder Hero*, for instance, is not one of his best novels yet it has one section that can challenge anything he has given us. It is the description of the ruined town Charlie returns to, after the brittle luxury of London's West End, to see his sick aunt. It is a picture of decay that is unnecessary, hopelessness that is heart-rending, a desperation that would be savage if the energies had not been sapped by malnutrition and destitution, injustice that cries out for revenge. It is impossible to give an accurate impression from a few random quotations, but anyone who is really interested in this country and its people and their history, instead of merely jabbering about power and devolution and taxation, should read Chapter Six, *This Other Eden*. As Charlie goes up the dark little staircase to his aunt's room he hears her calling him 'and he suddenly felt all weak and queer, as if the heart inside him had turned to water.' And the reader's heart will respond in the same way if he has any capacity to feel. And so it will when he reads about the courage which exists side by side with the desperation, the courage which (perhaps in the long run, unfortunately) made such conditions bearable. Imagine Mr Adderson, rotting away through unemployment (even in those days he noted bitterly that he was being referred to as 'redundant'), saying of his daughter who works in a toffee shop, 'Eighteen shillings she gets, and I tell her I bet she eats another eighteen shillings worth.'

It is odd how, as conditions improve, our society becomes more violent. JBP makes it quite clear why there was so little violence in the England of the thirties. Starvation is no foundation for it. But in any case, even in these more permissive days, when JBP has accommodated himself, descriptions of violence have no appeal for him. He admits its existence but he doesn't gloat over it nor present it unrealistically in what might be called a Gothic frenzy. (I hope the reader agrees with me that the prevailing 'realistic' description of violence is usually utterly unrealistic.) For JBP it is an event like many others but on the whole an obstacle in the path of the novelist's main duty, and therefore to be circumnavigated as quickly as possible. When his characters engage each other physically, their blows rarely land. If they do, it is with a muffled

thud which does no real harm; if there are signs of harm, by-
standers intervene. Then everyone gets on with the essential
business of the novel. This gentleness is so pronounced in
Benighted, where the combatants resemble bumbling elephants
more than angry human beings, it results in a reverse kind of
unreality. Such fights are probably ceremonial, like that of two
rhinos I once saw at the Zoo. They did no harm to each other
physically (God knows what happened psychologically) but the
moment came when it was agreed that one had won and the other
lost.

Another little trick JBP's characters like to perform is what I call
the Laughing Joke, when people begin to laugh without any clear
reason. Now this does happen, but JBP has in the past been too
anxious (in his impatient way) to show it happening again and
again, and to demonstrate that he knows all about it. The possible
origin of this may have occurred when he was travelling through
the American South-West (Death Valley, Boulder Dam, the Grand
Canyon) and he and his friends felt refreshed and started behaving
like schoolboys. He describes the incident in *Rain Upon Godshill*:

> If I could remember any of the jokes, I would not repeat them. Some-
> times it was worse then that. When the mechanical organ in Death
> Valley Scotty's Castle, that fabulous remote stronghold, suddenly
> assaulted us with a Liszt Hungarian Rhapsody, we went into corners
> and exploded. In the restaurant at Las Vegas, where we had buffalo
> steak for dinner, the idiocy rose to such a pitch that Pont finally put his
> head down on the table and cried with laughter.

This is both understandable and acceptable. But when JBP causes
his characters to behave like this in his novels, it becomes irritating.
It's not that it doesn't happen, it's the way he presents it. We are
always told there is no apparent reason for the laughter, but this
puts them apart and suggests that anyone outside the magic circle
is in some way inferior. And this runs counter to JBP's usual intention, which is to involve the reader and treat him as an ally in
the writer's investigation of the human mystery.

Chapter 23

Author and Reader

Priestley never forgets his reader, who sits before him as he writes. This leads to a degree of intimacy that is unusual in modern fiction though familiar to readers of the sentimental Victorians. It doesn't always work, or perhaps it would be more accurate to say that it often works in a reverse direction to the one intended. The Laughing Trick, for instance, appears to be thrown in as a bonus when it has no clear literary value. Take this example from *Three Men in New Suits*.

> Alan grinned and then suddenly began laughing, laughing until the tears ran down his cheeks. Gerald laughed too, his large red face turning almost purple. And this continued for a minute or two.
> 'I don't know what the devil we're laughing at,' said Gerald finally.

Now if this sort of thing is to be introduced into fiction it must be done with the greatest subtlety, otherwise it sounds like a mere space-filler. Gogol could say that one of his characters sat down and died without any reason because the idea is so outrageous it knocks us over — it's like being bowled first ball! But with JBP it happens far too often.

What I call the Bah! Joke (with its blood relation, the Humph Joke) is another example. Presumably it is to suggest the real world but its main effect is to come between the reader and the story. Many examples could be collected from JBP's fiction and it would be pointless to enumerate them. It goes like this. A character is annoyed or irritated, whereupon JBP either tells us that in fiction people often say 'Bah!' but never do in life or that on this one particular occasion X actually did use the expression. In *London End,* 1969, Tuby becomes JBP for a moment (though we have suspected the connection before) and says, 'I've always wanted to say *Bah* and now I do say it. *Bah!*' It could be a family joke, for JBP is a great family man, but it doesn't bear repetition. (Possible repetition is one of the pitfalls a prolific writer must face.)

At the back of this is a desire to communicate with the reader.

Black-Out in Gretley suffers more than most. Mr Perigo, we are told, sighed. That should be sufficient, but no, JBP has to add: 'People are always sighing in books but they rarely do it in real life. However, Mr Perigo sighed.' It is a mannerism that delays the pace of a story and *Black-Out* is the kind of story that depends to a considerable extent on the maintenance of its pace. 'People are always faking surprise,' writes JBP — 'lifting the eyebrows, widening their eyes, opening their mouths, and the rest of it — but if you are watching them closely they can't often take you in.' Isn't this merely a way of saying: I'm pretty clever at observing people, you know? And two pages later we get this: 'We're always reading about eyes lighting up, but this woman's really did then.' In *It's an Old Country* we have the Humph Joke. 'He had often read — and rather wondered at *Humph!* in print, but now he actually heard it . . .' Another example, from *Saturn Over the Water*. 'People in stories are always suddenly turning white, though I can't say I've noticed it in real life . . .' And again: 'He chuckled. I know people are often described as chuckling when they're not, but Mr Jones, being built for it, really could chuckle.'[1]

This is not a trivial matter. Fundamentally it spotlights something that any fiction reader soon learns and that JBP readily admits, that he is not a congenital novelist. Because he is a skilled and professional writer he can turn his hand to any literary form with a measure of success, but his natural talent is not for the novel. He can describe magnificently and he can manage narrative superbly but it is when he comes to character (which he himself regards as the cornerstone of fiction) that things go wrong. He cannot resist commenting and it is the comment that gets between the reader and his enjoyment, that causes irritation. When one reads a novel one should have to establish a relationship with one other thing and one only: the novel itself. The author's personality must not intrude, otherwise it becomes an embarrassment. But JBP's personality is always intruding. There is hardly a subject upon which he does not hold an opinion, and this opinion is usually strong and eager for expression. It is difficult for JBP to introduce a business man without remarking that he feels more at home with bank statements than with his employees. A politician will be viewed as a power-seeker, not as a worried man with difficult kids. Then, once his emotions become stimulated by the unsatisfactory nature of politicians and editors, a tension is set up, he thinks of himself, himself in contrast to these monoliths, and then comes the personal comment, usually too personal for its context. This self-consciousness invades all his writing (except the dramatic, where it has no outlet), and is often characterised by an unfortunate sourness. It is found, and mars, an otherwise excellent book, *Journey Down a Rainbow*, 1955, which he wrote with Jacquetta Hawkes. Invited to hear a Mexican singer, and expecting him to be no good, he admits he was wrong. He adds in parenthesis: 'Unlike many writers and all politicians and editors, I am often wrong.' One senses a great deal of personal irritation surfacing here. What he says may be valid (politicians in particular hardly ever admit a fault) but when stated in contrast to JBP's own admirable honesty the reader is liable to react unfavourably. He would rather deduce such things for himself. That this particular feeling rankles with JBP becomes clear when we find him repeating it in a *Sunday Times* article six years later ('I Had the Time', reprinted in *Encore*, 1962). He says he wrote very little about the first war. 'I think now that I was wrong but then, unlike most public men, I have often been wrong.' I can't help feeling that this is a cunning way of saying: I am usually right.

The sourness has many targets. When it appears in fiction it damages the flow of the narrative. It is recurrent in *Saturn Over the Water*. 'What good actresses most girls are,' we read, with the addendum, — 'if they're not on the stage.' This is paralleled by his frequently uncharitable comments on young writers. (Such statements are always generalised; JBP's targets are rarely mentioned by name.) The manuscript of this novel is supposedly written by Tim Bedford, a painter, but like JBP he cannot resist the temptation to make a disparaging remark about contemporary writing. 'I know it's out of fashion to describe anybody, so that we have whole long novels crowded with faceless people . . .' This is particularly unfortunate because although JBP does give us physical descriptions of his characters, in the manner of Arnold Bennett, they often remain faceless so far as an impression on the reader is concerned. It is the outstanding characteristic, the one that marks the character for what it is, that counts, and it is this that many modern novelists, such as Graham Greene, have concentrated on, replacing the traditional catalogue of features.

In short, the essayist is never far from the surface. JBP began his career as an essayist, whose main function is to discuss the world as seen from one absolute focal standpoint, the self. He deserted the essay, or altered its structure, when it fell out of fashion, and he took to the novel. *Adam in Moonshine*, his first novel, appeared when the transition was being made. It provides an object-lesson in the mutation of an essayist into a novelist. When Adam enjoys a landscape he thinks of Arden where they 'fleet the time carelessly as they did in the golden world.' This is a favourite quotation, the kind of thing that Shakespeare put into the mouths of the most unexpected people (in this case, a wrestler): 'and so contrived to keep you excited about him in spite of all that schoolmasters and professors and bad actors could do to make you lose interest.' This is the essayist. The story is momentarily forgotten, the targets are set up, and down they go: bang, the schoolmasters; bang, the professors; and bang, bad actors. And there is still plenty of ammunition left for editors and politicians and fashionable writers.

Chapter 24

The Later Plays

Hugh Walpole once told JBP that he was not a novelist and never would be. 'He admits it and says he loathes to write novels, loves to write plays.' These feelings often show through the writing.

He has written plays that are, in their way, perfect whereas he has never written a perfect novel. *An Inspector Calls*, 1947, is so well constructed and at the same time bears such a deeply felt social observation, where a fundamental realism is tempered by just the right degree of mystery and symbolism, that it is hard to fault the play in any way. It is not surprising that at times JBP's impatience and irritation with the English theatre wells up and spills into print, when we consider that this play was first produced in Moscow because there was no theatre available in London! Afterwards it went to the Old Vic and since then has been produced all over the world. Even if the play had no content it would induce a sense of profound satisfaction, the kind one gets from sitting on a well-made chair. It has the strength of a poem that is written at a single sitting. In the Introduction to Volume 3 of *The Plays* JBP wrote: 'Plays of this kind, in which one situation inevitably leads to another, and in which a certain uniformity of manner and tone is essential, are in my view best written quickly.' This one took him a week. It is also, incidentally, one of the best examples we have of his fascination with circularity, which I drew attention to in his essays. It ends as it begins.

It reinforces the message of *Desert Highway* but much more skilfully. We must all work together and consider the rights and needs of the other person if we are going to avoid disaster. The Inspector hammers this point home, but the hammering never becomes distasteful because it is in his character.

Just remember this. One Eva Smith has gone — but there are millions and millions of Eva Smiths and John Smiths still left with us, with their lives, their hopes and fears, their suffering, and chance of happiness, all intertwined with our lives, with what we think and say and do. We don't live alone. We are members of one body. We are responsible for each other. And I tell you that the time will soon come when, if men will not learn that lesson, then they will be taught it in fire and blood and anguish.

The conclusion is despairing as it is quite clear that the Birlings, with the exception of Sheila, don't want to learn the lesson. Sheila is one of JBP's generous-hearted young women, who always represent for him the main hope for our future. (May we take a tip from *I Have Been Here Before* and hope that, in the course of recurrence, Sheila will not have the young shop assistant dismissed?) As soon as her father discovers that the Inspector was not what he claimed to be, he decides that everything is all right. It's equivalent to the way we dismiss rape by saying the woman was provocative, or the way they dismiss unemployment in Eastern Europe by under-employing workers. The total effect is magnified by the mystery at the heart of the play: what was the Inspector? The mystery is integrated instead of being an excrescence put into the mouth of a character: 'I feel something queer is going on.' Gareth Lloyd Evans calls it a warning play, 'thrillingly communicated' and points out that what it warns 'emerges directly from the play's action and characterisation'. It makes no large statements about society, it does not pronounce on class or the financial system, it ignores politicians and does not sentimentalise the exploited or caricature the exploiters. In other words, it avoids all the faults to which JBP is sometimes prone.

This was certainly one of the two good periods in JBP's career as a playwright for in 1948 it was followed by *The Linden Tree*. But in the meantime JBP wrote a one-act play called *The Rose and Crown* and a play for the Toy Theatre called *The High Toby*. These are not of any theatrical importance but they indicate the author's involvement with the theatre. When a playwright is on the crest of his achievement it is unusual to find him writing short plays obviously intended for the amateur market or children. *The Rose and Crown* is a 'balloon' play: six characters in a pub, in the dreary post-war world, are approached by Death's agent. He will take one away. Who shall it be? They must make the choice. It is the only one of the six who declares himself satisfied with life — the others are afraid to die. It is a folk-tale and one might have considered the theme rather 'morbid' for the sensitive amateur theatrical world. *High Toby*, on the other hand, is a stirring eighteenth century tale of highwaymen, soldiers returning from the wars, fops, dishonest lawyers, embezzling uncles, beautiful languishing ladies and robust, healthy country girls. It is all served up with a sense of humour and cut-out scenery and characters by Doris Zinkeisen.

The Linden Tree was also written quickly while JBP was holed up in Billingham Manor on the Isle of Wight, where he was cut off from the rest of the world by heavy snowfall for a week. He refers to it as a 'smash hit'. The characterisation is of the type we have come to expect from the author — each person represents a trend or opinion or a strongly differentiated section of society: Labour England, aristocratic-cum-Black-Market France (the kind that seduced Nancy Mitford), Oxbridge, Redbrick, social conscience, personal hedonism. I feel it is one of those plays that should be guaranteed a production at least once in every generation because it is such an accurate mirror of its time.

The change that has occurred in the theatre since JBP's heyday is most apparent when we consider the stage sets. In nearly all his plays the stage is crowded with objects which take a full page to enumerate and describe. It is an earnest play and a sincere play but it represents a falling away from the *Inspector*. In a way it can be seen as the last fling of the didactic drama, where characters are lectured about society. In this extract it is at its worst, but I must insist that it does not fairly represent the general level of the play. The Professor is speaking:

> Young Dinah Linden, all youth, all eagerness, saying hello and not farewell to anything, who knows and cares nothing about Bavaria in the 'Nineties or the secure and golden Edwardian afternoons, here in Burmanley, this very afternoon, the moment we stop shouting at each other, unseals for us the precious distillation, uncovers the tenderness and regret, which are ours now as well as his, and our lives and Elgar's, Burmanley today and the Malvern Hills in a lost sunlight, are all magically intertwined . . .

Dinah is playing the Elgar Cello Concerto. When the Professor carries on like this JBP finds it necessary to have the cleaner say he's 'a lovely talker'. This is dreadfully mannered. It is not a trap easily avoided by realistic writers — the trap of poetic statement, which Shaw also fell into from time to time. The play contains a series of conflicts, between generations, sexes, ways of life and even historical periods. It is the latter which is finally dominant. *The Linden Tree* represents an incident in the struggle between two histories — that of the god and the altar on the one hand and that of the sword and the wheel on the other. It ends with the Professor reading a passage on this conflict from his 'book on history', as Dinah calls it.

Home is Tomorrow, 1948, was one of his best, according to JBP, and also 'a thumping flop'. No one seemed to like the play, the actors or the setting. 'Most of the notices seemed to us completely idiotic, as if the critics had gone to the wrong theatre,' he wrote in the Introduction to Volume 3 of *The Plays*. One critic called it a discussion on a desert island; another said it was not a play but a bunch of essays; a third that he was trying to write a thriller in the John Buchan manner. It is not one of his best plays but nor is it one of his worst. It is true that JBP, and any other playwright who was interested in ideas, was writing in the wash of G.B. Shaw. On the whole, he doesn't do it very well — compared with Shaw, the earnestness greatly out-balances the wit. He develops his plays of this kind through discussion, not situation, his characters are representatives (humours) and not living people, and stage directions are often used to describe what should have been elicited through dialogue and action. Nevertheless, this play suffers less from these faults than some earlier ones.

A United Nations team is trying to bring civilisation to a tropical island, but there are powerful forces ranged against it: particularly the inertia of the original inhabitants and the greed of international commerce. The conflict is objectified in the persons of the patient English civil servant who runs the team and believes passionately in its importance, and his wife who loves life and loathes discipline and constraint. In an outburst she attacks all her husband stands for.

> With the right sort of person I could exist quite cheerfully in one of these Port San Pedro waterfront slums or in a hut on the hills — just a good-tempered slut who didn't give a damn . . . But what I couldn't possibly do is to live a namby-pamby lower-middle-class suburban existence, stiff with third-hand culture and earnest idiotic committees and bloody-minded busybodies. And I just don't want Fundamental Education for natives and hygiene for everybody and a world society and UNO and UNESCO and UNUTO.[1] I despise three-quarters of it and absolutely loathe the rest.

Here we have one of the big debates of our time, along with the attitude that should be adopted to violence. Should we kill it by superior violence or should we apply the law? The ends-and-means discussion comes up for review in every generation. Are our ideals always twisted by national and/or ideological considerations? All these matters are debated in this play. It is a heavy load. It ends with the defeat of the international idea by political gangsterism yet before he dies Fortrose, the UNUTO boss, declares his conviction of final victory.

Summer Day's Dream, 1949, was again set in the world of public affairs. By 1975, after a ruinous Third World War, England has become an agricultural state that has lost any pretensions to world power or political significance. Shrewsbury is the largest town. There is no petrol and therefore no cars or tractors. Stephen Dawlish has neither a telephone nor television. The younger generation are deeply concerned with music and poetry. A Soviet official says that England, having lost her power, is now sunk in decadent romanticism. And how superior this kind of decadence is to the power-worship that preceded it, the author proceeds to tell us. His title hints at *Midsummer Night's Dream*, which is being rehearsed in the village, and which is quoted many times by two of the younger characters. A three-or even four-cornered argument takes place. It is the new English pastoral versus Soviet centralism versus American power concentration, while the fourth could be the internationalism of the Indian, Dr Bahru. The Russian, the American and the Indian form a team that is prospecting for minerals. If they find what they want the new-found way of life will be doomed. The new life is described by Stephen.

> We haven't time for anything that doesn't either free our bodies or refresh and rejoice our spirits. You might say we have two main problems — what to get for dinner, and what to do after dinner. So we grow things and raise stock — swap eggs for cheese, chickens for mutton — that's one level and it keeps us busy and interested. On the other level, what you might call after dinner, we write and sing songs, draw a bit, act plays, wonder and philosophise in our own way.

We must not forget that JPB is anything but an idle old scribbler who describes a world that he himself would loathe. He can paint more than a bit, he can read a score and pick out a tune on the piano, and there is plenty of evidence that he can write plays (and act in them!) and also wonder and philosophise in his own way. The people in this play have also ceased to bother themselves with foreign intrigues, trends, relations and all the favourite concerns of the media.

A lot of old but formerly lost knowledge is returning. They live in harmony with nature and do not fight against it. The human race is rediscovering its maturity while the specialists, on the other hand, behave like children: 'tearing about and plotting and being important about things that don't really matter — puts you at about ten or eleven years old,' says Margaret. The basic childishness of the self-important public man (far more often than woman) is one of JBP's favourite themes in his later work. Stephen sees them as still trying to rule thick lines across 'an old tried pattern, a faded map, offering some chance of happiness.' It was a kind of devil-worship, where the devils were Stupidity and Pride. In the end the experts are impressed against their will. They leave, promising to hand in a negative report and to leave the new pastoralists in their peace. Irina, the Russian, nearly succumbs to love.

This is the kind of play one wants to like but encounters obstacles. The *Times* critic put the matter fairly. JBP's special achievement in this play, he said, had been 'to create the atmosphere of a beguiling day-dream for his vision of an England which has come through atomic disaster to quiet wisdom. There is tenderness, there is humour, there is a floating magic in the gliding, desirable hallucination.' But the play that is inherent in its proper development just fails to appear. He wondered if it was basically a beautifully atmospheric short play spoiled by its extension into a full evening's entertainment. (*The Times*, 9 September 1949)

In the same year *The Olympians* was produced. This was an opera in three acts with libretto by Priestley and music by Arthur Bliss. Bliss is referred to in *Trumpets Over the Sea* as a friend, but to JBP's disquiet a friend who has a low opinion of his musical knowledge. It is set in 1836 and revolves round a mythical theme — the return of the Greek gods for a brief Midsummer's Night, with consequent bewitching and enchantment. It reads like a melange put together by Rostand and Bizet. It is theatre virtually devoid of content. In it one finds the emptiness to which obsessive fascination can lead a writer. The most significant thing about it, especially considering the period in which it appeared, is the suggestion that magic may return to our lives.

Three years later *Treasure on Pelican* came to the stage. This is yet another exotic island story, the third in a row — for *Summer*

Day's Dream had been set in our own island, but not the island we think we know. (The play before these three, *The Linden Tree*, had been written on the Isle of Wight.) *Pelican* is one of those plays that cause critics to refer admiringly to 'the old master (or wizard) demonstrating his magic again,' when they can think of nothing else to say. In other words, it is not significant as drama (in fact, in places it's a bit silly) but it is a model of professional dramaturgy. It is concerned with buried treasure but cleverly turns the usual treatment on its head. It's not about the search for treasure but the consequences of finding it. (How long had this idea been occupying JBP's mind? *Wonder Hero* had been about the consequences of finding treasure in modern terms; *Faraway* had been about the consequences of not finding the treasure.)

One of the strengths of JBP as a dramatist is his obvious desire to go half way to meet the producer. This is frequently apparent in the stage directions, as in this kind of thing: 'Nothing is said for some moments after the curtain is risen, to establish the atmosphere. When they speak, they do it out of this atmosphere, without a sense of real contact. Great care must be taken to suggest this cold, heavy atmosphere, quite different from that of the previous Act; but the sense of strain must not be too apparent at first.' He is inviting the producer to co-operate, and nothing is more calculated to please the producer and win his loyalty to the playwright. In fact, this attitude is more in line with modern TV practice where the ideal playwright is one who outlines his action, leaving details to the director, and keeping speech to a minimum. It is because JBP was so careful and skilled in these matters that a national newspaper asked him to write a model play for a competition. The result was good structure and poor psychology, and the same thing happens here. As it is also a thesis play, the normal demands of humanity tend to be squeezed out between the two rollers of message and technique. All the dirty pasts are revealed (as in *Inspector*) but crudely, the crimes and misdeeds being largely unrelated to the action. You could almost say that it turns out to be an adult *Lord of the Flies* (which in fact appeared two years later), with the adults revealing their base nature on a tropical island and being discovered *in extremis* by a Naval Officer.

In the following year JBP wrote another one-act play called *Try it Again*. As he has written a large amount of miscellaneous dramatic material, including one-acters for the amateur stage and radio and television plays, which are not available as they have not been published, I will take this opportunity to say a few words about some of them now. *Try it Again*, 1953, is about a man faced by his feminine triangle: mother, wife and mistress. It contains one of JBP's familiar recipes — a weak man and forceful women. (One recalls Alan Conway and his sisters.) A film director enters unexpectedly (another device — compare the Inspector!) and directs the situation as a show, suggesting a solution. He sees the parallel between life and theatre (another of JBP's favourite analogies) but says this is 'bad theatre . . . routine performances of routine parts.' He advises them to take it easy, to try for truth and sincerity, not act out 'mediocre comedy with tragedy waiting round the corner.' The problem is resolved by dramatic therapy. It is no longer the priest nor the psychiatrist who will suggest a solution but awareness of dramatic value, which must be based on sincerity. Probably hard going for the amateur theatre.

A Glass of Bitter, 1954, is another one-acter, appearing one year later. It has a neatly turned plot, as one might expect, for this is something at which JBP is an adept. The main characters are a married couple, the Grants, who present a self-satisfied front to the world yet conceal a high degree of insecurity. They are JBP's model of a typical middle class couple, and appear again and again in his work, from *Laburnum Grove* onwards.

Not all his longer plays have reached the stage, and some that have been produced have not been published. *The Pavilion of Masks* was produced in Bristol, but JBP did not like the production very much and it went no further. He says he intended to do some work on it but so far has not. (It appeared in a story version in *The Carfitt Crisis* collection.) *Take the Fool Away* was produced in Vienna but again he was not satisfied. He also wrote a play called *Time Was, Time Is*, which sounds like a return to one of his favourite themes, but he has not tried for a production, adding that he is 'old and lazy.'[2]

In 1955 the B.B.C. Light Programme gave a drama festival in honour of JBP. For the sixth and last of these productions he gave them a new stage play, *The Golden Entry*, which was adapted for broadcasting by Cynthia Pugh. The golden entry was the symbolic portal of an art dealer's gallery. People cannot afford to buy pictures. 'All we can manage now,' says the bankrupt dealer Harkfast, 'are a few atom bombs at fifty million pounds a time.' A man representing the creditors is suitably named Turpin: he is 'modern man without art — desperate as hell.' It never reached the stage but it sounds good vintage JBP, drawing on matters about which he felt passionately — the idiocy of nuclear armaments and the squalour of lives guided only by material considerations. It is impossible to give a full account here of the writing JBP has done for radio and television drama but he has always regarded the forms as opportunities for social criticism of the widest type — by which I mean not mere criticism of social systems but of the way men and women fit themselves into the business of living together. On the whole JBP has not made another reputation for himself here. The press has been cool. For example, the *Times* reviewer wrote of *The Stone Faces* (B.B.C. TV) that the plot might be acceptable if backed by passionate indignation, but one was chiefly aware of a reliance on coincidence. 'The play lacks energy. Its incidents are facile, its cynicism assumed and its sentiment treacly.' (*The Times*, 2 December 1957).

Returning to the stage, and in fact coming to the end of a distinguished career (it is twenty years since he had an original play performed), we note a move away from the public domain to the more personal matters that had engaged him at the beginning of his career. *The Scandalous Affair of Mr Kettle and Mrs Moon*, 1956, is not about the future of society or the best way to organise society but simply about two people who love each other in unfavourable circumstances. It is an escape play and obeys a well-worn formula: the lovers wish to find some kind of significance in life by running away together from the humbug, the deadly dullness and the crushing respectability that surround them. It is a well-meaning play but in its attack on the cliché of ordinary existence it is itself no more than an extended cliché. It suffers from situations and characters that, when they are not conventional, are conventionalised. It is the kind of play that attracts on the surface but niggles below it. Then what is wrong? People do get trapped into hyper-respectability and a wish to get out. Some do get out. But can this be handled in a play, especially one that observes the temporal unity of a single day? The move requires struggle, agony, courage, patience and immense subtlety of psychological presentation. These qualities are not present. The beginning illustrates two very typical aspects of Priestley's craft. First on stage is JBP's recurrent working woman, complete with duster, mournful looking and the embodiment of good kitchen sense. This may raise a subconscious groan — but how professional is JBP's method of getting the play started! The aforesaid woman oscillates helplessly between deafening radiogram and telegram and at the end of this by-play the audience must surely have settled down and prepared itself for the more serious matters to come.

As always, it is hard to fault the technical points. But the play fails in its general impact because it breaks most of the rules laid down by JBP himself in his lecture, *The Art of the Dramatist*, which appeared shortly after and which I will return to in more detail later. The playwright sees his material in terms of the particular convention, form or style he prefers to use. Each has its particular virtues and defects that must be accepted. He gives an example. You cannot have a play in which the action unwinds like a coiled spring and every single speech develops the situation, and where the characters are at the same time all created and exhibited in the round. 'Large characters in the round need plenty of space and therefore a certain looseness of construction, which immediately rules out any tight economical handling, any action uncoiling like a spring.' It seems to me that JBP tried for both in this play and naturally failed to achieve them.

His last play, *The Glass Cage*, 1957, was the most Ibsenish of all, for despite the experiments and the metaphysical by-ways he has explored, he is in the direct line of descent from Ibsen, treating serious matters in a realistic and often exhaustive and always earnest fashion. In this play family skeletons are revealed as mercilessly as in *Ghosts*. His careful stage directions and implied insistence that they must be followed exactly if full justice is to be done to the theme, is further evidence of this approach. But the play lacks poetry — although he sometimes aims at it, it is merely embellishment, it doesn't belong organically. This is an extremely restless play, as if his determination not to let it become static has led to over-reaction. It also reflects the novels he was writing in this period, in that the characters exhibit a psychological nakedness and the author reveals a disturbing clumsiness in presenting their mental processes. Despite these faults, however, it is one of his better plays, for it sustains interest.

Although I called *The Glass Cage* his last play he did in fact collaborate on another six years later. This was the dramatisation of Iris Murdoch's novel, *A Severed Head*. The choice of this novel is so unexpected that one wonders if JBP was yet again exercising his determination to try everything. Was he really attracted by the novel, which seems so utterly remote from his own view of life, and follows a type of fictional development that he had frequently derided? In this novel JBP, who considers character creation the necessary foundation of creative writing, found no character, twists and turns in place of a story, and a psychological level that was melodramatic and childish. Even Ivor Brown, one of JBP's steadiest admirers, in his British Council/National Book League pamphlet on Priestley, found it 'without affection and with little of the warmth of Priestley's usual approach to life.' In *The Magicians* Ravenstreet said he disliked going to the West End theatre because 'nine out of ten of the plays they offered didn't seem worth the time, trouble, money, spent on them, so many trashy novelettes printed on hand-made paper and bound in calfskin.' This could describe *A Severed Head*. Perhaps JBP was attracted by the presence of magicians in the cast. A psychoanalyst is called a magician: 'Watch it, brother. In real life magicians can be dangerous.' A sculptor is another. 'You gain power over people by making images of them.' But these would be tenuous grounds for adapting someone else's novel. I even wrote to JBP asking him how he came to make this choice, but received no answer. Perhaps it was none of my business.

Chapter 25

A Man of the Theatre

Gareth Lloyd Evans, author of *J.B. Priestley — the Dramatist*, 1964, claims that JBP wrote 'the most fascinating group of plays of any playwright of the twilit decade which we call the thirties.' It was certainly not a particularly interesting period in theatrical history, largely because there were so few playwrights who were prepared to break out of the conventions that had been established earlier — or did the fault lie with the managements, for the most remarkable playwright in the world will make no headway if the backing is not forthcoming. Priestley, however, was one of the very few who tried to introduce new methods and a new approach into a tired tradition. His unconquerable restlessness led him to write comedies, light entertainments and sociological plays, but it was in his Time-plays that his craft and imagination were most fully exercised. If he is not held in high esteem these days it is largely because he continued to write for the generation he belonged to when he started writing for the theatre. People brought up on Osborne and Pinter and Ionesco and Beckett were not likely to find the kind of sustenance they were looking for in Priestley. By the same token, however, Priestley is likely to be re-valued when these playwrights have also lost their major audience. Then will come the time to sort out the sheep and the goats. And the historians, including those who love theatre irrespective of its period, will probably think of Priestley as the author of some remarkable plays which managed to make drama out of speculation about the nature of Time. They may well see more clearly than contemporaries that these plays reflect a sense of loss which was one of the chief legacies of the first world war to those that survived it. I have already drawn attention to the rather mystifying fact that JBP, who spent so much of his youth in the trenches, has written so little about it. Perhaps the Time-plays were the delayed effect, the product of his trauma. There may have been a greater degree of sublimation than is normal, but the link is there. Put simply, we can imagine Priestley asking: Did I really lose those years — or is nothing really lost? Such an idea does not bear very close examination, but only because it is an emotional reaction and not a logical conclusion.

Balancing the introduction of ideas new to the theatre is his immense skill in dramatic construction. Sometimes there is overbalance — in his less successful plays the trouble is usually due to the form overwhelming the content so that the play is reduced to a 'box of tricks' — which is actually the term he himself applied to *Dangerous Corner*. Although this is superficially a Time-play the metaphysical aspect is specious, which is why I have paid so little attention to it. Guthrie, its first producer, said that the philosophy of the play was so limited that its impact was rapidly exhausted during rehearsal. Performances became more and more slick until they stopped altogether until the dress rehearsal. *Dangerous Corner* is the most obvious exercise among his plays of the art of construction (this is astonishing when one considers it was his first play) and yet it became extremely popular and had its own undeniably magical atmosphere. One of JBP's major skills is his sensitive reaction to audience reflexes. He knows, perhaps better than any other living playwright, that there is a paradoxical demand for illusion and reality at the same time. The audience demands relaxation, which implies a degree of fantasy, but will not accept more than a certain quota of unreality. It is in this mysterious unmeasurable no-man's-land that JBP is so proficient. Probably the best example in his work of superb construction allied with just the right degree of mixed reality-and-magic is to be found in *An Inspector Calls*.

In the lesser plays we often encounter a formula. (But has there ever been a playwright who did not resort to formula at times?) Priestley's favourite is to fling diverse people together and get them discussing, often social or political matters, and with a minimum of plot — but the plot must be sound, for JBP is a great believer in plot. Ideas are expressed idiosyncratically, emotionally and too often unrelatedly. There is a tendency to pomposity and sentimentality. These weaknesses are usually associated with the form — in other words, the form has overmastered the content. These faults can be usefully illustrated by an examination of the second volume of *The Plays*, which contains the following: *Laburnum Grove, Bees on the Boat Deck, When We Are Married, Goodnight Children, The Golden*

Fleece, How Are They at Home? and *Ever Since Paradise*. It will be noted that, apart from *When We Are Married*, this volume does not contain any of his better plays. In three of them (*How Are They at Home?*, *Bees* and *Fleece*) there is discussion which is too overt and tutorial. He is still adopting the Shavian method but without Shaw's wit or lightness of touch.

In the Introduction he says he finds it easier to plan and write a serious play than a comedy, as the latter requires more re-constructing and re-writing, and also extra rehearsals. It is rare to spot a weakness in JBP's dramatic equipment but perhaps he has been prone at times to regard serious discussion as a substitute for more dramatic qualities. He classifies three types of comedy. High Comedy (of which Maugham's *The Circle* is an example) has a particular appeal for Latin and Central European audiences but has never been very popular in England. The English preference is Light Comedy, depending on highly skilled star performers (the star system). He does not care for this type and although he had made two attempts at it he did not include them in this volume. His own choice was Broad Comedy, which is more farcical and less intellectual than High. It is easy to see that *When We are Married* is an example of this type. I might also add at this point that JBP doesn't like scene changes. All these plays have a single set.

Bees on the Boat Deck, 1936, is a Farcical Tragedy according to the table of contents and a Farcical Comedy according to the notes on the play. This may suggest the futility of labelling works of art. It includes a good deal of political satire. Its weakness is the familiar one, that the political ideas are expressed through discussion rather than presented through situation. *Goodnight, Children* illustrates a vein of obtuseness in JBP. He wonders why this play never became popular and ingenuously supposes the public dislike their broad-casting heroes to be made fun of. The truth is, it's a dull play, without a spark of human interest. You might call it a romp (some of his novels were romps, and succeeded better in that form) but it throws light on nothing save the nature of romping. All these plays are period pieces (therefore interesting to the historian) but only one of them, *When We Are Married*, transcends the moment and can claim universality. The sense of period is stressed by close adherence to contemporary manners, which receive close and careful treatment. For example, in *Fleece* Dr Alex Rothbury has met Veronica Frensham three or four times, is 'obviously in love

with her', and yet still calls her Miss Frensham. When he does
essay Veronica, he is snubbed. Yet he is represented as a rather
rebellious character. Of course, this is as it should be, the play is
set in the thirties. But there is nothing to set against it, to lift it out
of the mould of the formula play. The dialogue naturally suffers,
for formulas extend their dead hands to every department of the
play. Here is Veronica talking to the doctor, about male com-
pliments:

> They're amusing coming from you because they're so obviously against
> the grain. You're the kind of young doctor who loves being brutally
> frank — and rather rude. In fact, I heard one of these old women here
> — I think it was Lady Leadmill — complaining about you. She said she
> was going to warn your senior partner against you when he came back.

Standing by itself, taken out of context, that may not sound so
bad. But pages and pages of it — or, in theatrical terms, minutes
and minutes — can kill a play, as they killed so many by Pinero
and H.A. Jones.

Priestley is good enough to be a master of tricks and not their
servant. Of course, tricks do not make a play. The trick of
drunkenness (Slivers in *Bees*, William, Molly and the doctor in
Fleece) cannot make or save the play, nor would any playwright
imagine it could. But when used successfully, as with Ormonroyd
in *When We Are Married*, there can be no possible objection to it.
Another trick which JBP tended to resort to on various occasions
requires the telephone: the person who is speaking on the phone
addresses a remark to someone else in the same room, with consequent confusion at the other end of the line. These are small
matters but they are characteristic, and they correspond to the
fictional devices which I have already referred to: the Bah! Joke
and the Misheard Name.

Ever Since Paradise was experimental and even looks forward to
the Brechtian theatre that became popular in England after the
second war. In this play the method is not used very smoothly or
with sufficient flexibility. The original touring production was
superior to the London one, he says, and this may be significant —
perhaps the exigencies of provincial production supplied the in-
formality this type of play requires. In a note JBP shows that he
was obviously hurt by press hostility, and mentions one critic who
missed parts of the play yet condemned it. One has every
sympathy with JBP's contempt for failed playwrights who get their

own back through malicious and irrelevant criticism, yet without joining their ranks one cannot feel this was a success. It goes out of its way, in a manner that one feels can be best described as 'thirtyish', to avoid adultery and marital break-up, even when this seemed the only possible conclusion (and incidentally, the only humane one). It was the contemporary equivalent of the milkmaid being pulled off the railway line seconds before the express thunders past. The code must be upheld. But the code was unreal. This play was written in 1939 but did not achieve London production, in considerably modified form, until 1947, less than ten years before the explosion heralded by *Look Back in Anger*.

Whenever one discusses a playwright's craft one is inevitably drawn to consider his failures as well as his excellences. This is inevitable because a play is an organic whole and unless it is a masterpiece (and how many of those have there been?) it will contain both. Priestley knows how to manage the stage and its players and he has an excellent sense of timing. In the foregoing I have discussed his use of techniques in plays that were intrinsically below the highest rank. But now let us look at his stage craft in one of his better plays, *I Have Been Here Before*, and we will see how technique and content are completely in step with each other. This play is dominated by the ticking and chiming of a clock, and it is a clock which is intended to be invisible. It chimes at moments of recognition and high emotion. The symbolism is more pointed in this play than in the others concerning time, for the clock is materialised time. It is a play in which the director must be entirely sensitive to the playwright's moods. For example, at one point the stage direction reads: 'Janet looks out to the audience.' It is most important that she should in order to indicate a momentary escape from the time of the play, the now. This minute attention to feeling even extends to JBP's use of the curtains which, as Evans points out, reflect by their speed of fall the emotion generated on the stage.

It is not surprising that when the *News Chronicle* decided to run an Amateur Dramatic Contest in 1937, with a play specially commissioned for the purpose, it invited JBP to undertake the assignment. The play he wrote was called *Mystery at Greenfingers: a Comedy of Detection*. It underlined his right to be called a true man of the theatre. His 'Author's Note' to the Samuel French edition states that it was carefully devised and specially written as a test piece for amateur dramatic societies. The single set, properties and costumes are the simplest possible. (Incidentally, a big change has taken place in theatrical thinking about what constitutes simplicity since those days: for JBP it was represented by a fully-furnished hotel lounge — today it is a bare stage.) The Author's Note provides a useful summary of what JBP considers essential theatre. Notes on the character and set are supplied, presumably by the author. The six women and four men reflect the normal sex balance of amateur dramatic societies, a balance that is rarely reflected by the average play. JBP tells producers they are at liberty to make minor changes in the script, in adjustment to local conditions, so long as they do not interfere with fundamental movement and characterisation. In the copy I read he would have been pleased to see that 'big' had been changed to 'old' in the description of one character but displeased to find that a passage of social criticism had been cut.

It was not his first detection play, and would be surprising if it were, for JBP has tackled practically everything in the drama except verse. *Bright Shadow*, 1950, is sub-titled 'A Play of Detection'. It is a light-weight piece and has the usual over-informative air of the detective or mystery story, where the characters exist for one purpose only, which is to supply facts which can later be fitted into a pattern, but technically it is as faultless as anything he has written. *Greenfingers* is not a skilful mystery, even though the dramaturgy is beyond reproach. There are gibes against detective novels but they could equally be levelled against this play. Incredibilities proliferate and the final explanations to tidy up the plot are extremely tedious.

For Priestley the major difference between the film and the play has nothing to do with celluloid or 'flesh and blood' but everything with the comparison between a fixed form and a variable form. Once the film has been shot it is complete and cannot be changed, except by surgery. Every performance of a play is a new event. JBP is well aware of this and refers to it in *Margin Released*: '. . . if a film is well cast and skilfully directed it stays well cast and skilfully directed, whereas plays can be murdered.' Part of his success as a playwright is due to his awareness of this fact. One result is that he tries to present the director with a script that is clearly defined in its action but allows considerable freedom (with the guidance of the author) inside its established limits. I was curious to know how he decided whether an idea should be developed as a play or a novel and put the question to him, with especial reference to one of his later novels. His reply was characteristic:

> I doubt if your question about *Sir Michael and Sir George* is really justified, but I will answer it in a general sense.
> I happen to dislike plays that have a number of short scenes with varied backgrounds, and if I have an idea that seems to demand this, then I turn it into a novel and not into a play.

On the whole he has been perfectly consistent for most of his plays have only the one set — *Summer Day's Dream*, with two, is a rare exception. There is a strong contrast with many of the younger playwrights who seem to prefer plays presented in short snappy sections. The restlessness of *A Severed Head* makes its choice for dramatisation all the more surprising.

Ralph Richardson has praised JBP's dialogue. JBP believes that the English dramatist has a harder job of it than the American or Irish because his characters, if they are modern contemporaries, will do anything to avoid a scene and will keep clear of the picturesque and overtly dramatic like the plague. Again, this has proved excellent discipline. Whereas so many Irish plays dazzle first with their verbal brilliance and then bore with their emotional emptiness, JBP is compelled to concentrate on real situations and not pyrotechnic constructs. He has his own way of tackling the problem and gave an example in his speech, *The Art of the Dramatist*. (He had *The Linden Tree* in mind.)

> I open with absolutely flat realistic dialogue of the kind that any English audience knows only too well, and then gradually I begin to move away from complete naturalism, so that in the last half-hour the characters are using a far richer and warmer idiom, often making speeches that would be impossible to them in real life.

The dramatic experience is something JBP has thought about much more than the average playwright. His lecture, published as *The Art of the Dramatist*, gives us the fruit of this thinking. The phrase, 'dramatic experience', is not a very precise one in normal usage but JBP has a very definite idea of what he means by it. A play is experienced on two levels: you identify yourself with what is happening on the stage but at the same time you do not forget that you are sitting in a theatre. We allow our minds 'to function on two different levels at the same time.' The dual nature must never be forgotten by the critic. 'True drama is created by bringing life to the Theatre, and the Theatre to life.' There can be failures on both sides, by dramatist and playgoer. We often have to choose between plays that are lively and intelligent but suffer by not giving us what we want from the Theatre, and plays that are a clever box of tricks but bring no meaning to our workaday lives. The published version of the lecture has some appendices, the first of which reverted to this point. The child is often responsive on each level, appreciating what is happening on the stage but also being thoroughly aware that he is sitting next to mummy, although this does not always apply to the very young child, who either gets terribly excited or falls asleep. 'So it may well be that it is the child in us who makes us responsive to this magic. Men and women who are completely removed from their childhood, who for one reason or another have had to take the child in them and wring its neck, generally dislike the Theatre and are reluctant and un-responsive playgoers.'

Drama was once rooted in religion and we assume that these roots have been severed, but this is not true.

> I believe, strange as it may seem, that those roots were never cut, that the archaic religious foundation of drama has never been destroyed. Something remains, to give a curious sense of urgency, a devotion to their duty, to all players, directors, writers, who have not lost the last whisper of conscience.

This passage is taken from another talk, given in Manchester in 1961 at the inauguration of the new University School of Drama. It was printed in *The Moments* under the title 'What About the Audience?' and he calls it a sequel to *The Art of the Dramatist*. It is probably the most valuable of all the insights into his craft that JBP has given us. At first impact it astonishes the reader and even seems remote from contemporary life, but on reflection its truth becomes clear. It is also true of the audience. We are all our ancestors. The ancient myths may have been banished from consciousness but they still live in the dark of the mind. And one does not immediately recognise them in their new clothing.

Chapter 26

Experimental Drama

It would probably amaze the majority of today's younger theatre-goers (and writers) to be told that JBP has been one of the major experimentalists in the twentieth century English Theatre. Much of his work has been solidly in the realistic European tradition of which Ibsen and Shaw have been major landmarks, but one could name half a dozen plays which went outside the framework of this tradition, either in form or in content, and occasionally in both. 'Priestley is nothing if not an experimenter with form,' Gareth Lloyd Evans wrote in *J.B. Priestley — the Dramatist*. *Johnson Over Jordan* and *They Came to a City* both introduce the paranormal and symbolic; *A Summer Day's Dream* is futuristic; *Ever Since Paradise* dealt with realistic situations in a manner that owed a good deal to cabaret.

Priestley has made it quite clear that he is by no means satisfied with the state of the theatre in this country. His most damning indictment is to be found in the published version of *Johnson Over Jordan*. Too often the theatre has to struggle along without any of the sympathetic support which it should receive from authority and those who control the wealth of this country. The latter regard the theatre as just another commercial activity and the politicians (as is unfortunately traditional in this country) regard the arts and independent thinking with suspicion. Many countries on the continent of Europe put us to shame in this respect, and it is also true to say that the situation here is not so bad as it was, thanks to the activities of the Arts Council. Priestley has always put a great deal of his energy into fostering interest in and support for the theatre. He was, for example, chairman of a four-day conference held at Caxton Hall in February 1948, when several theatrical organisations (including the Joint Council of the National Theatre and the Old Vic, the Federation of Theatre Unions and the Shakespeare Memorial Theatre) put forward a plea for more Arts Council assistance.

Priestley diagnosed the sickness of the Theatre in volume 3 of

The Plays, referring specifically to *Summer Day's Dream*, which was withdrawn before reaching its fiftieth performance.

> The costs of production and the running costs of a play in the West End are at least twice what they were before the war. On the other hand, the prices of admission are only about ten per cent more than they used to be, and even these prices are now thought to be too high, especially by the hard-pressed middle-class public that probably forms the bulk of my special audience.

The situation in London was approaching that in New York where a few successes were surrounded by 'masses of lamentable failures.' Theatrical production was a wild gamble — you either hit the jackpot or you lose all. Serious dramatic work cannot exist in such an atmosphere; it is fatal to the author-director-team theatre in which he believes. Companies must either be subsidised or serious drama may disappear from London, and perhaps from the country, for London is our shop-window. Many of his plays, which could not find a secure home in England, have been immensely successful overseas. It is a matter of great shame for the English Theatre that such a fine play as *An Inspector Calls* was given its première in Moscow. An established playwright must have his work adequately produced in Britain. At the root of the problem lay the attitude of the Establishment towards the Arts. On a visit to Moscow, recorded in *Russian Journey*, 1946, he was impressed by the cheapness of theatre tickets. 'In Moscow, for less than the price of an ice-cream there, you can see theatrical productions of a perfection that not all the money in America can buy.'

The business man who backs plays sees a play as a commodity that will or will not sell. (This means, of course, that we should not expect our plays to be financed by business men.) For JBP the play was something much more personal and delicate. 'Since he wrote with an actor's approach to the theatre and to audiences,' wrote Susan Cooper, 'his plays were not so much scripts as records of a performance first played in his head' (*J.B. Priestley: Portrait of an Author*). This is important, for it explains the divided attitude of many people to the theatre. It has often been remarked that literature is less 'pure' than music, because of its social involvement; in the same way the drama appears to some people to be less 'pure' than fiction, let us say, because it requires flesh and bones to present it fully. There are in fact three forms of the play and JBP is thoroughly aware of this: they are the idea in the author's head, the rigid reproduction of the script, and the manifold interpretations of different directors in various performances. JBP stated in *Literature and Western Man* that 'the stage is a bad place on which to try to express the spirit of the age.' Anyone who has seen a Peter Brook production of Shakespeare or a Central European production of Chekhov will know the truth of this. The theatre is solidly objective. Tricks can be worked with make-up, decor and lighting to play havoc with the original idea of the author. And then the actors and actresses are so substantial; no spirit will survive their onslaught if they are opposed to it. Proust can make a subtle point quietly to a single reader — how can he make this point to a thousand people all at once and then pass on to the next point? JBP recognises that the film is the essential dramatic form of our time. We inherited the theatre but created the film, and we have a special feeling for this medium, which is a triumph of technology. The film removed a large section of the audience from the theatre, especially among the young. The serious Expressionists tried to bring the drama into line with the new movement, to overcome the theatre's obstinate objectivity, 'to give the drama both the breadth of the novel and the film and the subjective depth of poetry and the new fiction.'

What, he asks, should the playwright be trying to do? The answer must be: To make them feel. In his Introduction to *Two Time Plays*, 1937, he tried to illustrate this point in a discussion of *I Have Been Here Before*. What Lewis Casson, the director, realised and most critics did not, is that the important thing was not the dramatisation of Ouspensky's recurrence theory but the development and final conversion of Ormund's mind. In other words, the critics, instead of considering the dramatic action of the play were hung up by its philosophy. In JBP's view, too many critics who are failed dramatists or academic theorists or novelists earning something extra on the side concentrate on the ideas and forget the drama. (It is ironical that this is also the charge that some of them deliver, parrot-fashion, against some playwrights, including Priestley.[1]) The theatre is not the place to think in; it is the place to be dramatic in. It is also the author's job to make the audience feel. The feeling may influence their thinking later but that is a subsidiary matter. 'He can create in them a deep rich feeling that is, so to speak, tinged with thought.' JBP would like the Time-plays to be regarded as a contribution to the dwindling Theatre of

Ideas, not that he really believes in the existence of such a theatre but that ideas can 'play like summer lightning over a deep lake of feeling.' Naturally, he is not always successful; when he is not, the ideas dominate the feeling.

Ever Since Paradise, written in 1939 but not produced until 1946, is called a Discursive Entertainment. It is an experimental play, and is worth consideration for that reason for looking at it. The experiment lies in the employment of three couples, only one of which is the subject of the drama. Therefore there is one couple under review while another couple comments on situations and a third contributes atmospheric mood music. There is constant comment and cross-discussion, and one of the couples plays many roles in a manner that was quite unfamiliar and revolutionary at the time. The play's failure lies in the uneasy contrast between the novelty of its form and the nature of its content. The tone is decidedly bourgeois, and never rises above the level of conventional West End entertainment. One feels the experiment is an attempt to rescue it from its own weary theme: these are dreary people, with dreary problems, so let's see if we can inject a little interest by opening our box of tricks (which JBP, of course, handles so well). Almost symbolically, every new scene (there are many of them, set on a small interior stage) represents the corner of a sitting-room or a drawing-room. We feel imprisoned in domestic narrowness. The play expresses no more than woman's mag platitudes about life, love and marriage, and so we feel let down. It fails significantly to 'make familiar things new' as *When We Are Married* so triumphantly did, despite its orthodox form. One is reminded of the writings of that bourgeois prototype, Balzac, on love and marriage. JBP categorises the stages of marriage in this play, just as Balzac did in his marriage manuals. Undoubtedly, much of JBP's comment is shrewd. (A married woman whose husband is contemplating an affair says. 'It wouldn't be so bad if he'd found himself a *decent* woman.') What disappoints is that, although he analyses what is faulty in the marriage system of our society, he seems to accept it nevertheless. The tone is complacent. We get a weary flatness and no suggestion of an alternative. Here you are, he seems to say, and you mustn't expect anything better.

His success in theatrical experiment, then, came from his widening the scope of dramatic content rather than from technical innovation. He persuaded his audiences to feel the passage of time in a new way. I am not suggesting, of course, that he produced any permanent change in their attitudes, but that he persuaded them for a couple of hours to open their minds. There is evidence, for example, that some of the people who saw *Johnson Over Jordan* felt they had undergone a truly meaningful experience. But when he tried to do the same about society he was unable to work the necessary magic. Yet he knew what he was trying to do and was always ready to adopt any new technique that promised a closer relationship with his audience. It is therefore not surprising to find that he was ready to accept Theatre-in-the-Round, which came into vogue during the fifties, though with certain reservations. He tells us in *Journey Down a Rainbow* how he visited some theatres-in-the-round in Houston and elsewhere in Texas but found them too small. 'Actors and audience are too close and confused: they should be more obviously separated.' There was an advantage in cost reduction but no artistic gain that he could see. Two years later (1957), in a piece entitled 'Rough Sketch of a Lifeboat' in *Thoughts in the Wilderness*, he appeared to be more receptive to this technique. It occurred to him that it brought the theatre closer to the circus ring, a move that was guaranteed to rouse his interest. No sets, and the barest minimum of furniture and props, all in the most direct opposition to the normal cluttered Priestley play. Enthusiasts recommended it as being more imaginative, more intimate and more alive. JBP's main interest, however, still lay in its economic advantages, probably because he felt that much of his suffering in the theatre had been caused by high costs and lack of finance to cover them. Theatre-in-the-Round needed less space, it cost less to build, it could even be created out of a disused ballroom or the ground floor of a warehouse. It made touring much simpler and less expensive. 'If a dozen large towns had theatres-in-the-round, it would be possible to send out tours costing so little that a minority audience could keep them going.'

But JBP had his own candidate for a new and revised approach to staging plays. He called it the Platform Play and illustrated the method by writing *Dragon's Mouth* with Jacquetta Hawkes (1952). He got the idea after hearing a dramatic reading of Shaw's *Don Juan in Hell* by some leading actors in New York. The opening stage directions make it clear that this is to be no orthodox play. 'There are four stools; each has a microphone in front of it. The microphone stands may be linked together by a length of white rope which could suggest part of the rail of a ship. The four performers come on together, and they seat themselves before their respective microphones . . .' The four players represent Jung's four functions of Thought, Feeling, Sensation and Intuition. They learned their parts but remained static. One thing this method inevitably aimed at was the revival of rhetoric in place of the realistic muttering of modern drama. It was, of course, very cheap to produce. It toured the provinces and had a season at the huge Winter Garden Theatre in London during the summer of 1952, and it also went to New York. It made Priestley's point, that it could be accommodated in any kind of building.

But although the technique was modern and courageous and represents an adaptation to existing conditions it does not add up to drama. *Dragon's Mouth* is not a play as we understand the term but a heightened debate. Its main merit was that it gave actors the chance to show what they could do with the spoken word, a chance that does not often arise in a theatre dominated by the Method and influenced by television. The characters are part of the same situation and address each other, but the result is a symposium in the Greek style, to be read and not performed. (The later American play, *Kennedy's Children*, where the characters never tangle with each other, is actually more dramatic.) Even as a symposium it is not really successful, being an exercise in metaphorical expression rather than a developing, reasoned argument. The content seems very incoherent — the nature of man, especially woman, all the old metaphysical chestnuts JBP loves so much — and if there is a line of thought it is not clear. In some ways it resembles Virginia Woolf's *The Waves*, but lacks the clarity of the latter. JBP's first novel, *Adam in Moonshine*, was spoiled by 'fine writing'; this, one of his later plays, is spoiled by self-consciously vivid writing.

Ivor Brown, in his British Council National Book League monograph, *J.B. Priestley*, 1957, calls it Elastic Theatre. Priestley never followed it up. Theatre-in-the-Round was coming into fashion and attracting many of the new and younger playwrights, and it offered them more scope than Platform Theatre. But in any case, JBP is not a follower-up; the impatience that causes him to skimp his characters in his novels will not allow him to devote too much of his time to a single cause. There is always something else to attend to. While *Dragon's Mouth* was in production he was probably already working on *Treasure on Pelican* and perhaps trying to sort out his ideas for *The Magicians*.

Chapter 27

The Critic

Priestley's career as a critic has been chequered. During the twenties he wrote three books which can be classified as criticism, as distinct from essays or commentaries, and then came a long gap until the appearance of the ambitious *Literature and Western Man* in 1960. This is the reason why I have left it so late in this book to consider his status as a critic. It is not, one feels, his true *métier*. 'Of all the literary men I've known Jack Priestley is by far the best talker,' wrote Hugh Walpole. This sounds more like the essayist than the critic. And it is apt that he should have contributed a monograph entitled *Talking* in the series he edited called *These Diversions*. And yet he displayed certain qualities which would obviously be of value to a critic. He was a member of the original Book Society Committee in 1929, and acted as a useful counterweight to Walpole, who tended to see the best in everything, by being blunt and outspoken and not easily impressed. He was 'a boy with a man's wit and observation,' Walpole concluded, and this is the impression some of his early criticism often gives — insight allied with an occasional raw reaction. David Hughes summed this aspect of Priestley up pretty well in his *J.B. Priestley: an Informal Study of his Work*:

> . . . It is always possible to detect in his criticism those moments of uneasy perception or uncertain view which are the mark of the amateur, the man who loves books too hungrily to keep quiet across difficult territory. It is in my opinion no defect, for anything that is said about a book by an intelligent man is worth hearing, and if his feelings concentrate on a certain sphere of literature because they are naturally at home there, the conclusions he reaches about that sphere will be intense in their feeling and perhaps unique in their value.

Literary criticism is one of the few areas where the professional is inferior to the amateur. This is something that JBP instinctively expressed in his frequent attacks on academics and the 'professors'. By establishing rules and then sticking to them rigidly the professional often misses the values that lie within the interstices. After all, his rules have no divine sanction.

Priestley can at times be a very perceptive, even if hit-or-miss, critic because he has thought about what he, as a creative writer, is looking for. He doesn't write books on 'The Writer's Aim', but now and again he throws off a few hints as in *Rain Upon Godshill* when he praises a volume of Breughel, saying most of the details are comic but the total effect is beautiful and faintly tragic.

> Which is how most of us should see life and, if we are writers, record it. I see then in this Flemish painter of four hundred years ago a great artist with a broad appeal of the popular, tragi-comic, democratic kind, showing the crowd a vision of their own life; and those of us who ask to do nothing better than this, for we cannot see that there is anything better to do, whether we are painters, authors, producers of plays and films, should turn to him for refreshment and confirmation.

There is another very important point that he makes when considering an author's work, and one which is frequently ignored by those who should know better. Writing of Arnold Bennett, JBP points out that Bennett had already written more than fifty works, and if he was to be fairly examined, all of them should be taken into account.

> The real Mr Bennett is not the writer of this or that book, but is to be found somewhere behind all these books, perhaps buried beneath them, but buried alive. Moreover, it is dangerous to dismiss whole rows of these less important volumes, because Mr Bennett, being amazingly unequal, can suddenly fall to writing well in unexpected places just as he can fall to writing badly.

This is very well said and is (I don't know why) particularly applicable to academic critics. I can remember being reviewed by one who not only gave the impression that he had read no more than half a dozen books by the writer concerned but actually complained that I paid too much attention to lesser works! Well, there are no lesser works when you are discussing writers. In the case of JBP one must take into account *Wonder Hero* as well as *Bright Day*, *The Roundabout* as well as *The Linden Tree*. If we don't do this, we are not discussing the writer but a selection, and this seems pointless.

In his early reviews and essays JBP gave some indications of the direction his criticism would take when he gave it full rein. Reviewing *Moral Poison in Modern Fiction* by R. Brimley Johnson under the title 'Nasty Novels' (*The Outlook*, 26 August 1922), he makes it clear that he is determined to keep aloof from fashionable movements. There was no general movement to upset our common notions of morality, he said, but he saw 'a number of immature and not very original artists who are doing what such persons have always done, namely, follow a fashion.' No deep thought lay behind these trends. Looking back, you would see them in series — the Byronic hero, the cynical dandy, the emptyheaded guardsman, the ridiculous aesthete — and now we had the weak-kneed sexual maniac. In an article entitled 'Audacity in Literature' (*The Challenge*, 27 October 1922) he attacked the Spirit that lay behind the fashions. At worst, it was downright impudence, at best, an engaging sauciness, but whatever it was, it was not to be confused with originality. It is present when a writer shows contempt for the reader, by carelessness in matter and/or manner. He then lists those who don't have it: Hardy, Bridges, James, Conrad, Hudson, Galsworthy and Hewlett. Those who do have it are Shaw, Belloc and Chesterton (for their 'histories'), Beerbohm, Wells, Moore and Bennett (in their essays) and Drinkwater (in his plays). A familiar example of this audacity is the writer who makes a reputation as a story-teller and then sets up as a philosopher. It is difficult to take this analysis seriously, especially when his list becomes more and more inclusive, embracing a variety of figures from the past, going right back to Aristophanes. One feels that if one's sins place one in his company, they can't be too bad. And of course, a little later JBP would have come under his own ban!

There were moments during the early essays when a perceptive reader might have noticed that there was a mind at work capable of going beyond the cosy familiarities and self-admiring platitudes of the conventional essayist. For example, in the collection *I For One* there is a piece entitled 'In Praise of Normal Woman' which I would classify as good criticism rather than essayism. In it he says that the woman who lives a normal life can check the conceit and egotism of men. Her outlook is at the same time more personal and also impersonal; her interests are at once narrower and wider. What exactly does he mean by these apparent contradictions? 'She is primarily concerned with very little things, the minutiae of talk and behaviour for example, on the one hand, and with very big ones, the colossal elementary facts of life, such as birth, mating and death on the other.' This is not the trivial conceit of the essayist, who would be much more likely, when discussing women, to make feeble jokes about female tyranny in the home. It is fundamental observation and in fact parallels what Virginia Woolf (with whom he had little in common but whom he respected) was saying at the same time. It also deals with a subject that recurs again and again throughout his work, and is obviously important to him. It is a subject that we will consider more fully in a later chapter.

Apart from his books on Peacock and Meredith, JBP wrote two works of criticism which are of prime importance in understanding his view of life and letters, and which, occurring as they do at extremes of his career, bear a significant relationship to each other.[1] *Figures in Modern Literature*, 1924, tells us exactly who he considered important among his contemporaries. A Prefatory Note says he has avoided the usual Shaw-Wells-Galsworthy-Chesterton gallery. What we notice is that he also avoided the gallery that is now considered the most vital at that time: the Joyce-Woolf-Eliot-Pound-Yeats-Lawrence gallery. Some of these receive perfunctory mention. He considers nine authors, only two of whom (Arnold Bennett and Walter de la Mare) are likely to be read at all in the future, either in reprints or anthologies, except by Eng. Lit. thesis scholars. One of the others, Maurice Hewlett, unlike so many of his contemporaries (writes JBP) was 'an author and not an irritant.' Which tells us most of what we need to know of his opinion of the famous innovators.

He in fact belonged to the Georgian school of critics, by which I mean he exhibited the same characteristics and admired the same values as the Georgian poets. This sets the tone: Arnold Bennett has two faces, the second being 'nothing more (nor less) than a brilliant and delightful youth, not quite out of his teens, who has outgrown his tin soldiers and treasure islands only to make the Grand Babylon Hotel, golden, shining, the centre of his dreams and summit of his aspirations.' The approach is whimsical, slightly paradoxical and heavily metaphorical. The golden image carries all before it, its brilliance dissolving all accuracy. A.E. Housman's career as a poet, for instance, is summed up as follows: 'it was as if a man in a noisy crowded company had suddenly broken his silence with a few golden words, and then closed his lips for ever.' What does this add to our knowledge of Housman? On reading W.W. Jacobs: 'we have sneaked into the company of the old man at the "Cauliflower", and Bob Pretty and the rest, many a time when our reputations, bank-balances and families demanded that we should be otherwise engaged.' The Georgians liked nothing better than to be regarded as delinquents. And the overworked currency image inevitably appears, this time in an essay on Robert Lynd: 'to be able to make the ascent of Parnassus part of the day's work, frankly to accept the common coins of the market-place and then, by some mysterious means, to transform them into new bright mintage, etc., etc.' If only the Georgians could have used their copious mintages in a real market-place. The nearest they got to it was Woolworths.

The Georgian fondness for scolding the age was another winner. While they minted their coins, despite their inner roguishness, they existed in a sad, degenerate world — and didn't they know it! 'In an age that turns aside from contemplation and wise reveries, an age that delights in bludgeoning the nearest passer-by with the first idea it comes upon,' JBP booms, and goes on to tell us that Mr Santayana does none of these things. Yet despite the weaknesses, which he shared with so many of his contemporaries, these essays do not suffer from the over-personalised approach that spoils some of his later writings. They are more truly critical, they do try to establish a standard not irrevocably rooted in JBP's taste-buds. He has not yet developed the tendency to refer everything to himself. Here he shows a sensitivity that later can degenerate into a rather crude vulgarity (there are two kinds of vulgarity, as every alert reader knows), masquerading as directness. Too often, however, the perceptions misfire. He is, believe it or not, much too generous to most of his subjects, though he hints that he would be less than generous to many non-subjects. He is at his best when praising a writer who has never had justice done to him, Walter de la Mare, but it is noticeable that this is true only of de la Mare's prose. JBP doesn't know what to say about his poetry, except that he likes it, so he falls back on Georgian cliché, calling it 'the exquisite stammer of some elfin-hearted girl.' (Incidentally, when I say that JBP doesn't know how to express his feelings about poetry I am not saying anything to which he could reasonably object, for the critics who have written well on poetry in the whole English corpus are less than half a dozen.)

Philosophic imagination, says JBP, is necessary for all good art. This is where Arnold Bennett fails; he gives us an exhilarating picture of life but doesn't go that little bit further, as do Hardy,

Meredith and Conrad. But what does he mean by philosophic imagination? Without it, actions do not always proclaim their significance. It is necessary not only to enter into the character but also to see round him. Style has a threefold function:

> It expresses the thought by a logical arrangement of symbols; it contrives to intensify emotion by its undertones and overtones, suggestion and association of all kinds; and further it gives pleasure of itself merely as an arrangement, a pattern, a decoration.

It is folly to stress technique too much. He quotes Bennett with approval to the effect that Turgenev is the only great novelist who bothered his head about technique. 'The fact is, of course, that the art of fiction as practised by the great novelists *is* technique, and any other "technique" is either some inferior method or a mere catch-phrase of the pontifical critic.' JBP advances the interesting theory that the writer's imagination is rooted in one particular period of his life. Only the truly great, such as Shakespeare and Dante, fetch their images indiscriminately from all periods of their lives. Dickens and de la Mare call on childhood, A.E. Housman on early manhood, and so on. JBP echoed many other writers when he said that no one should expect cast-iron consistency from the critic. There is danger in insisting on a definition because it may become more important than the work under review. If a work is given a label it attraccts the 'horse-leeches' and the work becomes a vehicle for the label, and falls further and further into the background. This is particularly true today when certain poems and novels have frozen into their niches, more than at any time previous, owing to the scholastic industry represented by the multiplication of Eng. Lit. Departments. He approves Saintsbury's attack on the fallacy of 'this is beautiful but not to be tolerated.' It is impossible that beauty should be monstrous, says Saintsbury, and JBP agrees. It is scarcely necessary to add that JBP is against the Forces-, Tendencies- and Spirit-of-the-Time-mongers, who are upbraided mainly for being unfair to the individual author.

This is JBP's critical standpoint. It works better for prose than for poetry. With his wide interests and his determination to try anything, JBP had naturally tried his mind at poetry. The result, his first book, was called *The Chapman of Rhymes*. It was published in 1918 and the title page announces its author as J.B. Priestley, 2nd Lieutenant the Devonshire Regiment. The Dedication to 'P' begins

> *Belovèd, here's the book of laboured rhymes*
> *I garnered from the luteless, shifting times.*

It ends

> *You have my heart, here are my dreams, and now I live*
> *For naught but joy of you; I have no more to give.*

It is arranged in three 'Bundles'. The first consists of nine poems 'in which I listen to the evil whispering of Ancient Beauty and seek to lose the World'; the second of twelve poems 'in which I am swayed hither and thither and am moved by many things'; and the third of nine poems 'in which I come to the Broad Highway of Men and am a Good Comrade.' To give some idea of the quality of these poems I will quote briefly from the fifth poem in each Bundle. In the first, the poem is called 'The Hidden Life': The poet says he will go with his love to 'a great white peace in the sky;/Forsaking the world and the strife that kills.' In the second Bundle it is called 'The Song of the Man with the Weary Eyes' and consists of three stanzas, each with its promise; the beauty of Nature, the 'maiden honey-tongued and fair', and good comradeship at the inn — but each ends with the line, 'But there's never a leap of the heart now, whatever the time or place.' In the third Bundle the fifth poem is called 'The Rhymer of Witton Hill' and tells how a poet meets a fairy who asks him his desire. She tells him her gift will be a rhyme, but it will contain his requests; and now he lives among his treasures but the local folk are too blind to see them.

It is clear from the foregoing that JBP had been quite untouched by the new movements in poetry, including the work of the soldier poets. Therefore his criticism of poetry in *Figures in Modern Literature* is of little interest, though he does make some worthwhile points. The most important is that the treatment of poetry as philosophy in fancy dress is a false approach. (To some extent this covers practically every new poet since 1920.) 'If, when engaged in the hopeless task of disentangling the myriad threads of a poem's fabric, we make references to systems of belief, schools of philosophy, and the like, we do so for the sake of mere convenience . . .' Another pitfall is the resort to negative statements.

> It may be entertaining to be told the hundred-and-one things that a work of art is *not*, but it is not strictly necessary. But if one declares that So-and-so's poetry has such and such fine qualities, and contents oneself

with doing that, there are some people who are always ready to think that one has dowered So-and-so with every virtue known to letters.

JBP might have taken this argument further. The difficulty is that a critic of poetry must not base his views on the poem's philosophy; he must make positive statements; and these statements must be concerned with how the poet gets his effect, as well as on what he says; these statements must have body and not be mere Georgian evasions; and also (and this is the hurdle that brings nearly every critic down) he must make his criticism interesting and attractive, for any dullness rubs off on the poem.

JBP says, and quite rightly in my opinion, that a poet must follow in a tradition and not attempt a clean break. (We all know how the revolutionary Eliot shocked his disciples by insisting on the same point.) 'No artist should break away from tradition at all and fashion new forms until he knows the tradition and the old forms and is sure that they will not serve his turn.' (No one has illustrated this better than Picasso, who struck philistines dumb when he demonstrated in a film how well he could draw!) But the sensitive point is the point of departure, when the poet decides to beat a new path away from the main road, and equally when he fails to do so, not noticing that the road is full of potholes and rubbish. But there are two ways of failing, one of not knowing when to move and the other of moving at the wrong time or place. JBP was too easily swayed by the second-rate and in this volume he exhibited values which are embarrassing to report: 'one of the most original poets we have' of J.C. Squire (who had a pleasant facility but no originality) and some absurd praise of an inferior poem by Maurice Hewlett ('you have only to talk the poem and you are singing it, you cannot sing it without talking it; it is quiet conversation moving to a heart-breaking melody.') No inflation is quite as futile as the verbal inflation of the Georgians. Hewlett's 'The Village Wife's Lament' is 'the most adequate expression of simple grief in recent literature' and his *The Song of the Plow* is 'the best long poem of our time.' This alone tells us what JBP thought of *The Waste Land*. Hewlett's poem is a chronicle of Hodge, the English peasant — Hewlett insists on calling him a peasant long after he had lost his land, a social unreality which balances the orthographical unreality of 'plow'. It is possible to view Hewlett's poem as a revolutionary work in so far as Hodge is presented as the victim of ceaseless exploitation, but the form does not reinforce the new mood. The idea is naturally to JBP's taste. Technically, it is a splendid example of a tradition that was already on its last legs. It is clear that JBP identified with this rather than the new.[2]

His books on Meredith (1926) and Peacock (1927) were more successful (and even pleased the academics!) because they were concerned with writers of the past and no massive re-orientation was required. As critical works they need not detain us, except to state that they gave JBP a chance to exercise his undoubted facility as a phrase-maker. Claiming that Meredith is unique in the history of English fiction, he compared him to 'a man who cannot pass the salt without spilling it and yet is able to juggle with six plates and the whole cruet.' Such a comment tells us more about Meredith, and tells it truthfully, than most chapters in the average book of this kind. But now we come to a remarkable fact, the complete absence of any concern with criticism on JBP's part until the publication of his *Literature and Western Man* in 1960. It seems certain that for the greater part of his career JBP has shown little interest in criticism as a discipline. The early attempts were bread-and-butter works and the books on Meredith and Peacock were commissioned for the English Men of Letters series. Coming across his references to English literature and writers in some of the works that followed one would be justified in deciding that he lacked critical ability altogether. In a book like *Delight*, 1949, one is frequently impressed by the banality of his remarks. He throws out petulant gobbets of non-criticism, especially in his vendetta against the writing of his juniors. After quoting a rather tepid piece by Rupert Brooke he goes on: 'That — and pretty good writing too, much better than anything Brooke's critics offer us — is, etc.' Why did he have to snap this out? Was it because he knew, in his inmost regions, that it was simply pretty poor stuff after all, but he had adopted a position and had to defend it? He has opinions but (in this volume) rarely formulated his literary tastes in an acceptable way. This, for instance, after quoting from *As You Like It*. 'And — crikey! — call him Shakespeare, Bacon, Essex, Southampton or Uncle Tom Cobley — what a chap!' It makes one wriggle with embarrassment. One experiences the same kind of response in his comments on music, which he tends to describe as 'a glorious row' or something on that level. My point is that he could write much more responsibly than that but apparently didn't consider it worth the bother.

Before passing on to his one work of indubitable critical value I should like to say a few words about *Journey Down a Rainbow*, which he wrote in collaboration with Jacquetta Hawkes and which appeared in 1955. This is not literary criticism at all but it testifies to a mind (or minds) that is fully equipped in the critical sense. It is certainly one of his best books and it clinches yet another reputation, that of social commentator, to follow those of essayist, novelist and playwright. It is skilfully organised and presented, giving a stark contrast between primitive peace and harmony, found among the Pueblos on the Mesa (Jacquetta Hawkes's contribution) and modern hullabaloo and dissonance, experienced at a football match and in a Dallas night club (Priestley's contribution). In one way the whole book can be seen to illustrate the contrast between two principles, the feminine as demonstrated by the Indian's ties with the Earth, and the masculine, as demonstrated by the American's soaring into the skies. JBP's frequently repeated intuitions about women here find theoretical expression. At a night club a woman confesses to JBP that she loathes strip-tease.

> Here was yet another protest against a society in which masculine and feminine values were not properly balanced, harmonised. Strip-tease or equivalent antics existed of course in older societies, where feminine values were still deeply rooted, but they were offered to men on the loose, having a break from domestic life, knowingly playing truant. But a society in which a man takes his wife for a night out and they pay extra, out of their common stock of dollars, to see another woman undressing herself, is a society on which the male has completely imposed his values, and all talk of its being a matriarchy is nonsense.

This book contains some of JBP's best writing, of the controlled-venom type. 'Inauguration of Channel 13' is a little masterpiece. The stolid idiocy of the occasion (a new TV channel) is starkly recorded.

Literature and Western Man shows a tremendous advance on *Figures in Modern Literature*. Not only does the author exhibit a maturity and a confidence largely lacking in the earlier work, but here he is writing about something that he personally considers important. It is not just another book, written to satisfy a publisher. It is less a description of literature than a study of society. His main theme is that literature is running away from society.[3] It is his most sustained piece of criticism, and it also has a strongly contemporary feel about it. It begins with the introduction of moveable types and covers the whole of Europe plus its off-shoots — in practice this means North America, for South America and other European-speaking areas (including the whole of Eastern Europe, apart from Russia) are almost completely neglected. The first 300 pages are a little disappointing — that is, until he reaches the moderns. Although there are a number of valuable insights which one would not find in an orthodox history, not much is added to our familiar view of European literature. One wonders why he troubled to write down what had so often been written before. Probably his irritation with the academics and 'professors' got the better of him and urged him to set down a true portrait of the creative word. But his judgments seem remarkably like those of the professors! Of course, he does now and again score when he shows how a professor completely missed the creative point, but this would hardly justify a book of 500 pages. (He had often done it before in much shorter compass.) His themes turn out to be already rather hackneyed — the main one, the tension between the conscious and the unconscious is little more than a change in terminology (and not for the better) replacing classical and romantic.

There is a surprising lack of quotation. He is much stronger on the novelists than on the poets. There are omissions — there are bound to be omissions! — but the most serious seems to be the failure to mention Sade and the vast literary underground he represents. And one feels Mickiewicz was worth a mention. To get down to detail, he mentions in his first chapter the division, the psychological split, which only great art can heal, which became notable during the Renaissance and which dominates the whole of the modern literary output. This is his main theme. It can be seen in various ways — rationalism and the dream, the balance of masculine and feminine. Depth psychology has clarified much that used to puzzle our forefathers. 'Each misjudges the other: the Classical considers the Romantic unbalanced, childish, mad; the Romantic sees the Classical as drearily formal, tedious, lifeless.' He points out that the popular novelists of the nineteenth century are now considered our best. It is even true of the poets, for Tennyson, with all his faults, was Victorian England's greatest poet. Only snobs could deny the title to those very popular writers, Dickens and Tolstoy. In his later years JBP has in fact sprung to the defence of the Victorians, especially of Dickens, in

an illustrated biography, *Charles Dickens and his World*, 1961, and of
Tennyson in *Victoria's Heyday*, 1972. When writers became dis-
gusted with bourgeois codes they proceeded to break them
publicly. But the resultant literature was not the product of a wider
and deeper acceptance of life or an excess of vitality, but of embittered introversion and a sense of deficiency. 'In any event, an
artist does not gain freedom by this desire to shock stupid conventional people, for he is still compelling himself to accept their
standards and outlook by deliberately reversing them: he is only a
bourgeois type standing on his head.' This may be true, though to
some extent debatable. But in any case, it had all been said before.
A tragic result was that poetry, which ideally is the whole man
addressing other whole men, became specialised and set up a
barrier. Modern poetry, in its sincere effort to be more poetical,
lost most of its audience.

Nevertheless, it is in this part of his study that his idea really
comes to life. In a very interesting chapter introducing the
Moderns ('Background to the Books') he sees Georges Sorel as a
type figure through whom we can understand the new age. Sorel
was not the cause, although he helped the situation along, but he
reacted as thousands of others were reacting simultaneously. 'God
was dead, as Nietzsche had declared; and Man, alone and responsible, was busy cheating himself. So bring the whole edifice of
religion, philosophy, culture, education crashing down; make way
for the new myth; let the Life-Force, whose creatures we are,
shape the masses, rebellious and triumphant, as it wills and
pleases. And already we can hear the dictators screaming at their
hypnotised mobs, see the bonfires of books, and catch the stench of
concentration camps. Our own age has arrived.'

JBP, who in the past had been so cool on the subject of the first
War, now opens the escape valves. In an unusually impassioned
passage he sorrows over the loss of a generation. It is as though the
emotion has been pent up for half a century and now breaks its
bonds.

> The war cut Europe to the bone . . . No intelligent and sensitive
> European — and writers can hardly succeed without intelligence and
> sensitivity — could escape the terrible impact of those four years . . .
> The younger writers of the embattled nations who for one reason or
> another remained at home, but saw their brothers and friends fast dis-
> appearing, had the desperate choice of admitting the whole nightmare

into full consciousness or risking what deliberate suppression of it would do to their unconscious. As for the actual combatants, if they came out of it in one living piece, they returned to the civilian world like strangers from another life. They knew too many dead men too early; they were closer to them than to the living.

The war destroyed that mysterious but necessary connection between the two parts of the psyche, the conscious and unconscious. Brutality engendered coarseness. For example, the arrogance that had been found among a few before the war blossomed into a new absolutism. This particularly affected criticism. It became less relative, less ready to discover varying degrees and kinds of merit. There was a strong tendency to turn literature into Literature. Either you performed in the upper case or the lower case, and there was no association between them. Poets like Péguy adopted an austere stance that ruled out large areas of what had previously been accepted. His friend Rolland failed ultimately because he lacked the feminine creative power that resides in the male unconscious — he was simply one of many intelligent men who 'decided' to write fiction in the belief that a dominating idea was sufficient fuel to produce it. The situation was expressed in reverse when the intelligentsia and the avant-garde couldn't resist Hugh Walpole but were embarrassed by the association!

JBP is a great admirer of Yeats, one of the few who kept his head. Things fell apart and the centre could not hold because the old balance between introversion and extroversion was destroyed. Literature was introversion; extroversion belonged to another, lower world of experience. (At the end of this book JBP included a number of short biographies, compiled, I would say at a hunch, by an assistant but in each case ending with a snap judgment by himself. Of Fielding he writes: '. . . when younger English critics ignore him, it is usually because they have not read him.' JBP has no illusions: you don't trouble to read the worthless!)

By far the most valuable portions of this book are his evaluations of the novelists. His accounts of the Russians, Proust, Joyce and Kafka are superb in their brief compass. Sometimes a single word hits the nail squarely on the head, as when he writes that Kafka was not so much a writer as an 'atmosphere'.[4] At a time when so much important rubbish is written (usually in universities, I'm afraid) about symbolism it is refreshing to find a writer who knows what it means and what it does. Mann's *Magic Mountain*, for instance, is symbolic in the way Kafka is: 'it has not one meaning — and any criticism that declares it has is doing Mann an injustice — but meaning within meaning and, like all true symbols, a final one that cannot be grasped.' The value of that statement lies in its final clause. Like many readers, he finds certain aspects of D.H. Lawrence repellent but this doesn't blind him to his magnificent excellences. It's a pity JBP couldn't find time to write a book on Joyce so that the reading public could be helped to a balanced view of that fascinating writer. So far we have had mostly semi-hysterical adulation. The truth lying beneath all this is that JBP knows what he's writing about. How could Leavis, for example, despite his excellent critical equipment, apply it to something he knew only passively?

In conclusion, JBP deplores the decline of religion. Not the religion of the churches or the sects but an acknowledgment of mystery, an acceptance of a soundly based symbolism, and the restoration of guidance that is not merely the command of the conscious mind. 'We have no religion and, inside or outside litera-ture, man feels homeless, helpless and in despair.' It will be recalled that he believes that the religious impulse is still at the root of drama, even in its most modern and apparently secular form.

Chapter 28

Young Writers and the Avant-Garde

Priestley never showed much sympathy for his younger contemporaries who, after the first War, regarded themselves and were
regarded by the fashionable critics, as 'progressive' or 'avant-garde'.
His literary values were rooted in the past and were not to be upset
by new ideas imported by writers such as Ezra Pound and James
Joyce. He obviously did not object to dramatic experiment but he
showed no taste for literary experiment. What he seemed to object
to most in the modern movement was its insistence on introversion.

This has been a feature of his work from the earliest days. Even
his essays, which were rarely in any serious sense critical, tended
to lash out at times against 'younger writers' or 'modern novelists'.
No doubt much of this attitude could be attributed to the nature of
his war experience. When the war ended he was a military veteran
and still only twenty-four years of age. Many young men who
would have been his contemporaries had not survived. Others who
were beginning to write had just missed war service or had only
experienced it for a very short time, with few of the rigours JBP
had been exposed to. But we would have to look very deep inside
the individual to understand why Aldington, for instance, came
out a raging rebel while JBP tended to treat the new rebelliousness
with a pinch of salt.

One of the essays in *I For One*, 1923, is entitled 'The New
Hypocrisy'. According to JBP, the young novelist of the day was
likely to emphasise how selfish and vicious his heroine was, and
cowardly and snobbish his hero. But it was all a pose, he said. 'I
suspect that the people in the new novels are much better than
their authors would have us believe.' Another essay bears the
suggestive title, 'Those Terrible Novelists'. It begins: 'If I am
reading for pleasure, I rarely take up a modern novel. The fact is,
modern novels, our serious, intellectual, satirical novels, terrify
me.' He might have added another fact, that most of the new
novelists looked askance at the idea of pleasure in connection with

the novel, and tended to regard fiction as a branch of psychology or sociology. 'Our novelists frighten me because they are both omniscient and uncharitable,' he wrote. It was the omniscience of the scientist and the objectivity of the observer that many of them adopted as a cloak. Strangely enough, even the introversion of which he complained was often handled in a decidedly clinical way.

The result was often obscurity, either an admission of inefficiency in saying what one had to say clearly, or intentional, which was absolutely unpardonable. One of JBP's fictional heroes, Meredith, had often been accused of obscurity, and JBP made no concessions even to him. Meredith is said to have told a critic that, having inherited a little money, he was resolved to serve the critics with 'a strong dose of my most indigestible production,' which led to the opening chapters of *One of Our Conquerors*. 'If this statement is strictly true,' JBP wrote in his book on Meredith, 'if Meredith did deliberately make his later work obscure, then he ought to have been ashamed of himself.' Authorship should not be a standing feud with reviewers. Meredith was in fact guilty of some of the faults JBP discerned in the young progressives. His style mastered him, he felt impelled to give the appearance of subtlety and difficulty whether there was anything subtle and difficult to express or not. Towards the end of his career he was either 'the slave of his own mannerisms, or he deliberately covered up this interior simplicity with a surface complexity.' JBP asked himself the same question as he asked about his contemporaries: was it a pose, caused by the writer's refusal to come to terms with hostile critics and the public?

There was a kind of rawness about the youthful Priestley which was poles apart from the studied sophistication of many of the young men and women who were beginning to write at about the same time as himself. His ideal poet, for instance, was Chestertonian and Squireish, someone who wore outsize cravats and velvet smoking jackets and bawled his verses into the gathering storm. There are plenty of instances of this persona, bouncing through the early essays and novels, always a Georgian, always noisily extrovert. Penderel, the youthful intellectual in *Benighted*, 1927, is a good example of the type. He knocks at the door of an isolated mansion in the Welsh hills during a storm. There is no answer so he knocks again and says, ' *"Is there anybody there?" said the Traveller.*

That's why poetry is so good, he told himself, his hand on the knocker; at such time odd bits of it come shooting up in the mind like rockets.' There is a brashness here which is utterly remote from the new mood in poetry.

The 'young poet' figure comes in for a good deal of mockery in the novels. He appears in *The Good Companions* and again in *Festival at Farbridge*. This is not the chanting, bawling poet, who was admired but has now disappeared. It is the new style poet and he is remarkable for his preciousness. Peter Horlett in the play, *Music at Night*, 1938, is a fashionable young poet who pretends to be a proletarian poet. There are suggestions that he might be based on Auden. Katherine asks him why he doesn't write poems for the people, as he calls them, that the people will understand. This, of course, is one of the unexplained mysteries of the Left-wing poets of the thirties. But JBP is not entirely unsympathetic to young Horlett. He has a shallow, insincere side, like the rest of us, but in the course of the play he discovers his truer and better self. JBP was still prepared to be tolerant, even if his patience was wearing thin. Perhaps *Bright Day*, 1946, represents a kind of watershed between acceptance and downright rejection. 'I am told that the poetry that is being written these days is very fine but somehow you never catch a youth bellowing lines of it on a hilltop, and indeed I never find anybody wanting to quote it at all. I suppose it is no longer that kind of poetry.' Not only that; it was no longer a time when people wanted to 'bellow on hill-tops'!

From now on JBP was to show little sympathy with the new movement, which he still associated with the young , although its principal figures were in many cases of his own generation. He cannot bear the hoity-toitiness of some of the young men, especially in the theatre. In his Introduction to Volume 1 of *The Plays* he complains of the way they lounge about, making no contribution but referring patronisingly to the naturalistic play, hinting that they could knock one off any time they chose. He was discussing his own *The Linden Tree*. 'Well, let them try, for the need of the Theatre is pressing. Later on, having learned something in this humble field, they can attempt the new *Oedipus* or *Lear* on which they must be brooding on their distant heights.' It is not the only time he puts out a challenge of this type. It is a pity he feels it necessary to react so sharply to such pinpricks. Apparently the irritation is great but the response is, regrettably, futile. As a result it occurs in the most unexpected places, even in *Bright Shadow*, 1950, which is simply a play of detection. The only difference is that here the target is the novelist, not the dramatist.

> *Peter:*   Do you read detective stories?
> *Ivor:*   No. I prefer my fiction to be rather more intelligent and sensitive — to be literature.
> *Peter:*   Highbrow type, eh? Well, I've tried some of this new literature of yours, but most of it seems to be filled with people who don't accept any responsibility and run screaming when they remember any awkward question.

Ravenstreet in *The Magicians* also feels impelled to offer his views on the younger generation of writers. They certainly coincide with JBP's. Such writers 'either did something rather badly that older writers had done well or they tried to do something that didn't seem to him worth doing, were trivial, small-minded, cliquish, fancy boys and girls not writing for solid men of the world. Some of the most highly praised seem to whine like neurotic curates.'

Such passages do nothing to enhance the quality of the novel or play in which they appear. They are simply cases of letting off steam and it is steam which has no organic relationship with its source. Outside his creative work, JBP still expressed his irritation with the modern movement but had to do it more responsibly. In his published speech, *The Art of the Dramatist*, for instance, he referred to an imaginary dramatist who is working in the family convention and has to identify himself with all the characters in turn, including 'young Derek Jones, the Outsider, who cannot look forward to anything because he is so busy looking back in anger.' JBP has mixed feelings about Osborne, but this is a cheap gibe which does nothing to clarify the contemporary situation in the drama. There is another thrust which is equally unpleasing when, discussing verse drama, he says that it can be in rhymed couplets or Shakespearean blank verse or 'the much blanker verse favoured by contemporary poetic dramatists'. There is so much in this brief statement that does JBP no credit: rhymed couplets and Shakespearean blank verse are simply not possibilities for the modern playwright, as JBP well knows, and the dismissal of the remainder in a curt phrase is no contribution at all.

There is no doubt that JBP feels he has been neglected, and that many writers, with less talent and more pretentiousness, have won the acclaim of the critics. He states with a mixture of bitterness and satisfaction in *Margin Released* that he was outside the 'fashionable literary movement before I even began.' It was after the War, 'when the embittered introverts took over' that 'affection was banished from literature.' In this statement we have two of the most important clues to his attitude to his contemporaries. Introversion, an unhealthy obsession with the self and its workings, has ousted the objective tone of the great literature of the past which, in his view, gave a much more balanced view of humanity; and with it has gone a decline in the spirit of affection which used to rule creative literature. Writers used to love their characters, even the shady ones; now they despise them, especially if they display virtues. In his neglected *Over the Long High Wall* JBP writes of the 'life-shrinkers' who have played a large part in this unhappy development. The major ones are Marx, Darwin and Freud. They share responsibility for a society which most of us detest. 'They used the "nothing but" hatchet on a gigantic scale. They began to fence us in and then trim us down.' Some of their disciples have wisely moderated their views but others have been more dogmatic, more arid and more life-shrinking. To state publicly that you admire Dickens and still consider him our major novelist is to court disparagement — and this is exactly what JBP has done. But JBP is always ready to hit back. The modern critics and their acolytes who compose novels reject Dickens because his treatment of character is too extrovert. Of course, says JBP, they haven't read him, else they couldn't make such an egregious blunder.

> Lecturers in Eng. Lit. who 'teach' Joyce, Lawrence, Virginia Woolf, or other deeply subjective novelists, are entitled to turn up their noses at Steerforth and Little Em'ly and the machinations of Uriah Heep, but unless they salute Dickens's handling of David Copperfield's childhood they are so many ignoramuses. *(Victoria's Heyday,* 1972)

He calls it 'a marvel of subjective narrative'. As it is the subjective element that seems to impress modern critics, why aren't they impressed by this? Because, he says, they have no genuine principles but only follow fashion.

The feud between JBP and the younger writers was nicely encapsulated by the brush with Graham Greene which occurred as far back as 1932 but was not made public until Greene published his autobiography forty years later.[1] The character of Savory, the popular novelist, in *Stamboul Train*, seemed to be too close to Priestley for the comfort of Charles Evans of Heinemann, who decided that, if he had to choose, he would rather lose Greene as one of his authors than Priestley, and therefore insisted on deletions, particularly references to the novelist's pipe, his 'blunt fingers' and — his love of Dickens. According to the *Times* 'Diary' for 31 August 1971, JBP says he never thought the portrait had been intended as a lampoon of himself and that he had never intended going to law, as Greene alleged. Greene, for his part, made the unlikely suggestion that the description was a composite one built up from the author-manqué, Lord Baldwin, and the extremely unliterary Labour politician, J.H. Thomas, both conveniently dead by then. But the most interesting comment in the Diary was attributed to JBP: 'The popular novelist was referred to as "the new Dickens" and it happened that I'd rather (have) been referred to in those terms, against my wishes, as I never thought of myself in that way.'

Chapter 29

The Academics

Throughout his career JBP seems to have been fighting a running battle with the academics or, as he often calls them, 'the professors'. Naturally, he makes exceptions. He speaks of professorial friends and makes it clear that his condemnation is not of the blanket kind. It is also difficult to accuse him of sour grapes, for who, if offered the chance by some Good Fairy, would opt to become a Professor of English Literature at a university, however eminent, in preference to a career such JBP's? He also tells us that, after taking his Cambridge degree, he was offered an academic post but preferred to take his chance as a writer. It was surely the correct choice for him.

What is it about the academic function that he disapproves of so strongly? On the whole it is the tendency to establish rules governing judgment and critical approbation, leading to a mechanical and narrow view of the subject matter. In Priestley's case, of course, the concern is largely with literary values, although later he broadened his critical field to include other disciplines, especially those which we often consider as being on the margins of science. He deplored the obsession with analytical method which was particularly unsuited to aesthetic evaluation but also, when used to excess, stood in the way of a comprehensive view of phenomena and processes in general. Analytical ability is too often a mark of mental narrowness and has a special appeal to the inferior intelligence. JBP noted on more than one occasion that critical analysts were prone to accuse their opponents of 'woolly-mindedness'. This led him to a defence of the 'woolly-minded', which was simply an emotive term masking a broader view. The best expression of this standpoint is to be found in *Man and Time*.

> Sharp analysis and precision may trap us in a dead end. People who keep their minds open, never refusing what intuition and imagination may bring, are frequently dismissed as being 'woolly-minded'. There is in my opinion much to be said in favour of being woolly-minded. No doubt all kinds of nonsense may find their way in and be hospitably entertained, but so might a profound truth or two. Such a truth may easily be considered irrational, illogical and paradoxical, not worth a serious

examination, by the opposite of the 'woolly', the sharp and keenly analytical minds, determined to cram the universe into the limited human intellect and equally determined to ignore whatever has been left outside.[1]

It is well-known that JBP has engaged in a good deal of journalism during his writing career, and has been criticised for it. There was a time, not so very long ago, when the academic approach was the admired end of a spectrum that extended not very respectably to the quagmire of journalism at the other end. I doubt if this represents the view of most thinking people today. We are still aware of the less admirable aspects of journalism, its super-ficialities, its tendency to sensationalism and immediate response, its obvious errors in judgement enforced by the necessary speed of reaction — and yet journalism remains close to people, can never ignore people, lives and thrives on people. The academic opponent is much too prone to think in terms of abstraction. JBP attempts to answer the question: Why has he engaged in so much journalism? in *Rain Upon Godshill* and replies that, apart from earning a living, it enabled him to keep in touch with a large public, but also 'because it helps me to put my scattered thoughts and reflections and guesses at the nature of things into some sort of order.' The ordinary thoughtful man or woman has to make up his mind about a number of important matters, but he has to do it 'on the wing', so to speak, and not under laboratory conditions. The journalist is his representative.

> To write fifteen hundred easily-understood words, in a crisp dogmatic style, about the relations between men and women, the importance of education, the growing fear in the world, the nature of happiness, the problem of Time, or your fundamental beliefs, is to be compelled to take stock of such thought as you possess, hastily to reduce your mind to some kind of order, and to put yourself to a rather searching test.

There are two words in the above passage that are worth comment. One is 'hastily': it is the journalist's trade-mark — but it is also yours and mine, unless you have been awarded a Fellowship at All Souls. The other is 'dogmatic'; it is the one word in the passage that JBP would probably regret and which he would remove on revision, but which is the consequence of writing to a dead-line; concluded 'hastily'. But who do we mainly associate with the dogmatic utterance? The academic who works to rule.

Priestley tells us that he is never as certain of anything as he appears to be in a newspaper article, but this does not mean he is faking, only that the medium of communication demands a crisp, dogmatic *(sic)* style. It also helps him arrive at certain conclusions. Personally, I am not terribly impressed by or even much concerned with JBP's apologies for journalism because I think they can be made on a richer level. There is one level on which good journalism is superior to most academic writing, as I have said, and that is in the area of human value. I should explain at this point that when I refer to academic writers I am thinking of the invasion of the creative field by writers based on universities. In addition to this, the study of English Literature now has passed beyond what used to be regarded as the 'classical' and in many cases has become completely contemporary. (I know of one Drama Department that in 1979 'taught' Howard Brenton!) Between the wars the considerable advances made in the American novel were made by writers who had graduated through journalism. Since the second World War, both in Britain and America, they have been replaced by writers trained in academic disciplines. The result has not been encouraging. It may give the impression of being a more refined product but this is not true of what is fundamentally the most important aspect: human relevance. Wit abounds, realism abounds, cleverness abounds, but not the human dimension.

The claim that JBP makes for himself is that his writings contain a philosophy: it is ramshackle and amateur, a patchwork of beliefs, guesses, prejudices, nothing like a professional philosophy published by a University Press in two volumes, certainly not an insistent yea-or-nay approach to experience — but with life in it. So many philosophers taste like a mixture of hay and tin-tacks, although there are partial exceptions (he mentions McTaggart and Whitehead, I would like to add MacMurray) where the stir of life is contained, if not the whole thing. But best of all, of course, for JBP, was Dunne, and he was no professional. It is not my purpose here — in fact, it would be very foolish of me, when writing about someone like JBP — to decry the professional. But it certainly is my purpose to pick up JBP's point that the professional needs a proper environment in which to work and not merely a book of rules — or, as it would be called in the theatre — a box of tricks.

In view of all this, it is not surprising that on at least two occasions JBP was the target for the kind of verbal vitriol F.R. Leavis used to hurl at some (in fact, the great majority) of his contemporaries. In *Scrutiny* for September 1932 he wrote a piece entitled 'What's Wrong with Criticism?' In the absence of current standards maintained by the authority of tradition, the official machinery (and he referred specifically to the Royal Society of Literature and the B.B.C.) 'can only gear in with the mechanism of standardisation and levelling down.' And then, rather surprisingly, he adds: 'There could be no serious discussion of modern literature that should not be an implicit condemnation of Mr Walpole and Mr Priestley.' In 1934 he followed this up with a swingeing attack on JBP in the death-dealing style that Leavis and his mates have made notorious. It had been claimed that JBP shocked people out of their complacency. Not at all, said Leavis, it is impossible to sustain such an argument: what he gives us is 'tedious anecdotage', which is 'uninformed and shallow', and the item in the Index actually reads: '*English Journey* dismissed as incompetent sociology.' Nowadays Leavis's strictures are revealed as being much more infantile than they seemed to be at the time. But what is of major interest today is that he considered it worth his while to rebut Priestley. Leavis considered himself a most important critic and JBP never saw himself as one at all, at most a commentator. But the inference is that there nagged at the back of Leavis's mind the suspicion that Priestley and his kind had a good deal of significance. It should also be added that JBP, who is rather good at biding his time, later wrote an article in which he gave his own uncomplimentary opinion of Leavis.

He felt that there had been a change for the worse. In the past some of our best criticism had been written by professors of English, and he cited Saintsbury, Bradley, Ker and Raleigh — but the breed has passed away. They were really subsidised critics, more interested in literature than in the ambitions of their students. It might be said that Leavis, for instance, was chiefly concerned with having his students installed in places of academic power throughout the English-speaking world. 'When the old professors sat up late at night it was to talk and drink, read and write,' JBP wrote in *Midnight on the Desert*; 'but the new lot, teachers to a man, only sit up late to mark papers or to prepare a nice little lecture or two on the Romantic Revival.' This may be a bit peevish and at best only a half truth, but it is certainly difficult to name any academics who have produced criticism as vital and sensitive as Henry James, D.H. Lawrence and T.S. Eliot. He felt the same observations might be made in America. After his visit with Jacquetta Hawkes he wrote in *Journey Down a Rainbow*, 1955, that there were too many defeated men in academic life, 'or what passes for it.' Again, one does often notice the defeatism that characterises the speech and correspondence of many American academics. But it was not much better in England '. . . with the new and deliberate loutishness of the younger lecturers in provincial universities, with Fellows of ancient foundations offering to perform monkey tricks on radio and TV, all succumbing to *Admass*.' Watching a ventriloquist who has an exchange of talk with a head in a box he noted that the head 'was obviously a severe and pedantic type, reminding me strongly of some of our fashionable professors of literary criticism, who not only talk in the same manner but also seem to be merely heads in boxes.'

Although it is easy to sympathise with JBP's irritation with dullards who make use of their academic positions to pontificate on matters which require an insight they often do not possess, the frequency with which he returns to the charge and the nature of the abuse he levels at professorial heads may well be counterproductive in the long run. Agreed, they are often pompous, they invent rules to govern one's appreciation, they have no sense of style or a sense of style that is at odds with the matter they are discussing — but there is no point in repeating these charges *ad nauseam*. The only way to counter bad criticism is to produce good criticism, and JBP has been capable of this on occasion, though on other occasions his efforts are not superior to the professors'. Repeated insult proves nothing except perhaps what JBP himself might call a vein of loutishness. As early as 1925 JBP wrote this in a study of Shakespeare's Bottom: 'What would happen if one of the gentlemen who call Bottom "gross, stupid and ignorant", let us say the average professor of English literature, suddenly found himself in the arms of a very beautiful and very amorous fairy, even if his head were not discoverable by immediate sight but only by long acquaintance to be that of an ass.' (*The English Comic Characters*, 1925). We turn to the Introduction to Volume I of *The Plays* and after being told that drama is not simply a branch of literature but a separate little art we read: 'And one day, if I am spared, I hope to deal with this subject at some length, if only as a protest against the nonsense often offered us by literary professors and lecturers who write about the drama without understanding the Theatre.' *Man and Time*, a worthy book and one that does not need cheap sneers to embroider its message, tells us how JBP employed an 'emissary' to write to and if possible interview a number of distinguished physicists, mathematicians and philosophers on the subject of Time. (He is now moving well beyond the Eng. Lit. confines which had previously supplied him with his targets.) He quotes some of the replies and again is not always able to control his irritation: 'Yes, my dear Professor, but you must try to bear with us a little — that is, those of us who believe we have had certain experiences that cannot be fitted into your pattern.'

But this particular pattern, JBP's pattern, achieves its fullest expression in his ambitious novel, *The Image Men*, and it is perhaps one of the reasons why it is not the creative success JBP hoped it would be. Nearly all the academics in this novel, especially in the first volume, *Out of Town* — and there are a large number of them — are presented contemptuously. (Both Saltana and Tuby actually belong to the profession but have spent their teaching careers overseas. On their return they are not impressed by the home scene. This in itself is not objectionable — the number of returned teachers who have had a similar experience is large.) Vice-Chancellor Lapford has been scraping the bottom of the academic barrel to staff the University of Brockshire — and universities were going up like cinemas in the 1920s.' Tuby, speaking to Lapford's wife, says he understands the need for more scientists and technologists but is not enraptured by the thought of thousands of young men and girls, at enormous cost, sitting at the feet of a Professor Brigham or a Professor Cally — 'and Isabel, my dear, you know *damned* well what I mean.' Professor Steril is a good example of quaint uselessness. Late of Cambridge, now retired, he is brought to Brockshire to speak on *Notes Towards a Reconsideration of T.S. Eliot* (a title gravely borrowed from the master himself) and there is great excitement in the Department of English Literature. One needs only the barest knowledge of the academic world to know who is being satirised here. There are odd moments (very odd, perhaps, but they do exist) when JBP seems to reflect at a lower, earth-bound level, the notions of the existentialist philosophers — not the spurious ones, like Sartre, but those of genuine mintage, such as Kierkegaard and Chestov. This is never more true than when he inveighs against academics and materialist 'philosophers', sensing that they are not interested in reality but only a

custom-bred reflection of reality. It was Kierkegaard who wrote
'the don is the eunuch' but JBP might have done it for him.

Much of this is tasteless and even futile, especially when they have
little more significance than the sparks at a fireworks display. But
when JBP addresses himself more seriously to the broader aspects
of the academic mind, especially its unenterprising, hidebound
character, as demonstrated by the scientific positivist, we are on
more solid ground. Parts of *Over the Long High Wall* are in effect a
tirade against what he considers the decadence of science. His
argument comes very close to Charles Fort's. Establishment
scientists dismiss ideas, theories, even facts which do not fall
within the classic limits.

> They are right to defend a cool, scientific outlook, but if they ignore
> most of the evidence, they are offering us a display of prejudice rather
> than an example of the cool scientific outlook. If the early scientists had
> gone to work in this fashion, we should still be waiting for the triumphs
> of science.

A poet like de la Mare was being more truly scientific than many
scientists when he said to Sir Russell Brain: 'I believe that
telepathy is almost continuous. If you and I were not in telepathic
communication we couldn't carry on our conversation.' But the
Establishment attitude distrusts such independent ideas and prefers
to rely on what JBP calls 'consensus opinion censorship.' He
illustrated his challenge in the field of precognition, especially in
dreams. Whenever breaking or exploring new ground, one is
hampered by inadequacy of vocabulary. He uses the word *taste* to
describe a change in quality, for where the mind is concerned it is
often quality that comprises the variation.

The notion of necessary cause-and-effect has produced monster
inhibitions in our approach to our world. 'If I know something
strange happened, I don't have to surrender if the nearest scientist
tells me it couldn't have happened,' he writes in *Over the Long High
Wall*. The malaise extends far beyond the Eng. Lit. boundaries. A
new approach to phenomena has come into existence and been
widely accepted; it has replaced the orthodox scientific discipline in
many areas. The enquirer no longer appeals to the facts of
observation but to a theory about them. The scientist (JBP would
probably prefer to write 'scientist', for this is not how Newton and
Pasteur and Einstein set about things) says something is outside the
system of cause-and-effect he has been brought up on and which he

has, unaware, turned into a totem. Science has developed admirably within certain limits but is now bursting at the seams. The Aristotelian, Ptolemaic and Newtonian systems all permitted advances in knowledge up to a point, when they had to be partially abandoned. Another point of this kind has been reached. We must now be prepared to back evidence against principle, and the agent will not be a scientist or an academic, imprisoned as they are in their codes, but possibly a journalist. Chesterton, after all, hammered at this point all his life.

> We must try to notice, to remember, to ponder, to *take seriously*, what up to now we may have hurriedly dismissed. These are the little things that appear on the fringe of consciousness, the apparent strange coincidences, the flashes of intuition, the fragments of dreams that trouble the mind before it drives them out, the vague hauntings and premonitions and half-heard whispers that another life may be going on somewhere . . .
> *(Over the Long High Wall)*

He repeats again and again ('to the point of tedium') that we must back our own experience against the fiats issuing from labs and institutes. A situation is building up which parallels one with which we are already familiar in the field of politics and government: the 'us' and 'them' polarity. We, ordinary people who notice occasional odd fragments of behaviour, are beginning to be a bit more self-confident and aggressive in our attitude towards them, who tell us we are all suffering from mass delusions. To put it bluntly, that we're daft.

Chapter 30

The Feminine Principle

While reading Priestley's work in its totality one soon becomes aware of a Female Champion, half gallant, half protective. This is not a role greatly admired by many women these days but for most of JBP's career it has been an honourable one. He has always been convinced that the female contribution is as important as the male, but he shrinks from the Women's Lib. notion that women are a downtrodden race of men. (If a Women's Libber complains that this is not their standpoint, I can only reply that that's what it always sounds like.) Today some of JBP's championship of women may sound a little condescending but this is largely the effect of time. JBP admires some women for their qualities and condemns others for their lack of them. This is all rather un-seventyish, and so too is his lack of sexual intensity in portraying women.

There are, in effect, two women in JBP's fiction. The younger ones are all, to a greater or lesser degree, Susie Deans (*The Good Companions*). She is the most memorable of all his women perhaps because she embodies most completely those ideals JBP cherishes: she is pretty, she is light-hearted and she has little sexual personality. Her portrait is successful because he caught her at the right moment, and most of the others are less successful because Susie Dean disappeared from the social scene. She lived at a time when girls were not quite sure whether to be sporty or slinky. Later they made the decision. In his later novels of conspiracy the women are always useless to their organisations because they fall in love with the hero without any provocation. JBP is keen on love at first sight, and likes his girls, even the more controlled ones, to be a bit swoony from time to time. This is, for him, the right sexual make-up. But in terms of fiction it is as difficult to decide why they fall in love so easily as it is to explain why people confide in Snow's Lewis Eliot. In each case, they are theatrical properties, necessary for production. JBP's heroes are usually rather goody-goody. They are prepared to go to bed with a girl but they always need per-

J.B. Priestley welcoming Canon & Mrs Collins
to his 75th Birthday Party at the Savoy

suading with good reasons. They will never do it for the hell of it or just because it's fun. This is a bit sick because you know they'll succumb but they've got to be talked into it. The girls don't decide these matters. This sort of thing used to be considered decent but is in fact rather inhuman.

Although JBP has written a great deal about women and their qualities he is very scathing about 'experts' on women. This was demonstrated as early as 1927 in *Benighted*, when Margaret sharply tells Penderel he knows nothing about women. He agrees, and says he doesn't pretend to, and he doesn't like the fellows who do. Philip then puts in, 'It's a funny thing, but the men who write little books about women, or lecture about them, or pretend to specialise in them in their novels are always complete bounders.' In this connection JBP is walking on a knife-edge. He comes perilously close to pontificating about women at times, though I would normally give him the benefit of the doubt. Philip, of course, is referring to bar-room philanderers, who know everything because they have a vast sense of superiority towards the other sex. JBP insists that in many ways women are superior to men, but this attitude can also take on a patronising aspect if pressed too far.

JBP's attitude to women is made very clear in *Angel Pavement*. He finds women rather more impressive than men in the Anglo-Saxon world. They adapt better to changing and often unfavourable conditions, they often have more guts and determination — though this may have deleterious results, as was illustrated in *English Journey*, where JBP showed the women knuckling under to factory life more cheerfully than the men. The women show up well in this novel when the crunch comes and everyone is threatened with crisis. Of course, there are horrible old battle-axes and there are insipid minxes, but the major characters rally splendidly to distress signals. Instead of moaning for the rest of her life, Miss Matfield decides to get down to it and make a career for herself; Mrs Smeeth is prepared to give up her longings for excitement and help her stodgy old husband find his feet again; and Mrs Dersingham, a model of suburban ineffectiveness, even gives the impression of welcoming disaster, which will enable her to play a role more exacting than that of a mere comforter. In her case JBP resorts to his favourite theatrical metaphor: 'the footlights had blazed out, the curtain had shot up, and she had responded at once to the call of the drama.' And in a sentence the difference between the sexes is made clear (though JBP does not go so far as to suggest that it has universal application): 'unlike her husband, who appeared to be only half the man he usually was, a listless lump, she felt twice her customary self.' This brings us to the second type of woman who constantly re-appears in his fiction. She is usually fortyish, neat and energetic, apparently nervous but basically full of a justified confidence in herself — and she has a rather low opinion of men although there is a sentimental attraction. She needs a crisis to bring out her full potentialities. In *The Good Companions* she was named Miss Trant. Another typical portrait is Mrs Atwood in *The Doomsday Men*. Like the others, she takes the opportunity to remark on the stupidity of men.

When JBP's American travels started he came up against a new dimension in the sex equation. He admitted the vitality, courage and enterprise of American women — 'but how they must have to draw on these qualities!' he exclaims in *Midnight on the Desert*, and goes on: 'It is a bad business being a woman in most places, but in the United States it must be hell. No relaxation. No letting up for a second. Never relieved from the front-line trenches. Never dropping out of the race till Death rings the bell . . .' He looks through magazine advertisements. His American friends laugh at them, as though they have nothing to do with the real America, but he doubts if vast fortunes would be spent on guesswork. 'They showed me very clearly that the ordinary American woman, whose custom they are soliciting, is an unusually competitive being. She has only been freed from most of the drudgery of the European woman in order to lead a still more strenuous life. She has to compete all the time.' She must get her man and then she must keep him — if she slacks for a day he'll be gone. Then there are the children, she has to manage them, she can't afford a moment's carelessness. She must cultivate her body, poise, charm, personality, her mind. In *Journey Down a Rainbow* he returned to this theme, stating even more explicitly that in America the woman is expected to adapt herself to a masculine world and its demands.

Priestley has shown himself on more than one occasion to be the answer to a publisher's prayer whenever a special job has to be done, whether it be the editing of a book on the countryside or the English heritage, or an appreciation of a topical subject. When in 1943 a British publisher decided to honour the part played by women in the war effort, it was to JBP that he turned. The result was *British Women Go to War*. In it his championship of the women's cause was expressed in two ways. First of all he said quite flatly that it was the women who defeated the *Luftwaffe*. If their morale had cracked, so would the nation's. Secondly, women's war work brought them into the mainstream of guidance and control of the nation's affairs. He ends his account with these words:

> The world has long been suffering from an overdose of the masculine values and a lack of the feminine principle, with its realistic outlook and its care for the individual human being . . . Woman is the natural conserver of life, and if she helps us to fight our battles it is only because she knows that beyond victory there is the chance of more abundant life.

The term 'feminine principle' may be used to gloss over all kinds of values which may remain vague unless clearly stated. Briefly, it seems to mean two things to JBP: it includes the idea of woman as the 'natural conserver of life', as expressed in the foregoing passage, and it also contains the belief that women have a closer grasp of reality than men. (This of course is the obverse of the generally held opinion that men are more at home in the world of ideas, abstractions and general principles than women.) It was remarked of a female character in *Faraway* that, '*as a woman*, she may have thought it her duty to defend the solid reality of life' (my italics). In *Lost Empires* JBP's hero, Dick, goes much further. He meets the suffragette, Agnes Foster-Jones, and is impressed by her courage and gaiety. 'I began to feel then, what I have believed ever since, that given equal opportunities women are *better than ordinary men*, only extraordinary men rising to their level — and after all, most extraordinary men appreciate and enjoy women as few ordinary men do.' And in this case the italics are JBP's.

Cissie in the same novel was a very ordinary woman, but she experienced a deep joy, rising from the very depths of her heart, which most women feel when they are with their men and those men are happy. JBP now adds a parenthesis: 'It is an argument, I suspect, for the essential superiority of Woman, able to be entranced not by pursuits but states of mind.' He felt women wished to defy rationality, logic, evidence and to welcome any sign of the unpredictable, the marvellous, the miraculous. 'I have come to believe this is a good and not a bad thing in woman, helping to prevent us from being imprisoned by our rationality and our theories of cause-and-effect.' It is an interesting point, pursued in JBP's account of Mr Micawber in *The English Comic Characters*, where he treats Mrs Micawber as a humorist in her own right, her special quality being the supplier of logic to underpin her husband's hare-brained schemes. Thus the logical woman is comic because she goes against her presumed nature.

The advance of women has been one of the few social gains made by the human race during this century. We have already seen that for JBP the pre-first-War period reached a civilised peak, but he made an exception in the matter of sex. He disagrees sharply with those moralists who think society has been sliding to perdition in that respect. 'Indeed, one of our clear gains among many that are dubious, is the emergence since then of women and girls far more attractive, lively-minded and companionable, than their mothers and grandmothers were. If only women could have transformed our public world, now one-sided to madness in its male aggressiveness, as they have transformed their appearance and style of life,' he wrote in 'Fifty Years of the English' (*The Moments*, 1966). Later in this same article he makes a facile comment about female suffrage which is the kind of thing that even an intelligent writer can let slip when he is tired or writing to a deadline. 'What England has had since female suffrage is life on the dole, appeasement, World War II, the Atom and H-bombs, and now irresponsible advertising-agency politics. I still think women have more common sense than men, but not when they have to mark a ballot paper.' This compares with the kind of silly remark Shaw was capable of making, as when he said that women would vote for the most handsome politician, which meant Ramsay Macdonald.

All in all, JBP sees women in the contemporary world as being uncertain of themselves, not always knowing how to adapt to a world made by and for men, and not too often making the wrong choice. In *Out of Town* (Volume 2 of *The Image Men*) Saltana remarks on the lack of self-confidence exhibited by many women in our new societies which are dominated by the masculine principle. Behind their show of brisk efficiency they are often anxious and humble. In older societies, where the feminine principle is still respected, the women pretend to be humble and passive but are in fact proudly self-confident. To use a metaphor, women don't like machinery but are coming to terms with it. In JBP's account of the 1850's, which he called *Victoria's Heyday*, 1972, he quotes Jane Welsh Carlyle and adds a revealing comment of his own. Jane went to the Great Exhibition of 1851 and confessed in her diary that she didn't like it. (Most visitors seemed to regard it as the most exciting event in their lives.) Jane witnessed a lot of well-dressed people looking at things that were for the most part tawdry; it was very fatiguing and she personally would have got more enjoyment out of reading a fairy-tale. (This was a reference to the much touted Arabian Nights aspect of the Exhibition.) And JBP's comment is this: 'this must have been what a lot of women secretly thought, after trying to avoid all that machinery.'

Women are faced with a dilemma and JBP risks a generalisation. In 'Do They Overdo It?' (*Outcries and Asides*, 1974) he writes: 'Most women with brilliant academic records, whether in the arts or sciences, women who become fairly well-known "intellectuals", work harder than men at suppressing the irrational and instinctive sides of themselves.' They wish to get as far as possible from the illogical and intuitive image of femininity, perhaps to prove that they are better men than their husbands. This, at least, is what JBP seems to fear. In *Found, Lost, Found*, 1976, Tom Dekker tells Mrs Dragby he's an old-fashioned feminist but not a Liberator. 'I think you're in danger of exchanging the feminine principle, which I revere, for the masculine principle,' he says. 'It's like a racehorse wanting to be a rhinoceros.'

Chapter 31

The Universal Mind

Priestley has always shown a marked interest in the question of personal identity. This has become a catch-phrase with many writers, containing little real meaning, and too often the product of reading trendy articles in the 'progressive' press. JBP was working from experience. He could feel no certainty about his own self: what it was, who he was. At the back of his mind there lay the feeling that a something, even a someone, was keeping watch, at times controlling, possibly lending a little guidance. It could be no more precise than that; it was supremely 'woolly-minded'; and to that extent it was real, much more real than the exact definitions and lineaments of the 'professors', who need have no doubts because a scientific-positivist scheme of things made everything crystal clear. Priestley was never converted by Dunne. Dunne brought him something which he immediately recognised. It was called at times the Super Mind, at other times the Universal Mind. It had an affinity with Oriental metaphysical thought but was the fruit of experience and self-questioning and not, as is true of so many Western disciples, of an excited confrontation with the unfamiliar mannerisms of Oriental thought.

Perhaps the first time that JBP felt that an X-quantity was intervening in his experience was during the war. He tells us in *Instead of the Trees* that he was a casualty three times in the first War. On each occasion he noticed that, when terror was apparently at its height, calmness supervened. Something seemed to take over, something that wasn't frightened or panic-stricken, and the empty feeling in the stomach vanished. Mild curiosity took its place. Being of a curious turn of mind, he began to ask himself what it was that actually took over. If it was a mechanism, who or what put it to work? One thing he was certain of, and that was that it couldn't be the ego, operating on itself. I think this point is worth noting carefully, for it demonstrates JBP's independence of mind. It is a commonplace among modern writers to describe the Self or Ego as an object of itself.

I think it came as a shock to many readers to discover that this apparently objective and down-to-earth writer of popular novels should bother his head about matters which might be termed mystical or supernatural or metaphysical, depending on your line of approach. *The Good Companions*, for instance, seems entirely remote from any unseen or mysterious forces that might be held to shape life. It is romantic, certainly, but in the prosaic mould, not the mystical. But because ordinary people do sometimes have these unfamiliar thoughts about the nature of life (though they would never use such a term in expressing their wonder) we should not be surprised when one of the characters in this novel has the feeling of being manipulated by unknown beings. This is Mrs Joe, when she congratulates Susie on her good fortune. She speaks in capital letters of the Big Chance and the even Bigger Chance. Something told her it would come. 'It — it — a thing like this — makes you ask yourself, Where Are We? — if you see what I mean.' She loses herself in these profundities, says JBP. They are profundities of a kind JBP himself referred to more and more frequently as time went on. The growing interest in the paranormal these days is based less on the research of people like Professor Rhine and his Duke University team than on the shyly-held conviction of ordinary people that there is 'something else'. It is the feeling expressed by Shakespeare in his players-on-a-stage metaphor, one which had a particular attraction for JBP. In his play, *People At Sea*, he makes use of a variation when the novelist, Valentine Avon, while playing bridge, wonders if higher beings could play with him and his colleagues as they play with the cards.

The leap forward in JBP's thinking came with the fertilising encounter with the theories of J.W. Dunne. 'The bit of divided universal attention which is interested in your world-line is *your attention*,' Dunne wrote in *The New Immortality*, 1938. 'The bit which is interested in my world-line is my attention. Your mind and my mind are simply marked places in the Super-Mind, marked by the world-lines which determine the presence of sensory phenomena.' Attention does not occupy a point but covers a very wide area with a central focus. 'Attention focused about your part of the Super-Mind must have a fringe overlapping the attention which is focused about my part of that mind. Since your attention can re-divide (i.e. possess several foci), it can concentrate one of these foci upon the point where my attention is focused. And that, of course, is mind-sharing or, as it is called so absurdly, "telepathy".' Add to this that the Super-Mind can divide attention in every direction in its larger field of view, and you have a concept that goes a long way to explaining JBP's 'something somewhere'.

Can this explain the sudden arrival of what seems to be a wonderful idea, often bringing with it a state of genuine ecstasy? May it be the result of a temporary union with a greater mind? These are the questions he was asking in *Rain Upon Godshill*, which appeared in the year following the book by Dunne from which I have just quoted. Sometimes we feel, he says, especially when we are exhausted and drained of energy, that we are being sustained by something outside us. He had already considered the ancient idea of inspiration and rejected it. Yet the Muse could be merely another name for the Greater Mind, and a less portentous one. This awareness of inspiration has haunted not only poets but also scientists through the ages. It is agreed that it happens, but how it happens and what it is has baffled the keenest intelligences. One can hardly accuse JBP of slackness in not taking the investigation any further. It is a field in which many come together to share their bafflement: Shelley with his 'The mind in creation is as a fading coal, which some invisible influence . . . awakens to transitory brightness;' Yeats with his 'Our most characteristic thoughts, elaborate purposes, precise emotions, are often, as I think, not really ours, but they on a sudden come up, as it were, out of hell or out of heaven;' and the mathematician Poincaré with his 'These sudden inspirations are never produced except after some days of voluntary efforts which appear absolutely fruitless, in which one thought one had accomplished nothing, and seemed to be on a totally wrong track' — all attest to the same mysterious process.

Inevitably the idea arises, at some time or other, that we are subject to manipulation. It is, of course, a notion that has supplied the science fiction writers with plenty of scope for the exercise of their ingenuity. JBP dropped a few hints in his plays. In *Home Is Tomorrow* Riberac just waits for something to happen: 'It is a moment of quiet, of emptiness, before the unknown chess player makes his next move.' Chu, the Chinese, finds this unconvincing in a Westerner. A little later Riberac says, 'Though we may still talk and talk, we will now act according to the mysterious plan already laid down for us.' In *Summer Day's Dream* Margaret, the new-style

Englishwoman, whom the Russian accuses of being a mystic, has the sense of a higher type of humanity. Bahru has been through this phase and now regards science as a saviour — he and Margaret reverse the roles usually assigned to Westerner and Easterner. He will have nothing to do with Margaret's mysterious forces because he can't see, hear or touch them. 'How many insects,' asks Margaret, 'are there in your jungles that know anything about the Chemical Research Department of the South Asia Federation?' Who, she might have added, are certainly manipulating the insects' destiny.

Most of the later works contain passing references to this effect — they cannot be more than passing, for he has no idea how it works, only a suspicion that there is a Super-Mind which may intervene from time to time. He tells us in *Trumpets Over the Sea*, 1968, how, while trapped in a store in Daytona Beach he discovered that one woman who served him was a Cockney, another had spent some time in London, and round the corner was an Oxford student working there during his long vacation. It might be objected that such occurrences are both commonplace and trivial, yet they worry JBP and bewilder him. None of these people were connected with the visit of the L.S.O., which had brought him to Daytona Beach. Was there any connection between him and them, apart from a casual encounter? 'What determines these odd migrations? Are we being moved by demiurges playing chess with us?' The master-question is this: how independent is the Ego? In that stimulating book of odds and ends which he calls *Outcries and Asides* his mind darts back to the problem of the creative act. What happens when we write well and fluently? he asks in 'Western Answer'. Does somebody or something take over? This is repetitive, but in my case deliberately so, for this is how one encounters it in JBP. He is not, as he has so often told us, a professional philosopher. But he is alert, he is curious, he has what Sterne used to call a hobby-horse. Do we escape from the prison of the Ego during creative work? 'Perhaps this might be our Western answer to the Eastern mystics, our enlarging of consciousness in a cold climate.' And it must be done in the Western way for the Westerner who tries to follow Eastern paths usually finds the task exceptionally futile. One must take it in with mother's milk. In 'A Teasing Riddle' he tells us how his mind wanders while reading, he feels sleepy, and then a train of thought enters his mind. It is usually quite sensible but it has nothing to do with him. It's just as if he had picked up a strange programme on his receiver. It's how Klee used to go for a walk with a line. He was led but by Whom or What he never knew. And then the Dream, always the Dream. A number of people enter a room, chattering, and among them is an old friend, now dead. He hangs back, which is unusual for him. JBP goes to him, claps him on the shoulder, says he's glad to see him and then wakes up. 'As I have suggested elsewhere, it seems to me that consciousness is not contained within passing-time and so survives in some measure the death of the body.' Outside time, bodyless, perhaps confused, his old friend knew he was still alive and wanted to tell JBP. This is simply called 'A Dream'.

Here is a possible plan. It will do to take the place of the outmoded plans we grew up on, until it in turn is set aside. One of the major metaphysical ideas that has exercised man's mind since he started to think about origins and destinies is that what we are and what we experience are so many fragments in a whole that must have meaning, though it is hidden from us. The Super Mind pulls the pieces together. JBP is a thousand active particles, pulling in a dozen directions — romancing with Yorkshire councillors, soberly attending Football League matches, deploring the wretched pension schemes for broken-down workers, looking back to the Future and forward to the Past, writing Hollywood scripts out of industrial fantasy, seeing Dostoevsky and Proust and Lawrence plain and not distorted by prejudice, knowing that society is an intricate web that cannot be abstracted from, dancing a gay galliard on the beds of drowsy professors, delighting in pipes and jokes and saying Bah! — when and where does one stop? It's all there and it's happening all the time.

It needs a Super Mind to decree that there is one person and not an anthology or a series or . . .

NOTES

Notes to Chapter 1

1. This day, and the memory of it, crops up constantly. For example, in *Lost Empires*: 'But their life lines, now exactly parallel, were soon to rush away from each other, for while Edmond vanished in the mud and mire of Passchendaele . . .'
2. This has been confirmed by JBP in a private letter.
3. 'I was supposed to be very good at school, always coming out at or near the top, but most of the time there I suffered from an appalling boredom I have only known since at UNESCO and other conferences.' ('Life, Literature and the Classroom', *The Moments and Other Pieces*, 1966)
4. One of his favourite humorists, Stephen Leacock, a selection of whose work he edited as *The Bodley Head Leacock*, wrote an essay entitled 'Are the Rich Happy?' when he made fun of the propensity of people on high incomes to protest they cannot keep up with the rich.

Notes to Chapter 2

1. In his *George Meredith*, JBP passes this comment on Meredith's contributions to the *Ipswich Journal*: 'Some of these contributions, unsigned of course, but showing unmistakeable traces of Meredith's manner, have been dragged into the light by those well-meaning enthusiasts who contrive, before they have done, to make the object of their veneration wish they had never been born.' I only hope my recovery of some of Mr Priestley's early journalism does not have that fatal effect on him.

Notes to Chapter 3

1. But see Chapter 27, 'The Critic'
2. Chesterton, who resembled Priestley in being a writer who had a great deal to say, yet was trapped by the essay for much of his career, is an excellent exemplar, with his *Tremendous Trifles* and *All Things Considered*.
3. Just as there is only one James Joyce, with the same consequence —

those who follow the Master only achieve boredom.
4.   Although he has never regarded himself as a soldier, in the Introd-
     uction to *Literature and Western Man* he wrote: 'This is not a work of
     scholarship. If it had been, my name would not have been attached to
     it, for among my dwindling pretensions there is no pretence of scholar-
     ship.' But what, then, is scholarship?

Notes to Chapter 5

1.   In 1926 JBP had included *Reading* by Walpole in a series of
     monographs called 'These Discussions'. Other titles had been *Talking*,
     by himself, and *Laughing*, by Martin Armstrong.
2.   'I will admit that this is largely a novel of happy escape, but I will not
     admit that it is at all a deliberate falsification of life,' (Introduction to
     Collected Edition of *The Good Companions*, 1931).

Notes to Chapter 6

1.   *An Experiment With Time*, by J.W. Dunne. 1939

Notes to Chapter 7

1.   Both *Dangerous Corner* and *Laburnum Grove* appeared as novels, in 1934
     and 1936 respectively. They were not written by Priestley but by
     Ruth Holland with JBP's co-operation, and issued by his own
     publisher, Heinemann.

Notes to Chapter 8

1.   For example, *People at Sea*.
2.   JBP's admiration for the old music hall performers is well known and
     will be illustrated abundantly. As for cricket, he wrote a tribute to
     Herbert Sutcliffe, already referred to, and he wrote an Introduction to
     The Golden Age of Cricket by David Frith.
3.   In 1937 *Two Time Plays* was published, comprising *Time and the
     Conways* and *I Have Been Here Before*. *Three Time Plays*, 1947, comprised
     those two plus *Dangerous Corner*, and not *Johnson Over Jordan*, which I
     have treated as a third Time play in this chapter.

Notes to Chapter 10

1. The essay had in fact been published some years earlier in a periodical but reached a wider audience in this volume.
2. And has since disappeared, in true pantomime fashion!

Notes to Chapter 11

1. *The Long Mirror*, 1940, appears to be an exception, but it was certainly planned and probably written before the outbreak of war.

Notes to Chapter 12

1. Not yet a dirty word.
2. In this connection we may also consider *They Walk in the City*, 1936, which is more a political documentary than a satisfactory novel.
3. The contrast is used fictionally in *Wonder Hero*.
4. A reference to an influential book of the period, *The End of Economic Man*, by Peter Drucker.

Notes to Chapter 13

1. But in *Midnight on the Desert* JBP wrote that the truest classless society he has encountered was among the cowboys of Arizona.

Notes to Chapter 14

1. The muddle is not always his own invention. In 1932 JBP was scheduled to give a radio talk entitled 'To a Highbrow', but the script was lost by the BBC, leading to a gap in the programme! This caused great hilarity among journalists and Sir John Foster Fraser used it as his text in his reply to the toast of 'Journalism' at a literary luncheon.

Notes to Chapter 16

1. JBP's view of the Golden Age is an *idée fixe* and has never varied. Its latest expression is to be found in his Introduction to David Frith's *The Golden Age of Cricket*, 1978. 'Most of us have our own private Golden Ages,' he says. 'My own is roughly from 1910 to 1914 when I joined the Army and began to lose so many friends, when I entered another sort of world, which could never again be trusted.' Cricket's Golden Age, according to Frith, was 1890-1914, thus overlapping JBP's.

Notes to Chapter 17

1. The jogging craze (will it last?) came later and may be a challenge to the spirit of Admass.
2. The situation of the writer given here is paralleled by his place in the Public Lending Right controversy. He writes the book and the major pickings go to the publisher, agent, bookseller and librarian. Librarians in particular are shocked that writers should expect to earn a living wage.
3. For a balanced view of America, *Midnight on the Desert* cannot be bettered.

Notes to Chapter 19

1. This didn't only apply to theatre business men. Shortly after this I worked on a committee in Dorset concerned with local education and artistic facilities. Another member of the committee was Jack Longland, director of education, who was making a reputation as a speaker and debater on the radio. I suggested that we might subsidise a travelling theatre and added that most people had little opportunity to see anything beyond a leg-show at Weymouth. Longland's reaction was the very one Priestley deplored, a kind of man-to-man, saloon-bar 'Lucky fellows, eh?'

Notes to Chapter 20

1. Except for *Jenny Villiers*, which was set against the rehearsal of a straight play.
2. There is an excellent appreciation of Little Tich in *The Balconinny*. 'He did not really act a man telling you something funny about his mother-in-law, but a man pretending to be a man telling you something funny about his mother-in-law.
3. The funny man may be encountered outside the theatre. Mr. Fred Mitty, in *Angel Pavement*, is described as 'a funny man, a determined wag.' He is absolutely unbearable and symbolically as well as actually, is thrown out.

Notes to Chapter 21

1. *J.B. Priestley: an Informal Study*, by David Hughes. 1958.
2. He made this very point about Charles Reade in his book on the English Novel, 1927. 'He wrote a good many plays and preferred

them to his novels, with the result that a passion for purely theatrical situations, a melodramatic habit of mind, was forever leading him astray.'

3. And also Kenneth Young, who wrote the second British Council National Book League pamphlet on Priestley.
4. They bark at each other. Was JBP trying to imitate Mr. Jingle in his beloved *Pickwick Papers?* If so, it's an interesting example of how the original can succeed and the copy fail.
5. Nevertheless, four years later JBP wrote in *Charles Dickens and His World* that *Our Mutual Friend* was 'unquestionably one of his best.' He expressed the view that you have to grow into the excellence of this novel, and this may be true of *The Image Men.*

Notes to Chapter 23

1. 'Very few people chuckle, except in print, but this man did' (*Found, Lost, Found,* 1976).

Notes to Chapter 24

1. In this play, United Nations Undeveloped Territories Organisation.
2. The information in this paragraph is taken from a private letter.

Notes to Chapter 26

1. Of course, they are sometimes right — but whether they have the moral right to make such charges is another matter.

Notes to Chapter 27

1. There are also valuable critical insights, of the kind we get from a creative writer turned critic rather than the academic, in *The English Comic Characters*, 1925, which consists of eleven studies, including four Shakespearean and three Dickensian. *Fools and Philosophers*, an anthology published in the same year, serves as a kind of supplement
2. *The Book of Bodley Head Verse*, edited by JBP and with a Preface by J.C. Squire, 1926, is surely one of the most undistinguished anthologies ever published! In fairness to JBP it should be noted that his choice was limited to Bodley Head publications.
3. Illustrating this very point, I would like to refer the reader to my own study, *Six Novelists Look at Society.*

4. I can still remember the effect my first encounter with Kafka, on reading *The Castle*, had on me. For a whole day normal relationships seemed to have been suspended, and I moved in a world where the irrational alone seemed normal.

Notes to Chapter 28

1. See Chapter 1.

Notes to Chapter 29

1. Perhaps this explains fundamentally why I am attracted by JBP. It must date from the time when I was reprimanded by a receiver for not having a 'point of view'. Point!

BIBLIOGRAPHY

In all cases the Publisher referred to is the British Publisher

Verse

The Chapman of Rhymes, 1918. (Privately printed).
The Olympians, 1949. (Opera Libretto) William Heinemann.

Essays

Brief Diversions, 1922. (With sketches) Bowes, Cambridge.
Papers From Lilliput, 1922. Bowes, Cambridge.
I For One, 1923. Lane.
Talking, 1926. Jarrolds.
Open House, 1927. William Heinemann.
Apes and Angels, 1928. William Heinemann.
The Balconinny, 1929. William Heinemann.
Postscripts, 1940. (Broadcast Talks) William Heinemann.
Out of the People, 1941. William Heinemann.
The New Citizen, 1944. (Pamphlet) Council for Education in World Citizenship.
Letter to a Returning Serviceman, 1945. (Pamphlet) Home & Van Thal.
The Secret Dream, 1946. (Pamphlet) Turnstile Press.
The Arts Under Socialism, 1947. (Lecture and Pamphlet) Turnstile Press.
Delight, 1949. William Heinemann.
The Writer in a Changing Society, 1955. (Pamphlet) Hand & Flower Press. Aldington (Kent).
Thoughts in the Wilderness, 1957. William Heinemann.
The Art of the Dramatist, 1957. (Lecture and Pamphlet) William Heinemann.
Topside, or The Future of England, 1958. William Heinemann.
The Moments and Other Pieces, 1966. William Heinemann.
Essays of Five Decades, 1969. (Selection) William Heinemann.
Outcries and Asides, 1974. William Heinemann.
Particular Pleasures, 1975. William Heinemann.

Criticism

Figures in Modern Literature, 1924. Lane.
The English Comic Characters, 1925. Lane.

George Meredith, 1926. (English Men of Letters) Macmillan.
Thomas Love Peacock, 1927. (English Men of Letters) Macmillan.
The English Novel, 1927. Benn.
English Humour, 1929. Longman.
The Romantic Period, in the article on English Literature in 14th Edition of Encyclopaedia Britannica, 1929.
Theatre Outlook 1947. Nicholson & Watson.
The Story of Theatre, 1959. Rathbone Books.
Literature and Western Man, 1960. William Heinemann.
William Hazlitt, 1960. (Pamphlet) Longman for British Council.
Charles Dickens, 1961. (Pictorial Biography) Thames & Hudson.
Anton Chekhov, 1970. International Textbook.
English Humour, 1976. (Not a re-issue of the 1929 edition.) William Heinemann.

Novels and Other Fiction

Adam in Moonshine, 1927. William Heinemann.
Benighted, 1927. William Heinemann.
Farthing Hall, 1929. (In collaboration with Hugh Walpole). William Heinemann.
The Good Companions, 1929. William Heinemann.
The Town of Mayor Miraucourt, 1930. (Short Story). William Heinemann.
Angel Pavement, 1930. William Heinemann.
Faraway, 1932. William Heinemann.
Wonder Hero, 1933. William Heinemann.
Albert Goes Through, 1933. (Short Story). William Heinemann.
I'll Tell You Everything, 1933. (In collaboration with Gerald Bullett) William Heinemann.
They Walk in the City, 1936. William Heinemann.
The Doomsday Men, 1938. William Heinemann.
Let the People Sing, 1939. William Heinemann.
Black-Out in Gretley, 1942. William Heinemann.
Daylight on Saturday, 1943. William Heinemann.
Three Men in New Suits, 1945. William Heinemann.
Bright Day, 1946. William Heinemann.
Jenny Villiers, 1947. William Heinemann.
Going Up, 1950. (Stories and Sketches) William Heinemann.
Lost Empires, 1950. William Heinemann.
Festival at Farbridge, 1951. William Heinemann.
The Other Place, 1953. (Stories). William Heinemann.
The Magicians, 1954. William Heinemann.
Low Notes on a High Level, 1954. William Heinemann.

Saturn Over the Water, 1961. William Heinemann.
The Thirty-First of June, 1961. William Heinemann.
The Shapes of Sleep, 1962. William Heinemann.
Sir Michael and Sir George, 1964. William Heinemann.
Salt is Leaving, 1966. William Heinemann.
It's an Old Country, 1967. William Heinemann.
The Image Men: Vol. 1 *Out of Town*, 1968. William Heinemann.
                   Vol. 2 *London End*, 1969. William Heinemann.
                   (Also published in one volume).
Snoggle, 1971. (Mainly for youngsters) William Heinemann.
The Carfitt Crisis, 1975. (Stories) William Heinemann.
Found, Lost, Found, or the English Way of Life, 1976. William Heinemann.

Drama

The Good Companions, 1931. (Dramatised with E. Knoblock) Samuel French.
Dangerous Corner, 1932. William Heinemann.
The Roundabout, 1933. William Heinemann
Laburnum Grove, 1934. William Heinemann.
Eden End, 1934. William Heinemann.
Duet in Floodlight, 1935. William Heinemann.
Cornelius, 1935. William Heinemann.
Spring Tide, 1936. (Original edition was by George Billam and Peter Goldsmith. The latter was a pseudonym for JBP.) William Heinemann.
Bees on the Boat Deck, 1936. William Heinemann.
Time and the Conways, 1937. William Heinemann.
Mystery at Greenfingers, 1937. William Heinemann.
I Have Been Here Before, 1937. William Heinemann.
People at Sea, 1937. William Heinemann.
When We Are Married, 1938. William Heinemann.
Johnson Over Jordan, 1939. William Heinemann.
The Long Mirror, 1940. William Heinemann.
Goodnight, Children, 1942. William Heinemann.
Desert Highway, 1944. William Heinemann.
How Are They at Home?, 1944. William Heinemann.
They Came to a City, 1944. William Heinemann.
Music at Night, 1947. William Heinemann.
An Inspector Calls, 1947. William Heinemann.
The Rose and Crown, 1947. (One Act) Samuel French.
The Linden Tree, 1948. William Heinemann.
The High Toby, 1948. (For Toy Theatre, with D. Zinkeisen) Penguin

The Golden Fleece, 1948. William Heinemann.
Home is Tomorrow, 1949. William Heinemann.
Ever Since Paradise, 1950. William Heinemann.
Summer Day's Dream, 1950. William Heinemann.
Bright Shadow, 1950. William Heinemann.
Dragon's Mouth, 1952. (With Jacquetta Hawkes) William Heine-
    mann.
Private Rooms, 1953. (One Act) Samuel French.
Treasure on Pelican, 1953. William Heinemann.
Try it Again, 1953 (One Act) Samuel French.
A Glass of Bitter, 1954. (One Act) Samuel French.
Mr Kettle and Mrs Moon, 1955. William Heinemann.
The Glass Cage, 1957. William Heinemann.
A Severed Head, 1963. (In collaboration with Iris Murdoch) Chatto &
    Windus.

Sociological

English Journey, 1934. William Heinemann.
The Man-Power Story, 1943. (Written for Ministry of Labour).
British Women Go to War, 1943. Collins.

Personal

Midnight on the Desert, 1937. William Heinemann.
Rain Upon Godshill, 1939. William Heinemann.
Margin Released, 1962. William Heinemann.
Instead of the Trees, 1977. William Heinemann.

Travel

Russian Journey, 1946. Writers' Group of Society for Cultural
    Relations with U.S.S.R.
Journey Down a Rainbow, 1955 (With Jacquetta Hawkes) William
    Heinemann.
A Visit to New Zealand, 1974. William Heinemann.

Speculation

Man and Time, 1964. William Heinemann.
Over the Long High Wall, 1972. William Heinemann.

Social History

The Prince of Pleasure, 1969. William Heinemann.
The Edwardians, 1970. William Heinemann.
Victoria's Heyday, 1972. William Heinemann.
The English, 1973. William Heinemann.

Collections and Selections

Self-Selected Essays, 1932. William Heinemann.
Four in Hand, 1934 (contains *Adam in Moonshine, Laburnum Grove, The Roundabout* and a selection of essays) William Heinemann.
Three Plays and a Preface, 1935 (*Dangerous Corner, Eden End* and *Cornelius*) William Heinemann.
Two Time Plays, 1937 (*Time and the Conways, I Have Been Here Before*) William Heinemann.
Three Plays, 1943 (*Music at Night, The Long Mirror, They Came to a City*) William Heinemann.
Four Plays, 1944 (as in *Three Plays*, plus *Desert Highway*) William Heinemann.
Three Comedies, 1945 (*Goodnight Children, The Golden Fleece, How Are They at Home?*) William Heinemann.
Three Time Plays, 1947 (as in *Two Time Plays* plus *Dangerous Corner*) William Heinemann.
The Priestley Companion, 1951 (selected and introduced by Ivor Brown) William Heinemann.
The Plays of J.B. Priestley have been published in three volumes, as follows:

Vol. 1: *Dangerous Corner; Eden End; Time and the Conways; I Have Been Here Before; Johnson Over Jordan; Music at Night; The Linden Tree.* William Heinemann.

Vol. 2: *Laburnum Grove; When We Are Married; The Golden Fleece; Ever Since Paradise; Bees on the Boat Deck; How Are They at Home?; Goodnight, Children.* William Heinemann.

Vol. 3: *Cornelius; People at Sea; They Came to a City; Desert Highway; An Inspector Calls; Home is Tomorrow; A Summer Day's Dream.* William Heinemann.

These volumes do not contain the whole of JBP's dramatic opus.

Three Novels contains *Bright Day, Angel Pavement, Sir Michael and Sir George.* William Heinemann.

Introductions, Contributions, etc.

It is impossible to list all JBP's work under this heading but here are some of the more interesting items.

The Diary of Thomas Turner, 1925. (Ed. JBP)
Essayists Past and Present, 1925. (Ed. JBP) Jenkins.
Fools and Philosophers, 1925. (Ed. JBP) Lane.
Thomas Moore's Diary; a Selection, 1925. (Ed. JBP) Cambridge University Press.
Book of Bodley Head Verse, 1926. (Ed. JBP) Bodley Head.
These Diversions, 1926. (A series of monographs, ed. JBP, including *Reading*, by Hugh Walpole, *Laughing*, by Martin Armstrong, and *Talking*, by himself. See Essays) Jarrolds.
What I Believe, 1937. (With W.R. Matthews and others) Muller.
Our Nation's Heritage, 1939. Dent.
Beauty of Britain, 1950. (With A.G. Street and others) Batsford.
All About Ourselves, 1956. William Heinemann.
Bodley Head Leacock, 1957. (Ed. JBP) Bodley Head.
Coming to London, 1957. (Ed. John Lehmann) Phoenix.
Encore: the Sunday Times Book, 1962. Michael Joseph.
The Golden Age of Cricket, 1978. (Ed. David Frith) Lutterworth.

Biographical and Critical Studies of JBP

J.B. Priestley and the Theatre, by Rex Pogson. 1947. Triangle Press.
Priestley the Dramatist, by Gareth Lloyd-Evans. 1947.
Introduction to J.B. Priestley, by Eric Gillett, 1956. (With a selection) William Heinemann.
J.B. Priestley, by Ivor Brown. 1957, revised 1964. Longman for British Council.
J.B. Priestley: an Informal Study, by David Hughes.1958. Hart-Davis.
The World of J.B. Priestley, by Donald G. MacRae. 1967. (With a selection) William Heinemann.
J.B. Priestley: Portrait of an Author, by Susan Cooper. 1970. William Heinemann.
J.B. Priestley, by Kenneth Young. 1977. Longman for British Council.
J.B. Priestley, by J.G. Braine. 1979. Weidenfeld & Nicholson.

INDEX

There is no entry for J. B. Priestley in this index as the book is not a biography and there are very few biographical references. Information about his connection with C.N.D., for example, will be found under that head. His publications are listed in alphabetical order in the main body of the Index.

Names followed by (F) are fictional characters. This is not meant to be comprehensive and in many cases information about characters will be found by reference to the title of the novel or play in which they occur.